Teaching America about Sex

Teaching America about Sex

Marriage Guides and Sex Manuals
from the Late Victorians to Dr. Ruth

M. E. Melody
and
Linda M. Peterson

NEW YORK UNIVERSITY PRESS
New York and London

NEW YORK UNIVERSITY PRESS
New York and London

Library of Congress Cataloging-in-Publication Data
Melody, Michael Edward.
Teaching America about sex : marriage/sex manuals from the late
Victorians to Dr. Ruth / M.E. Melody and Linda M. Peterson.
p. cm.
Includes bibliographical references and index.
ISBN 0-8147-5532-1 (cloth : alk. paper)
1. Sex instruction—United States—Handbooks, manuals,
etc.—History. I. Peterson, Linda Mary, 1947– II. Title.
HQ56.M365 1999
613.9'5—dc21   99-6300
                        CIP

New York University Press books are printed on acid-free paper,
and their binding materials are chosen for strength and durability.

Manufactured in the United States of America

10 9 8 7 6 5 4 3 2 1

*For Edward A. Goerner
and Frances S. Parker*

Contents

Acknowledgments

Professors Melody and Peterson wish to acknowledge the assistance of J. Patrick Lee, Ph.D., provost and professor of French at Barry University, who introduced us to the work of [Pseudo] Aristotle. Hugh Ripley, dean emeritus of library services and university librarian, along with the able members of his staff, provided valuable assistance. Among Barry's librarians William Patrick Morrissey deserves special recognition, as does Isabel Medina. The former can track down any obscure reference, while the latter works miracles with inter-library loan. Susan M. Widmayer, Ph.D., and Martha Widmayer, Ph.D., read an early draft of the text and provided valuable suggestions. Our editor at New York University Press, Niko Pfund, a man of foresight as well as a sensitivity to currents in several disciplines, provided support and encouragement as we labored on the text and fussed over it. Jane Goggin provided secretarial assistance during the inevitable last-minute computer crisis. Priscilla Rankin of the Gainesville Junior College Library in Georgia facilitated the inter-library loan process so that we acquired a copy of Hanchett's book in record time. Without the synergy of our friendship and the gender politics class that we team-teach, this text could not have been written.

Professor Melody also wishes to acknowledge the National Endowment for the Humanities for a Summer Institute grant from the Women's Studies Department at the University of Cincinnati, which allowed time to study writings in women's social and political theory. Professors Hilda Smith and Berenice Carroll provided skillful guidance to a neophyte whose graduate training muted the voices of women. Professor Carroll has also provided encouragement and support over the years as well as the benefit of her own many insights on these issues. Barry University provided a sabbatical that allowed for much of the background reading necessary for this book. Professor Laura Armesto, dean of the School of Arts and Sciences and associate vice president for undergraduate studies, graciously supplied release time that allowed for the actual writing of the text. Jeffrey Seibert, Ph.D., Jeffrey Ehrlich, M.D., and Richard Beach, M.D., Ph.D., selflessly provided hope, support, and encouragement.

Professor Peterson wishes to acknowledge Professor Clyde Hendrick, whose graduate seminar in women's studies showed her that women's voices need not be muted. Laura Armesto, Ph.D., dean and friend, proved steadfast in her faith that this book would get finished, and Susan Widmayer, Ph.D., was generous with her time, her criticism, and her love.

Introduction

Sex matters. Everyone knows it.

Scholars, however, have been reticent on the subject until fairly recently. Perhaps this reflects an inbred reserve or justifiable fears of tenure committees. Academia consigned sex and its corollary concerns to sociologists—John Gagnon is one example—or anthropologists like Malinowski or Mead. Anthropologists studied people who were several times removed from modern societies and thus nonthreatening to prevailing norms.[1] Michael Gordon notes this scholarly silence in his survey of American marriage/sex manuals (1978, 59), as do Porter and Hall in their more recent survey of the British literature (1995, 3). In fact, all the authors surveyed in *Teaching America about Sex* note America's general sexual silence. Despite the works of all her predecessors over the past century, Ruth Westheimer in her *Sex for Dummies* in 1995 writes that Americans still remain ignorant about sex.

Gordon (1969, 1978) observes that the domestic advice genre developed in England as early as 1487 with the publication of Caxton's *Book of Good Manners*. Marital advice literature evolved from this genre by the nineteenth century in America, and early on it typically consisted of printed sermons drafted by clergy.[2] Late in the century, medical doctors published as many marriage manuals as the clergy. In the 1890s, according to Gordon, members of the clergy published five marriage manuals, while doctors produced another five. All these works targeted the middle and upper classes. The medical writers even focused on intimate matters. In these early manuals written by medical doctors, theological and philosophical premises inform their work as much, if not more than, scientific ones. Medicine had yet to become fully developed as the science we know today. Gordon terms these works "conservative," in that they sought to keep sex bound tightly within the confines of marriage. By the 1930s medical doctors like Theodore Van de Velde and Hannah and Abraham Stone dominate the marital/sexual advice genre.

Several decades later other medical doctors like David Reuben and Alex Comfort transform marriage manuals into more explicit sexual ones. The cultural revolution of the 1960s fostered open discussion of sexuality as well as a pleasure ethic that permitted issues of sexuality to be divorced from marriage. Marriage manuals, in this sense, mainly restrict legitimate sex to marriage. Sex manuals, on the other hand, primarily focus on erotic techniques without much concern for legal formalities. Reuben's *Everything You Always Wanted to Know about Sex, but Were Afraid to Ask* and Comfort's *Joy of Sex* are sex manuals that focus on pleasure as an end in itself. Reuben's other work, *Any Woman Can! Love and Sexual Fulfillment for the Single, Widowed, Divorced*, however, represents more of a marriage manual, while Comfort's *More Joy: A Lovemaking Companion to the Joy of Sex* and *New Joy of Sex* are sex manuals (see also Gordon and Bernstein 1970).

Gordon, certainly a pioneer in studying this genre, selected the texts he reviewed in 1978 from a random sample of titles from the *Cumulative Book Index* in the decades from 1900 to 1939. He adds other titles that had an important impact. Avoiding the theology of random samples and regression analysis (Kuhn 1962), we selected texts noted in authoritative works like D'Emilio and Freedman's *Intimate Matters* (1988) as well as those that had several printings spanning a decade or more. Gordon may have gotten a random sample of what was published within a decade, but this does not mean that anyone paid serious attention to these texts. We, of course, must deal with the same problem (Gordon 1978, 60).

Most of the texts we selected went through several printings and were usually revised and then reprinted. Van de Velde's *Ideal Marriage*, for example, was first printed in America in 1930, and Random House reprinted it at least thirty-seven times before a revised edition was published in 1965. After World War II, readers purchased more than five hundred thousand copies of *Ideal Marriage*. Alex Comfort is an example of an author whose work spans decades. He began his series with *The Joy of Sex* in 1972, published *More Joy* in 1974, and ended with *The New Joy of Sex* in 1991. His earlier editions sold more than eight million copies. Likewise, Dr. Ruth's work, an ongoing enterprise, started in 1983 with *Dr. Ruth's Guide to Good Sex* and extends at least until *Sex for Dummies* in 1995. Like Porter and Hall (1995), we searched for authoritative texts, what they term "canonical" texts, that express the sexual zeitgeist of the time. The length of the run as well as continued sales indicates that these texts struck a responsive chord among the public and not just within the medical community. As this genre evolves from Van de Velde in the 1930s to Reuben in the 1960s, marital/sexual advice authors court a popular audience, and the common apologia for writing about the subject disappears from their prefaces.

Like the works of Gordon and Porter and Hall, *Teaching America about Sex* does not deal with the actual sexual practices of Americans. D'Emilio and Freedman remain authoritative on this issue, and in reality much remains to be recovered. George Chauncey's *Gay New York* (1994), for example, provides an ingenious social history that utilizes a variety of sources, from newspaper clippings to reports from anti-vice societies. Our aim, then, is to track America's sexual zeitgeist through the marital/sexual advice literature over the decades from the 1880s to the new millennium.

Everyone acknowledges that sex matters. Gordon argues that his study of the literature from 1900 to 1939 begins the task of differentiating between the content of sex manuals and the actual practices of Americans. He aims to note shifts in expert opinion and provide a brief social history (Gordon 1978, 82–83). Weinberg and Hammersmith (1983) in their study of manuals from 1950 to 1980 state that the advice literature certainly influenced public opinion and presents what they term "legitimate" views of sexuality. The literature also demonstrates, especially for the period they are considering, the influence of therapists and the linkages between women's status in society and dominant sexual scripts. We agree, but also acknowledge the insights suggested by Porter and Hall in *The Facts of Life.*

In subjecting marriage/sex manuals to scholarly interrogation, *Teaching America about Sex* seeks to analyze the sexual politics of these works. The text aims to discern the evolving pattern of permissions and prohibitions and to note mechanisms of enforcement, from God to electroshock. Like the work of Porter and Hall, *Teaching America about Sex* accepts Foucault's basic insight that "sexuality [is] . . . produced by the production of knowledge about it" (1995, 8). Writing in this sense evokes doing. Sex is a contested field of conflicting identities, norms, and sanctions. Porter and Hall compare their effort to (re)constructing a history of dancing. At different times certain steps are de rigueur, and they must be performed precisely. Sanctions await those who fail and awards are given those who execute the moves marvelously.[3]

Most of the authors discussed here are medical doctors, and two of them are psychiatrists. *Teaching America about Sex* thus becomes a history of the medical profession's construction of sexuality from the 1880s to the present. Dr. Ruth is the most famous exception. She received a doctorate from Columbia University Teachers College in the study of the family. Following several years of work with Planned Parenthood, she studied to be a sex therapist at New York Hospital-Cornell Medical Center. For the most part, however, medical doctors are the ones who define sexual norms in the advice literature and enforce their dictates. Medical science makes sex a discipline in Foucault's sense; in analyzing this, we move beyond the approach of Porter and Hall.

As Foucault argues in *Discipline and Punish* (1977), the nature of power changes in the modern world. It no longer primarily consists of the power of a sovereign to punish a particular person or utilize torture to gain a confession. Foucault employs the example of Damiens, a regicide, for the former mode of power. Power acts on Damiens's body to torture it, to pull it apart, to kill it. Modern power, by contrast, is relational and consists of a type of physics located in the individual. Sex as a discipline establishes norms to which individuals must conform, and the essential enforcement mechanism is rooted in consciousness. This power can be exercised through books that construct norms or even through consultations with physicians or psychiatrists. The marriage/sex manuals approve some techniques and stigmatize others. Similar to Foucault's analysis of the manual of arms, *Teaching America about Sex* will delimit the correct use of the body in sex. Ironically, the manual of arms corresponds somewhat to marriage/sex manuals. The texts under consideration construct an approved ideology of sex, which becomes enforced as normal. The aim of this discipline is to exercise power over a population, and the medical profession along with psychiatrists largely enforce it. Some specialized institutions such as reform schools can also be involved.

Marriage/sex manuals, in this sense, provide an example of the penetration of disciplinary power into the most intimate details of life. Power constructs the gender binary and stigmatizes difference. In marking certain activities as approved, the advice literature makes the intimate visible and subjects private activities to scrutiny and classification. These norms become inscribed in consciousness and largely self-enforcing. Thus, as Foucault notes, the perfection of power makes its actual use unnecessary. Dr. Ruth's celebrity status suggests that the power of the medical profession over intimate matters might be eclipsed by other professionals/masters.

Teaching America about Sex also examines the linkages between sex, reproduction, and marriage. Like D'Emilio and Freedman in *Intimate Matters*, the text charts the evolution of this trinity from the 1880s to the present. *Intimate Matters* deals mostly with sexual behavior and its historical context; it does not focus much on the advice literature. D'Emilio and Freedman do suggest, however, that the advice literature varies with the times. *Teaching America about Sex* will deal with the extent of this variation. What changes and what remains? What fundamental premises inform these works and how do they change over time? *Teaching America about Sex* begins with the assumption that America experienced two sexual revolutions in the twentieth century, which dramatically transformed behavior. The text, then, seeks to chart these revolutions through the marital/sexual advice literature. The advice literature, we surmise, should correlate with the major findings of D'Emilio and Freedman's historical study. Over time, the literature should advocate less sexual repression, endorse birth control, especially with the advent of the birth control pill in 1960, and eventually sanction sexual intercourse within relationships, not merely marriage. The advice literature's portrayal of lesbians and gay men serves as a barometer of change. D'Emilio and Freedman make the same assumption, but chart the changes historically. They focus on lesbian and gay organizations, their drive for legitimacy and consequent changes in social and political systems. As sexuality is divorced from reproduction, the advice literature should show greater acceptance of sexual diversity. Since lesbians and gay men transgress gender norms, lesbian and gay sex manuals potentially offer a glimpse of ungendered sex. *Teaching America about Sex* begins with late Victorian writers so as to measure the extent of the changes in America's sexual zeitgeist through the twentieth century.

As noted above, Gordon studied several decades of the literature and suggests that it tends to be conservative. *Teaching America about Sex* will test this finding over a much longer time span. Millions bought copies of these marriage/sex manuals, and they undoubtedly did influence behavior, as Weinberg and Hammersmith suggest. Following insights of Foucault, *Teaching America about Sex* seeks to discern the disciplinary nature of the evolving sexual regime. As the advice literature makes the private public and the intimate visible, it allows the authors to construct socially sanctioned identities. Even the explicit sex manuals of Reuben and Comfort construct masculine and feminine identity within the context of their erotic engineering. *Teaching America about Sex* seeks to discern the norms that all these authors load into consciousness as if loading an operating system onto a computer. Like an operating system, norms make everything else work and generally run in the background. Just as computer crashes make one well aware of the operating system, *Teaching America about Sex* assumes that sexual revolutions call constructed identities and sanctioned behaviors into consciousness and thus allow the possibility of change and even rebellion.

The work of several feminist authors leads us to more complex issues. Judith Butler, an academic gender theorist, persuasively argues in *Gender Trouble* (1990) that gender consists of a performance, an act in some ways.[4] In the long gender play called life, everyone has a part, even though there are only two approved roles. Susan Brownmiller, a journalist and well-known feminist author, analyzes the accepted role for women in *Femininity* (1984). As Brownmiller sees it, femininity ultimately consists of niceness and deference. It means subordination to patriarchal power in myriad ways—from hair and makeup to nonfunctional clothing, walking, and emotion. The Victorian corset is a classic example. Brownmiller's earlier work, *Against Our Will* (1976), adds a profound level of complexity to her later articulation of the feminine. Based on her exhaustive study of sexual assault, she suggests that America has come to eroticize masculine dominance. In its common form this manifests itself in the belief that men must initiate and take the active role in sex, and it marks much ordinary discourse about female sexuality. At the extreme, this power manifests itself in sexual assault, primarily an act of brute force that is expressed sexually. Gang rapes, as Brownmiller demonstrates, are as much about male bonding and displays of potency/power as sex.

Lenore Walker, a professor of psychology and a national advocate for battered women, argues in her definitive works *The Battered Woman* (1979) and *Terrifying Love* (1989) that eroticized masculine power can reach toward further extremes enacted in battering and even murder. Some women, she argues, who need to kill in self-defense are hindered by "learned helplessness." Though "learned helplessness" is a psychological condition, it corresponds somewhat to Brownmiller's concept of the feminine. Alice Walker and Pratibha Parmar in *Warrior Marks* (1993) deal with female genital mutilation, a common practice in some cultures; this marks the extreme case of attempts to control women's sexuality. Little of this would surprise Catharine MacKinnon, a professor of law and feminist theorist who suggests that the pattern Brownmiller discerns is rooted in many male arousal systems. In *Toward a Feminist Theory of the State,* arousal itself is an expression of power: "Force is the desire dynamic, not just a response to the desired object when desire's expression is frustrated" (1989, 136). Naomi Wolf's more recent update of Brownmiller's *Femininity* supports both Brownmiller's and MacKinnon's theoretical observations. In *The Beauty Myth* (1991), Wolf reports a 1986 survey showing that 30 percent of college men would commit rape if they could escape any punishment. When the question was reworded to say, would you "force a woman into having sex," 58 percent said yes. In a different survey of 114 undergraduate men, over 80 percent reported that they liked to dominate women, considered conquest part of sex, and thought some women asked to get raped (1991, 165).[5] Though Wolf includes an important chapter on sex, her primary focus lies elsewhere. Her basic concern is the plasticity of the female body and how cosmetic surgery and constant dieting, among other things, trap women in a destructive beauty myth. The ideal, as Wolf sees it, can never be achieved, and for many women can result in the horrors of anorexia and bulimia.

Taking gender as performance, *Teaching America about Sex* interrogates the marital/sexual advice literature to discern the script and how it relates to intimate behavior. To achieve this end, the chapters will address many of the same issues. Each chapter, for example, will discuss the constructions of masculinity and femininity and compare them to traditional models. *Teaching America about Sex* seeks to discern whether masculinity is defined primarily in terms of power and dominance. If the authors understand masculinity this way, we seek to uncover the corresponding view that sex consists of an act of conquest. If the literature changes, when does this happen? The chapters will also inquire into the authors' treatment of male arousal. Is it charged by dominance, power, actual violence (even if "playful"), or related fantasies? Each chapter will directly address female pleasure and its centrality to intimate matters. If early authors consider female pleasure secondary to maternity, when does the literature change? This, of course, necessitates a discussion of birth control in all the chapters. Following D'Emilio and Freedman, *Teaching America about Sex* assumes that acceptance of birth control leads to an emphasis on sex as an expression of love between partners and an endorsement of pleasure as central to the event. Each chapter will explicate how the authors define the central elements of marriage. The text also assumes that the advice literature changes after the 1960s sexual revolution to endorse sex outside marriage. Does the literature endorse "casual" sex or restrict sex to long-term relationships? Feminist theorists like Butler typically distinguish between the penis, an organ, and the phallus, which is embedded in a social structure called patriarchy. In a later work, *Bodies That Matter* (1993), Butler discusses the phallus almost as if it were a Platonic form. Men participate in the phallus by possessing a penis, but no particular penis fully embodies the form. Ordinary male discourse in its discussion of endowment may actually represent a claim to greater participation in the phallus. In ordinary discourse the penis is also considered the basis of manhood, which means that participation in the phallus lies at the core of male identity. Each chapter will search for the phallus disguised in discussions of the penis.

The text is organized by decade and then author, even though the works of any one writer might span several decades. This corresponds to the organization of the other commentators and allows for direct comparison to the work of Gordon and Weinberg and Hammersmith. This approach also corresponds to D'Emilio and Freedman's *Intimate Matters* and facilitates the consideration of historical and cultural factors. Authors whose works span decades include Theodore Van de Velde, Hannah Stone and Abraham Stone, Alex Comfort, and Dr. Ruth. To understand the contending or comparable views across decades, one can read several nonconsecutive chapters together. Chapter 4 deals with the second edition of Van de Velde's *Ideal Marriage*, published in 1965, and can be read in conjunction with Reuben's works in 1969 and 1971, which are dealt with in chapter 6. Chapter 7 discusses the last volume in the *Joy of Sex* series, published in 1991, and can be read alongside Dr. Ruth's *Sex for Dummies*, discussed in chapter 9.

Some authors write in a question-and-answer format, while others employ case histories. Some authors use both techniques. The question-and-answer format allows speedy access to particular items of interest while breaking up the monotony of long chapters. Case histories supply a note of realism to what can seem abstract points. Reuben's *Everything You Always Wanted to Know about Sex* presents a long series of questions and answers in which the reader, presumably, is asking the questions. Dr. Ruth got her start with a radio program where she answered questions from listeners in New York City. Since these authors invite dialogue, we have interrogated some of them in a question-and-answer format and pose questions that arise from their works. The answers, of course, are ours, but reflect the particular author's point of view.

Teaching America about Sex adopts language suitable for the text under discussion. With the late Victorians, for example, our diction remains indirect and circumspect. For Van de Velde we continue with circumspect language ("acme" for "orgasm," for example), along with an emphasis on physiology. Reuben invites franker, if not ironic, discourse. We deal with Comfort's salty and sassy language by quoting him frequently. In adopting the literary voice of these authors, we seek to convey the spirit of the work under discussion as well as its point of view. We refer to lesbians and gay men mainly in the terms employed by the authors. In early works, if there are any references at all, authors typically use the term "homosexual" or "invert." When we discuss works written after the Stonewall rebellion in 1969, discussed in chapter 8, we try to use the term "gay" for both women and men. Later, the appropriate designation becomes "lesbians and gay men." To make this book more readily accessible to general readers, the intended audience for almost all these marriage/sex manuals, we have kept the scholarly apparatus to a minimum and placed citations at the end of paragraphs or sometimes sections.

Chapter 1 opens with an analysis of Henry Hanchett's *Sexual Health*. Hanchett, a medical doctor, represents a moderate voice among Victorians. Unlike some of his colleagues, he writes that women do experience sexual desires, though to a much lesser extent than men. Like all the late Victorians he sees masturbation as an evil, but he does not obsessively focus on it or generalize from individuals to the nation. Like his colleagues, Hanchett conflates theology, natural philosophy and medicine. His Christian worldview predominates, much as it will in the work of his colleagues. Counterbalancing Hanchett is John Harvey Kellogg's *Plain Facts for Old and Young*. Kellogg, another medical doctor, seeks to change the tone of marital advice literature by divorcing sexuality from sensuality. In Kellogg's view reproduction is part of God's plan for humankind and provides a way to share in the divine power of creation. Human nature, however, is prone to evil, and this is especially the case in sex. Since women have little, if any, sexual desire, his admonitions are directed mainly toward men. Kellogg, following traditional teachings, even regards mental unchastity as a sin. Nature punishes sin by visiting illness upon individuals. In Kellogg's understanding, semen serves as an élan vital and must be preserved. Due to this he calls for continence in marriage and suggests that intercourse take place monthly. Though women do not really experience sexual desire, they engage in intercourse as a marital obligation and to fulfill their maternal destiny. Just as sinners get ill, so do nations. Thus Kellogg's admonitions serve not only to redeem individuals from corruption but also to save nations from ruin.

Henry Guernsey's *Plain Talks on Avoided Subjects* is mainly congruent with Kellogg's work. Humankind has both a spiritual and animal nature, and the task of life consists of living in harmony with one's higher nature. As in Kellogg's work, moral evil manifests itself in physical maladies and can even be discerned in a person's countenance or gait. Intercourse exists solely for the purpose of reproduction, and semen must be preserved. Guernsey's discussion suggests a bank account metaphor, but this particular bank does not accept deposits; withdrawals cannot be replaced. Guernsey praises the feminine mental state, characterized by subordination. He believes that women, if properly educated, lack amorous feelings or any sexual propensities. Women must sacrifice their feelings upon marriage and bow to the laws of God and nature. Both Kellogg and Guernsey believe that desirable characteristics can be transmitted to the next generation; thus they share a view of potential human perfectibility. Their shared view of sin, however, prevents them from postulating a perfected race.

[Pseudo] Aristotle's *Masterpiece* provides a different understanding of sexuality, especially with its emphasis on orgasm. This text illustrates the role of folk wisdom divorced from canonical texts as well as the fact that conceptions of sexuality can be (somewhat) contending. The folk wisdom of the *Masterpiece* does not reappear in the canonical literature until the 1920s.

Chapter 2 focuses on Margaret Sanger, a central figure in the evolution of America's sexual zeitgeist. Sanger gave the birth control secret to less privileged classes and thus had a major and enduring impact on the relationship between sex, reproduction, and marriage. She stands at the forefront of those demanding sexual pleasure for women, which in her terms meant the end of sexual servitude. She almost reached a radical feminist viewpoint, and certainly broke with the class-based analyses of the socialists of the period. Sanger, like the late Victorians, also sought to remake the world. She shares their belief that human improvements will lead to a new morality and spirituality. Though she never gets very specific on how this will happen, she postulates that liberated women will somehow create a new age.

Sanger not only spilled the secret, but also facilitated the funding for research for the birth control pill. Thus, from her early days of smuggling diaphragms to her work in the 1960s, her life spans a period of sexual change in America. As the linkage between sex, reproduction, and marriage became strained over time, Sanger was always ready with one device or another as well as funding for new research. Her powerful argument that marriage is about relationships as much as having children has had an enduring influence. In her view, sex is as much about rapture as pregnancy. Sanger quite consciously seeks to turn the celebration of eros into a new religion, and Alex Comfort in the *Joy of Sex* series accomplishes this with his understanding of sex as a peak experience. Sanger, in other words, is a prophet both in her proto-feminist insights and in her role in the evolution of the zeitgeist.

Sanger, of course, caused controversy in her day and is still vilified in some circles. Even her most sympathetic biographer, Ellen Chesler, accuses her of inconsistency. Sanger, however, certainly wrote under the effects of persecution, and her works must be read accordingly. She often lapses into silence, especially on the issue of eugenics. She never manages to get around to defining the difference between fit and unfit. Though she continued to use eugenic rhetoric till the end of her life, her overall aim was to co-opt the movement and bend it to her own purposes. In her personal life, Sanger's demand for open relationships as well as sexual pleasure prefigures the sexual eruption of the 1960s.

The Great War—really the great slaughter—as well as the new psychology propounded by Freud and Ellis, among others, shattered old ideals among the elite. Chapter 3 addresses these issues. The avant garde in New York City came to celebrate Negritude, that is, blackness as an embodiment of the primitive. Family size among the privileged declined, while it remained high for laboring classes. Lower-class dating patterns spread throughout the culture. All of this combined with the essential engine of a capitalist system produced, as D'Emilio and Freeman put it, an economy of pleasure and gratification.

In 1926 Joseph Collins, a psychiatrist, published *The Doctor Looks at Love and Life*. Collins views procreation within marriage as the norm, but he rejects religious justifications in favor of scientific ones. In general he favors less sexual repression and accepts social Darwinism. Unlike his predecessors, Collins does not bewail a birth crisis, but merely teaches that societies experience a succession of ruling stocks. Collins argues for women's equality and emphasizes that gender reflects what is today termed a social construction. His text is most curious not for its emphasis on gender equality, but rather its vision of the elimination of homosexuals. Collins promises that psychiatry can protect society from inverts and launches a war against lesbians and gay men that continues in David Reuben's *Everything You Always Wanted to Know about Sex* in 1969.

Marriage in the Modern Manner, by Ira Wile and Mary Day Winn, offers companionate relationships that dwell on aesthetic and spiritual realities. Progressive in some ways, the text advocates teaching sex education in the public schools and frankly acknowledges that the American norm has become plural, consecutive marriages.

What Is Right with Marriage, by Robert Binkley and Frances Binkley, attempts to create a science of marriage, while Ernest R. Groves in *The Marriage Crisis* directly confronts the problem of divorce at the time. The masses, as Groves sees it, have come to understand intercourse primarily as a pleasurable thing, due to the availability of birth control. This time of social ferment witnesses a pattern that is repeated later in the century. When sexual norms are challenged, some authors take pen in hand to defend marriage. Some attempt to modify the institution to better suit the times, while others search for a new foundation for it. This "defense of marriage literature" defines the various times in this century that sexual mores have changed or have been perceived to change so as to threaten marriage itself. The defense literature represents a reaction to challenges to the reproductive trinity.

Chapter 4 opens with a consideration of Theodore Van de Velde's *Ideal Marriage*. He insists that husbands satisfy their wives, and he supplies graphs to explain the different arousal systems of men and women. His exhaustive table of contents foreshadows the menu approach later adopted by Alex Comfort. Unlike Comfort, however, Van de Velde remains circumspect in his language even when he legitimizes sexual activities previously reserved for bordellos. Van de Velde, a gynecologist and a married man, wrote *Ideal Marriage* in exile from the Netherlands, since he absconded with one of his married patients (Porter and Hall 1995, 214, 278).

Ideal Marriage is not only a marriage manual, it is also an example of the defense of marriage literature. Van de Velde, perhaps for the last time, unifies medical science, reason, and theology to support reproductive sexuality. He is clearly aware that orgasms are mainly clitoral, so he valorizes penetrative intercourse on grounds other than pleasure. Women, it turns out, need sperm. This late Victorian idea permeates his work, and even survives, though in a truncated form, in the revision of *Ideal Marriage* in 1965. Women need this élan vital, and the initial jet of sperm against the vaginal wall can trigger orgasm. All of *Ideal Marriage* presents an argument against birth control. We glimpse the traditional gender norms that pervade the work when he notes that in the supreme moment men experience power while women feel tenderness. His *Sexual Tensions in Marriage*, published in 1931, explicates the implicit gender norms that inform *Ideal Marriage*. This work acknowledges the existence of homosexuals, but proves less hostile than Collins. Overall, Van de Velde defends the gender binary with a passing acknowledgment of bisexuality. In this volume, Van de Velde argues that nature designed things the way they are, and without any suggestion of irony he notes that nature does, indeed, have a double standard. In *Fertility and Sterility in Marriage*, also published in 1931, Van de Velde recants. Though he changes his views on birth control and religion, he remains blind to his own misogyny. Women still need motherhood.

Insofar as Van de Velde demands that husbands provide pleasure for their wives and legitimizes a variety of new pleasures, *Ideal Marriage* appears somewhat progressive. Overall, however, the text has more in common with the late Victorian literature than it does with modern works like *The Joy of Sex*. Van de Velde retains a belief in the spermatic political economy, and insofar as his first volume received the most attention, he rejects birth control. Thus he retains the linkage between sex, reproduction, and marriage.

Chapter 5 deals with sex and pleasure as conceptualized by marriage manual writers in the 1950s. During World War II social roles had loosened. Women went out to work in record numbers to help the war effort. Sexual behaviors, too, became freer as large numbers of young men and women found themselves far from the regulating eyes of parents. With the end of World War II, relaxed standards were replaced with more traditional approaches to life. This included a clear reinstatement of gender roles for men and women, strongly reinforced by TV sitcoms such as *Father Knows Best* and *The Donna Reed Show*. These rigid gender roles extended to sexual behavior.

One of the most popular marriage manuals of the era was Hannah Stone and Abraham Stone's *Marriage Manual: A Practical Guidebook to Sex and Marriage*. Written in a question-and-answer format, it was far less explicit about technique than Van de Velde's book. The popularity of a book with so little actual instruction is, perhaps, not surprising in an era when every married couple on TV slept in twin beds. Birth control information is promised early on in the text, although as in the case of sexual technique, little actual information is forthcoming. Since every normal couple will want children, birth control is for planning and spacing children, not preventing conception. Sex should be mutually satisfying and confined to the marriage bed.

Eustace Chesser's *Love without Fear* does not stray very far from the Stones' example, although at first glance it might seem to. Granting women some equality, at least in the workplace, Chesser then decrees that the double standard may be unfair, but violating it for women is a disaster. He believes that sex for women is part of a chain of events including wooing, courtship, the sex act, conception, pregnancy, childbirth, lactation, and maternity. Sex for men, on the other hand, may be a "mere incident." He not only implicitly condemns birth control as interrupting the natural chain of events for women, but he also reinforces the double standard. Yet Chesser's work also looks forward to the coming revolution of the 1960s, albeit obliquely. His notion that couples should take a vacation together before marriage to ensure sexual compatibility both shocked 1950s sensibilities and suggests that birth control is needed after all. His confusion over women's sexuality is characteristic of other work of the 1950s. He regards women as having a pent-up sexuality that, if unleashed, can be truly frightening.

Chapter 6 deals with America's second sexual revolution of the century. The media made much of San Francisco's Summer of Love in 1967. Unlike the sexual exuberance of the 1920s, this challenge to the sexual regime was amplified throughout the country by the media, and the pill made sexual freedom seem possible in new ways. Sex without the burden of marriage or the responsibility of children seemed possible. *Playboy* undressed the wraps of the old norms and at the same time purveyed consumerism linked to good sex. Not to be outdone, Helen Gurley Brown in *Sex and the Single Girl* slashed and burned old notions of femininity. She applied the new norms to women and suggested that they too join the party. Other cultural and political events also undermined traditional authority structures.

The civil rights movement along with the antiwar movement brought many younger men and women to see the government as repressive. A few called for revolution, many others advocated change, even radical change but by nonviolent means. In all of this, the sexual mores as handed down from the 1950s appeared as part of a repressive, if not murderous, system of social control. Rebellion against an unjust war and racist institutions came to be associated with a lifestyle of drug use and free love. Women, having had their consciousness raised in the antiwar movement, began to organize. Critiques of patriarchy and gender norms began to circulate and led to the formation of liberal and radical activist groups, the National Organization for Women as well as Redstockings. All of this combined with the first gay riot at the Stonewall Inn in New York City seemed to portend radical changes in sexual mores. Curiously, David Reuben, a major writer in this period, does not celebrate this sexual revolution. In most ways his texts reinforce traditional norms.

In 1969 Reuben published *Everything You Always Wanted to Know about Sex, but Were Afraid to Ask*. Reuben, like Van de Velde, acknowledges multiple purposes to sex. It can be for reproduction, love, or even fun. He does not, however, emphasize the latter choice, and the tenor of his work asserts that sex as a recreational activity is a bad option for women. Reuben valorizes vaginal intercourse as a transcendent experience. Instinct, according to Reuben, demands vaginal penetration, and it also provides for emotional involvement. Everything else he stigmatizes as perversion. Reuben notes side effects of the pill and gives it limited acceptance.

Reuben's *Any Woman Can* more fully delineates his traditional agenda. Much like Van de Velde, Reuben argues that reproduction is a basic instinctual drive in women. Orgasms focused in the clitoris satisfy pleasure needs, while those resulting from penetration gratify the maternal instinct. Sex, as far as Reuben is concerned, should be restricted to marriage. In fact, premarital sex removes a powerful incentive that supports the institution. Reuben continues psychiatry's assault on homosexuals. Condemned to misery, they search for what they cannot have. His work is homophobic and derisive, and hurls accusations as medical fact that will preoccupy the authors of the various editions of *The Joy of Gay Sex*.

Chapter 7 focuses on Alex Comfort's effort to carry through on the logic of effective birth control. In Comfort's works reproductive sexuality and its linkage with marriage get tossed aside for a heady hedonism. Published in 1972, *The Joy of Sex* espouses carefree sex. Reflecting the general exuberance of the 1960s, Comfort postulates that "there are no rules." This obviously includes the norm that authors use indirect references and even Latin. In this world of carefree sex, Comfort envisions sex as a play activity, and a therapeutic one at that. Unlike Reuben, who first published in the 1960s, Comfort embraces promiscuity. Comfort explicitly endorses relationships, but he notes that they can last fifty years or merely fifteen minutes. Fidelity, in this formulation, remains merely one option to be worked out with one's partner.

Though Comfort celebrates the sexual revolution and implicitly sets himself up as its prophet, he continues the tradition's assertion of phallic privilege. Though sperm no longer serves as an élan vital, Comfort considers the penis a dominance signal and the root of a man's self-esteem and identity. It even has a personality all its own. The vulva, on the other hand, causes anxiety in males. Thus dominance and power remain firmly linked, and sex becomes playful violence, which, of course, is therapeutic.

Since Comfort celebrates the uncoupling of sex, reproduction, and marriage, he is more sympathetic to lesbians and gay men. Yet his toleration proves limited. Lesbian and gay sex violates one of his few norms because it limits one's scope to same-sex partners. Bisexuals, really accepted for the first time in this volume, can become "stuck." The imprecision of these concepts allows for Comfort's endorsement of heterosexual relationships and deep vaginal penetration.

In *More Joy*, published in the same heady time, Comfort hears the death knell of marriage off in the distance. In this volume Comfort elaborates on his valuation of deep vaginal penetration. Men, as he puts it, experience penetration as violence, and the biological nature of gender demands it. Elaborating on his fascination with violence, Comfort turns hostility into love. But even Comfort acknowledges that the sexual revolution is over in *The New Joy of Sex* in 1991. AIDS (acquired immune deficiency syndrome) ruined the party, and by implication might even save marriage. New sex toys, much more role playing, saucy language, and titillating illustrations set his work apart. Comfort, however, does not challenge the prevailing gender norms, though radical feminists offered handy critiques at the time.

None of the gay sex manuals discussed in chapter 8 offer any real alternative to Comfort's fundamental views. *The Joy of Gay Sex*, published in 1977, proclaims a more explicit political agenda than *The Joy of Sex*. In *The Joy of Gay Sex*, Charles Silverstein and Edmund White must deal with a disempowered group that first awakened on a large scale after the Stonewall rebellion in 1969. Hence the authors promote coming out as a necessary act to validate the self, assert identity, and enlist as (what Dr. Ruth will later call), "soldiers in the gay army." The text implicitly gives testimony to the havoc caused by psychiatrists like Collins and Reuben and the medical model of homosexuality that they espoused. Silverstein and White reject this model and celebrate with a great deal of exuberance the new gay identity. This new identity, as the text makes clear, revolves around libidinal pleasures. Like Comfort, Silverstein and White emphasize role playing and suggest that some gay men do not think in terms of dominance and submission. Despite this and other disclaimers, they mainly substitute a new nomenclature for the traditional gender/power distinctions. Top/bottom replaces the older male/female dyad with its corollary of powerful/powerless. The *New Joy of Gay Sex*, published in 1992, downplays the political content of the first edition and, reflecting tragically changed times, takes AIDS into consideration. Thus in the new edition Silverstein and Felice Picano deal with insurance issues and living wills. On the whole, the revised edition proves consistent in its core teaching with the earlier one. Silverstein and Picano's discussion of rape makes this clear. They distinguish rape not as an act of force or power, but as one that lacks consent. In other words, force and power inhere in sex and are ultimately reflected in deep penetration. Like Silverstein and White they do emphasize role playing, but the core of their approach focuses on penetrative sexuality as an act of power and conquest. Both editions distinguish gayness mainly as a matter of orifices to be penetrated. Gayness is defined as the same-sex object choice, which reinforces the binary as well as traditional gender distinctions. Early declarations of the Gay Liberation Front promised otherwise, but this was not to be the case. Sexual orientation proved a weaker bond than gender.

With some glee, both editions celebrate the uncoupling of the reproductive matrix. Like Comfort they delight in sex as a means of pleasure as well as a means of building and maintaining a relationship for those who choose such a commitment. Sex, whether in a bedroom or a back room, for eight hours or ten minutes, is a value in itself. In this both editions agree with Comfort and like the *Joy of Sex* series break with their predecessors. Pleasure, if not lust, becomes the norm.

The Joy of Lesbian Sex takes a different tack. While Emily Sisley and Bertha Harris also celebrate sex for pleasure, they reject both the power/dominance theme and the necessity of penetration. Relationships of all types are based on negotiations rather than dominance and submission. Like the earlier *Joy of Gay Sex*, this volume encourages multiple sexual relationships, but with an important qualification. Sisley and Harris assume that lesbians are likely to have one primary relationship. They further assume that at least one partner will occasionally have sex outside this primary relationship. They regard this as perfectly fine and possibly even enriching as long as one is honest about it. There is also a political subtext. While Sisley and Harris devote a great deal of time to the issues of coming out, lesbian motherhood (they dimly approve), and consciousness raising, the majority of the book provides a celebration of sexual pleasure divorced from its reproductive aspects. Female sexuality is finally unleashed. Desire is not only a given, it is a constant.

Published just seven years later in 1984, *Lesbian Sex* presents an entirely different view. Sex is no longer the main issue, and readers are encouraged to give up the tyranny of orgasms. Because JoAnn Loulan is writing a self-help book, she primarily addresses problems. As a problem-solving book it is useful, although it gives a grim picture of lesbian life, particularly lesbian sexual life. *Lesbian Sex* insists on expansion of the definition of lesbianism to include more than just choice of sexual partner.

Chapter 9 deals with the sexual counterrevolution following the cultural upheaval in the 1960s. As her views evolve over the years, Dr. Ruth becomes an exemplar of the reassertion of traditional norms. In *Good Sex*, an early work published in 1983, she remains largely within the orbit of the *Joy of Sex* series. In this work, she does, however, endorse consensual, non–disease-transmitting sex. She qualifies this by noting that relationships make sex qualitatively better. Two years later in *First Love*, Dr. Ruth emphasizes the importance of relationships. As she notes, sex remains part of love and marriage. Her *Guide for Married Lovers*, published in 1986, belongs to the defense of marriage literature. She makes tolerably clear that sex should occur within a marriage relationship. Dr. Ruth notes that most orgasms are clitoral and that the majority of women do not experience them in vaginal intercourse. Unlike some of her predecessors who extol the joys of orgasm, Dr. Ruth suggests substitutes such as gifts of jewelry. In 1992 her *Guide to Safer Sex* picks up the theme that in the age of AIDS and herpes, penetration is not the only goal of sexual intimacy.

Sex for Dummies, published in 1995, brings many of her earlier themes together and presents her most developed view of sexual intimacy. Sex exists for the purpose of reproduction, while pleasure serves as an inducement, not the purpose of the act. This position accounts for her equivocal views regarding lesbians and gay men. They do not reproduce; thus their sexual expression must be frustrated in its fundamental goal. AIDS and other sexually transmitted diseases ended the sexual revolution, and Dr. Ruth continually notes that condoms do break. Unlike the more permissive *Good Sex*, she hesitantly approves one-night stands, provided that they occur only once or twice in a lifetime, and she emphasizes the medical dangers of such liaisons. This work also forms part of the defense of marriage literature.

With her radio show Dr. Ruth brought the marital/sexual advice genre before a new, larger audience. She also undoubtedly helped many individuals and couples. Radio shows that offer marital/sexual advice have become more common over the years, and television now offers its own variants. Dr. Ruth pioneered all of this as she sought to educate the public about good sex.

1

The Late Victorians and the Spermatic Political Economy

As the nineteenth century progressed, America underwent profound social changes. Urbanization went hand in hand with industrialization as well as increased social mobility. In urban centers sons and some daughters could find employment and lodging outside the family sphere, and parental authority was eroded. Cities like New York had rentable furnished rooms along with services like cafeterias for single men and women. Clusters of unmarried men and women could be found in the Bowery and Times Square areas, among other places. Social isolation in burgeoning cities also lessened the traditional moral authority of churches. The shame that grounded their moral power depended on people living in small communities where moral transgressions would be known and pressure brought to bear on recalcitrant individuals or couples. Governments, as D'Emilio and Freedman note, had less interest in enforcing family and sexual mores and turned instead to property issues.

Men and women as well as doctors and health reformers wrote tracts filled with marital and sexual advice. Some writers focused on the importance of sexual intimacy for building relationships and attaining spiritual transcendence. Health reformers emphasized fears of venereal diseases and even cholera, which swept through New York City several times in this period with devastating effects. The emphasis on being master of one's domain resonated with men seeking their fortunes through thrift, industry, and self-improvement. Sexual self-control seemed merely one more discipline along the way to success. Dr. John Cowan, for example, explicitly linked self-control with success in commerce: "for the doing of this not only enables him to lead a continent life, but it as surely guides to success in all business undertakings." Many writers believed in a spermatic political economy, focused on the retention and spending of sperm, which led them to decry the horrors of masturbation, since it depleted male energy that could be better utilized in commerce. Masturbation preoccupied many writers: John Harvey Kellogg, for example, urged marital continence. But some writers, like Henry Hanchett, did not apply the concern over the loss of vital fluid to marital relations.

Late Victorian writers urged men to direct their sexual desires toward procreation within the marital relationship. They stressed that sexual congress constituted a spiritual bond between husband and wife and (in procreation) between God and man. Some authors thought that women experienced no sexual desire, while others taught that they merely had much less than men. All the advice literature emphasized controlling desire and managing sex. In the same period, the middle class discovered romantic love, which quickly became a reason to wed and produced a renewed emphasis on intimacy as the basis of marriage (D'Emilio and Freedman 1988, 66–73; Chauncey 1994, 78, 136, 158).

Health and Sex

Henry Hanchett, a medical doctor, published *Sexual Health: A Plain and Practical Guide for the People on All Matters Concerning the Organs of Reproduction in Both Sexes and All Ages* in 1887. A popular book, *Sexual Health* went through three editions. The elaborate subtitle indicates that Hanchett intended the work for a general audience, both women and men. In a comment typical for authors in this genre, he states that he will not apologize for dealing in plain terms with "delicate subjects." Decades later Theodore Van de Velde, another medical doctor, will express similar sentiments. By the 1970s, as the marital advice literature evolves into much more explicit sex manuals, medical doctors like Alex Comfort will no longer apologize or express reticence. In his preface Hanchett suggests that ignorance leads to vice, which in turn can cause disease. By implication, *Sexual Health* will lessen ignorance and, hence, disease. Parents, as many authors of the advice literature note, neglect to instruct their children in "delicate subjects." In a remark that suggests that Hanchett views women as temptresses, he states, "Young ladies do not know that by exposing their persons in evening dress and allowing intimacies and even receiving caresses from young gentlemen, they often awaken passions in the latter which sends them to brothels for gratification." In keeping with the need to restrain male desire, he adds that circumcision is necessary to prevent constant irritation of the glans, which can ignite animal passions. Hanchett quotes Emerson on the strength of such animal passions. For the sake of preservation, nature "immensely overloaded passion at the risk of perpetual crime and disorder." He then cites St. Paul to the effect that God ensures that men can triumph over temptation. As Hanchett sees things, education about disease, sin, and shame juxtaposed with consecration, self-denial, righteousness, and honor can provide a check on animal passions (Hanchett 1887, 4–5).

Hanchett addresses male sexuality first and suggests that a boy's erotic life begins long before puberty. In terms of sex education, he advises parents that the early years are the most important ones. Circumcision prevents dangerous stimulation and provides for cleanliness. Though Hanchett does not dwell on the evils of masturbation to the same extent as some of his medical colleagues, he does add that it can lead to "nervous disorders," bed wetting, stammering, headache, and epilepsy. To avoid all this, parents should keep their boys physically active with a multitude of playmates. Keeping boys exhausted makes it less likely that "morbid tendencies" will ensnare them (9, 11, 13).

When a boy reaches puberty he should be taught that "nature has determined that the species shall be preserved at any cost" and reminded of the insidious dangers of masturbation. The sexual organs have only one use in light of nature's purpose. Both nature and revelation teach that marriage remains the proper state for intimate activities. Pleasure, according to Hanchett, cannot be divorced from duty, though many temptation await. "The grade of his manhood is established by the amount he can overcome, and that his value in the world depends much on the question as to whether he will rule his body, or his body him." Unlike some of his colleagues, Hanchett does not regard the occasional loss of vital fluid as a serious medical problem. To forestall masturbation, one should follow a diet rich in grains and vegetables and take meat in moderation. Gymnastic exercise helps, as do a hard bed and a cool bedroom. Cold sponge baths every day before breakfast or bed also help. Overall, "the more completely the . . . [genitalia] are left alone the better." Intimate behavior "exhausts vitality" rapidly, so young men must be warned not only about masturbation, but also about prostitution, which is degrading and results in disease almost all the time. Prostitution also strikes at the family, which is the core institution of society (15–21).

Hanchett, as is typical of the time, views intimate matters within a theological and philosophical context as well as a medical one. Scientific medicine had yet to take charge of the profession. Hanchett believes that nature intends man to govern and master his animal impulses in light of his higher obligations to society and posterity. In this context, he takes a hydraulic approach to male sexuality. The buildup of seminal fluid influences the mind. As pressure increases, men will desire sex. If no other relief is available, the energizing fluid will be discharged during sleep. If this occurs, on an occasional basis it poses no problem to either morals or health. If a man ignores the erotic tensions caused by the accumulation of vital fluid, his body will produce less of it over time. Hanchett reserves normal discharge for the "only right, natural, and healthful course . . . of marriage," and in this state women get raised to the "lofty pinnacle of motherhood" (22–24).

Hanchett goes on to attack prudery within the marriage relationship. "Any attempt . . . to deny to . . . [the sexual organs] their full dignity and activity, can only result in local excitement but little better than masturbation, save that it can result in offspring of a puny, bloodless, half-vital sort." On the other hand, discharge outside the confines of marriage causes "moral poison" and probably disease as well. Such forbidden activity with prostitutes

> involves the soul-consuming excitements of law-breaking, of skulking from discovery, and of spasmodic, irregular, and inordinate sexual activity; costs health, strength, wealth, self-respect, and virtue; sacrifices purity and the restraining and purifying power of a true valuation of womanhood; exchanges liberty for the domination of a creature too vile to be called a woman; barters useful citizenship for the state of the criminal sapping the foundations of society by striking at marriage and the family.   (24)

Sex exhausts men, it saps their vitality. Semen is an "expensive" fluid for the body to produce and so spending decisions must be made carefully. Some of his colleagues, like Kellogg and Guernsey, will elaborate on the horrific fate of spendthrifts. Men do differ on how often they can drain this "nerve force." A long period of fatigue following intimacy indicates excess. Hanchett goes on to discuss diseases of the sexual organs, and he adopts a theory of innocent transmission, venereal *insontium*. Some nineteenth-century physicians believed that venereal diseases could be transmitted without any intimate contact at all. The usual culprits included public water fountains, towels, bedding, and eating utensils. This theory, of course, afforded privileged women who utilized doctors the status of innocent victims without any taint of sin or corruption or any suggestion that their husbands might be the source. As one woman put it,

> At first it was unbelievable. I knew of the disease only through newspaper advertisements [for patent medicines]. I had understood that it was the result of sin and that it originated and was contracted only in the underworld of the city. I felt sure that my friend was mistaken in diagnosis. When he exclaimed, "Another tragedy of the public drinking cup!" I eagerly met his remark with the assurance that I did not use public drinking cups, and I used my own cup for years. He led me to review my summer. After recalling a number of times when my thirst had forced me to go to the public fountain, I came at last to realize that what he had told me was true.

This woman lived in fear of discovery and was horrified by the thought that she could pass on the odious contagion. A meal with a friend could do it.

> Every day I expected to be accused of unspeakable things. . . . Even though I was not discovered I had perhaps a more dire possibility to face. Daily, hourly, momentarily I was haunted by the dread of passing on the disease to another. . . . Every act of my life was carefully weighed under the influence of that feverish fear. . . . I was strained, tense—afraid, afraid. Night and day, day and night I bore my burden of fear.

Hanchett goes on to describe treatments for these conditions and discuss venereal diseases as well as impotence and sterility as impediments to marriage for men (Hanchett 1887, 21, 25–34; Brandt 1985, 9, 21, 22 for the quotations; brackets in the original).

Unlike some of his colleagues, Hanchett believes that women can experience some sexual feelings. A girl's sexual life, like that of young boys, begins before puberty, and parents must be vigilant against nurses who will sometimes stimulate the genitalia to quiet a child. Though young girls can experience sexual feelings, they remain less likely to be "awakened" in them. This pattern holds throughout life; "distinctly sexual desires are, on the average, less imperious in the female than in the male." Hanchett notes that society, reasonably enough, is organized on the basis of this difference in arousal systems since women lack men's "mainspring" of passion. The hydraulic understanding, in other words, does not apply. Hanchett pities girls without any sexual feelings and considers this an abnormal condition. Parents should teach their daughters about delicacy, modesty, and the necessity of activity. They are not to touch their private parts except for washing. Though girls do masturbate, they do so less than boys, but they too can experience mental, moral, and physical disasters as a consequence (Hanchett 1887, 36–41).

Again Hanchett criticizes prudery. "It is no shame to have organs which can house and nurture a budding human life; it is no shame to study those organs and learn how they can best serve the new being that will be dependent upon them and their healthy condition." On the other hand, "it is a shame to consider those organs either nuisances, able to put unwelcome responsibilities upon us, or mere sources of animal gratification and pleasure." In puberty young women should check their ambition, work, or studies to deal with the body's new demands. Every month during her period, a girl gets a reminder that "she is responsible to posterity for her habits and daily behavior, and that the important relations of her sexual life to every other part of her being, show that she should never fail to consider whatever she does in the light of its possible influence upon her children." Hanchett also introduces the concept of vicarious menstruation: he believes that nature can discharge the egg by way of the nose, lungs, or some other route. Impediments to marriage for women include a lack of sexual organs, an unyielding hymen, and some diseases (41, 42, 44, 47).

Having discussed the sexual organs, Hanchett devotes his attention to marriage. He begins by asking what he considers a perennial question. Why do women marry? Hanchett notes that new possibilities in the professions and business complicate the issue. Some women, as he says, marry to achieve motherhood, which proves "the most exalted office open to humanity." Earlier in the text Hanchett linked biology with destiny. "Every part of her body and every facility of her mind is in subtle communication and sympathy with the organs in which sexual life centers." Marriage accords with divine intention, brings a woman glory, and satisfies feminine nature. On a more practical level, he adds that often a woman marries because some man has asked her (37, 41, 60).

Parents should teach girls to avoid the blunder of marrying for money and instruct them about the disgrace of divorce. Contrary to what many believe, romantic love as portrayed in novels does not provide a sound basis for marriage; what is crucial is "that devoted, pure, self-sacrificing love which the Master's command makes it the duty of each of His creatures and disciples to feel for all his fellows." The real basis of marriage, as Hanchett puts it, resides in the development of character. Marriage also includes parenthood, which "the all wise Father has seen fit to associate with this institution." Though God implanted the sexual instincts and they are honorable and beautiful in their proper use, these instincts do not merit the "sacred name of Love." The sexual instincts, however, prove necessary to drive men into marriage. Hanchett enjoins women to enjoy sexual relations and suggests intervals of three to four days (61–63, 65).

According to an often repeated story, an English novelist, Captain Frederick Marrayat, on a tour of America in 1837, reportedly saw piano legs covered by pants at an academy for young women (Lystra 1989, 56). Hanchett does not endorse such prudery. He teaches wives that the sex act is a duty to their husbands, but this particular obligation can provide pleasure for both of them. He recommends nakedness as well as "endearing caresses" during the act. He also endorses the American custom of sharing the same bed—unless restraint proves impossible. Hanchett does supply a practical basis for these recommendations. Women need to satisfy their husbands to keep them faithful as well as to engage the very forces that ensnared them into marriage in the first place. Women also need to stop thinking of the sex act as one marked by shame or disgrace (1887, 66).

Hanchett rejects what he terms the "avoidance of offspring." More than thirty years later Margaret Sanger will popularize the term "birth control" as a substitute for such awkward expressions. According to Hanchett, the only proper way to avoid children is to either remain single or live together as if single. Hanchett condemns interference with nature's design and condemns abortion as a "cowardly crime, if it be not actual murder" (70–71).

Hanchett reserves his highest praise for the chaste life defined by active charity, that is, working for the betterment of humankind. "This is undoubtedly the highest ideal and gives best promise of health, happiness, and usefulness." Not everyone can live up to this ideal. For these people—the majority actually—Hanchett teaches that marriage remains both natural and proper. Hanchett relies on 1 Corinthians, chapter 7 for his statement of the ideal. As St. Paul wrote,

> An unmarried man can devote himself to the Lord's affairs, all he need worry about is pleasing the Lord; but a married man has to bother about the world's affairs and devote himself to pleasing his wife: he is torn two ways. In the same way an unmarried woman, like a young girl, can devote herself to the Lord's affairs; all she need worry about is being holy in body and spirit. The married woman, on the other hand, has to worry about the world's affairs and devote herself to pleasing her husband.

Though Hanchett rejects prudery for the married, he explicitly proclaims chastity the ideal, and this ideal can be readily transformed into marital continence.

As is typical of this period, Hanchett roots his work in natural philosophy as well as theology. Adopting a standard approach drawn from ancient Greek philosophy, Hanchett postulates that humankind possesses both an animal nature, which he identifies with the sexual instinct, and a faculty of reason and will, which distinguishes homo sapiens. The latter faculty comes into play when women and men reject the evils of masturbation or live a chaste life in God's service. Though women in his view do experience some sexual desire, men feel much more of it as seminal fluid builds up in the system and ignites sexual desire. Sooner or later, release must be had. Masturbation—a form of release—can lead to various evils, but Hanchett views this mainly as a personal issue. Several of his colleagues, like Kellogg and Guernsey, will add a political dimension and argue that masturbation engages the fate of the nation. Like Kellogg and Guernsey, Hanchett views masturbation in terms of self-control, the need to be master of one's domain. Reflecting ancient Greek thought, Hanchett believes that reason should govern the body. Though Hanchett remains well aware that caresses, among other things, can ignite a man's passions, he sees this resulting only in visits to bawdy houses. Some of his colleagues who view these issues in political terms will see the fate of nations involved in caresses and thus will urge much more caution than Hanchett. When great issues are involved, prudery becomes prudence. In a common view that others will elaborate into a spermatic political economy, Hanchett notes that seminal fluid is costly for the body to produce. Rather than romantic love, Hanchett celebrates the self-sacrificing form, which draws its inspiration from scripture. Hanchett's references to St. Paul underline the Christian premises that inform his work. Hanchett does encourage women to be sexually responsive, which, of course, ensures their own pleasure. He also supplies a practical reason. As sexual fluids build up and men must have release, women can ensure the faithfulness of their husbands by engaging in sexual relations, not avoiding them.

Sexual Restraint and the Fate of Nations

John Harvey Kellogg, M.D., of breakfast cereal notoriety, first published *Plain Facts about Sexual Life* in 1877. A revised edition dropped the explicit reference to sex and was simply entitled *Plain Facts for Old and Young*. In *Plain Facts*, Kellogg explicates the natural laws regulating human sexuality as well as the penalties for their transgression. Like other late Victorians, he remains reluctant even to discuss the subject and writes in such a way as not to appeal to prurient interests. Even so, he calls for judicious circulation of his book. The "cordial reception" that greeted the original edition (about one hundred thousand copies were sold) required a new one with additional chapters written especially for boys and girls.

Kellogg laments that previous books functioned as parts of advertising schemes and were filled with "misrepresentations" and "falsehoods." Illustrations in these works aimed to stimulate "animal propensities" and had a corresponding "pernicious influence." Kellogg approaches the subject differently. Unlike previous authors, he will often divert the reader's attention with examples from the animal and plant kingdoms, an appeal (in his understanding) to innocence and loveliness. His goal is to discuss human sexuality divorced from its "sensuality." He even aims to bring this difficult subject before youth. He argues that children already have some sexual knowledge before puberty and that it is better to supply a proper understanding rather than let them get "distorted images" and "exaggerated conceptions" from "evil sources." On balance, he finds partial knowledge more dangerous than full knowledge. Kellogg advises parents to teach their children "just and religious views of the nature and purpose of the relation which the Creator has established between the two sexes." Hanchett would agree. Parents should supply information in reaction to their children's natural curiosity and should avoid sparking "sexual excitement" (Kellogg 1888b, v–32).

Early in the text Kellogg heralds his vision of creation: "The universe of life presents the most marvelous manifestations of the infinite power and wisdom of the Creator to be found in all his works." Man, as noted in Genesis, stands at the apex of creation. Women, in this traditional view, are derivative, literally from a rib. Nature itself testifies that the Creator "gave to certain bodies the requisite arrangement or organization to enable them to perform certain functions, and delegated to them the power to transmit the same to other matter, and thus to perpetuate life. The Creator alone has the power to originate life." As a result of Eve's sin as detailed in Genesis, women justly suffer in giving birth, but bad habits and modern civilization add to the required quotient. Monogamy, marriage, and family all derive from divine law (34–35, 42, 76–77, 139).

In Kellogg's traditional Christian view men and women have both an animal nature (which he also terms human nature) and a soul or spiritual nature. To overcome our natural tendency to evil—a result of the Fall as told in Genesis—as well as "unseen agencies," we need divine grace. Unaided human nature would only rarely gain victories over evil. Prayer can indeed help but will not ensure victories. "The struggling soul beset with evil thoughts, will find in prayer a salvation which all his forces of will, and dieting, and exercising will not, alone, insure him." To gain victories, one must add faith and works to prayer. "All that one can do to work out his own salvation, he must do; then he can safely trust in God to do the rest, even though the struggle seems almost a useless one." Sin consists of thoughts as well as actions. "It is vain for a man to suppose himself chaste who allows his imagination to run riot amid scenes of amorous associations." Such "mental unchastity" scars the soul, and is "photographed upon the books of heaven, they each appear in bold relief, in all their innate hideousness" (166–67, 169–70).

In Kellogg's view physical imperfections can cause many vices. "When the full bearing of physical influences upon the mind is allowed, it is difficult to avoid pleading extenuating circumstances in the case of the greater share of transgressors of both moral and civil laws." But culpability remains, and only emphasizes the necessity of grace (194).

Human nature, as previously remarked, is prone to evil. In Kellogg's view, modern living adds to this innate propensity. Public amusements, fairs, sedentary employment, and superheated rooms all cause "abnormal excitation and precocious development of the sexual functions." In fact, modern living makes "absolute chastity" almost impossible and calls for additional help from Providence. People engaged in physically strenuous occupations such as agriculture have somewhat of an "antidote" to their inborn tendency to evil. Turning away from evil is what cures individuals of maladies. "When a sick person gets well, it is usually because he has reformed from his evil ways, and nature has ceased to punish him for his physical sins." Health and morality are thus linked; illness can be the physical manifestation of sin. Kellogg then links ill health, morality, and crime. "We have long held that a great share of the crime among civilized people might be fairly charged to bad physical conditions, which by impairing the physical health, lower the nerve tone, and then the moral tone, so that there is not a proper appreciation of moral principles and obligations." Though Kellogg at times seems to strike a Rousseauan note about the goodness of unsullied nature, his Christian view tends to predominate; all nature is fallen. Even though

"Indian [Native American] boys do not masturbate," natural peoples share a corrupt human nature. Modern living only makes things worse (196–98, 247, 635, 636).

God delegates the divine fructifying power to humankind. According to Kellogg, nutrition and reproduction constitute the two main functions of life. Nutrition he views as a selfish function, while reproduction is unselfish—though humankind can make it selfish. The great purpose of marriage is to pass along life as well as to improve the race. In his view, "the perfection of the new being, then, must be largely dependent on the integrity and perfection of the sexual elements [from the parents]." To achieve such perfection, couples must practice continence within marriage. Hanchett, on the other hand, rejects marital continence, but as a man of faith holds the chaste, single life in service to God as the ideal. Being a student of the Bible, Kellogg must be aware that God commanded humankind in Genesis to be fruitful, multiply, and fill the earth. Kellogg does not deny this, but he postulates a view of physical and moral illness that requires even marital continence (118).

The early exercise of the sexual function by men, usually through masturbation, saps vital energies. Lacking energy to put into maturation and growth, the mind as well as the body become "dwarfed." The masturbator cannot look another man in the eye. Over time, improvident use of the sexual function leads to degeneration of the testes, the inability to have healthy children, impotence, and sterility. Nocturnal emissions in men (which seem normal to Hanchett) actually reflect sexual excess or mental incontinence. Other factors such as stimulating foods and the use of feather beds and pillows also help to spark nocturnal emissions. If such emissions are infrequent and are experienced by a "robust" person, Kellogg is not all that alarmed, but if they are relatively frequent and occur in a "feeble" person they create "great injury." Lassitude, languor, despair, and even suicide mark such men. "Headache, indigestion, weakness of the back and knees, disturbed circulation, dimness of vision, and loss of appetite" are other effects. Losing semen more than once a month, even in marital relations, should cause alarm. Hanchett, on the other hand, endorses intercourse every three or four days.

Kellogg, like Hanchett, views seminal fluid as a kind of élan vital. "The seminal fluid is the most highly vitalized of all the fluids of the body, and that its rapid production is at the expense of a most exhaustive effort on the part of the vital forces, is well attested by all physiologists." In Kellogg's view, the male body uses semen internally to repair damaged tissue. He goes on to cite medical authorities who argue that all emissions are injurious in that they lead to nervous exhaustion and debility. Whether through marital excess or masturbation, a man comes to find his "manhood lost, his body a wreck, and death staring him in the face." Imbecility, insanity, idiocy, melancholy, and suicide await (250, 253, 266–72, 276–77, 283–84). Sexual excess, whether masturbatory or marital, has related effects in women. Though women do not experience seminal losses, they do experience "nervous exhaustion," which serves as a common cause of hysteria. Like other "higher animals," women also undergo "the rut." His argument at this point rests on an animal analogy. Right after menstruation, women may experience sexual feelings. Citing medical authority, Kellogg notes that "the majority of women, happily for them, are not very much troubled with sexual feeling of any kind. What men are habitually, women are only exceptionally." Sexual desire, insofar as it exists at all, comes only temporarily after menstruation. "She submits to her husband, but only to please him; and but for the desire of maternity." This, of course, corresponds to Kellogg's recommendation that sexual relations be experienced once a month. Monthly intercourse, then, fulfills a man's duty to beget children and lets him experience pleasure with minimal semen loss, while it also corresponds to a woman's cycle of desire, if she has any at all. The purpose of intercourse is to conceive children, and this also fulfills a woman's "motherly instinct" and serves as the "noblest function of womanhood." Maternity, according to Kellogg, "is the most sacred and elevated office which a woman can perform in the world" (89, 287, 401–2, 462–63, 473–74).

Semen loss and excessive rutting have drastic consequences not only for individuals, but also for future generations. In an implicit riff on Lamarckian genetics, Kellogg believes that acquired characteristics, even a propensity to sin, can be transmitted to the next generation. As he argues: "it is in this way only that we can explain the early and apparently almost irresistible propensity in generation after generation to indulge similar habits and feelings." In Kellogg's view, then, some people inherit a propensity to indulge sexual passion, and this inheritance is inflamed by modern living. "The children of libertines are almost certain to be rakes and prostitutes." Thus parents can commit a "crime against the race" by producing less than healthy offspring. Criminal classes increase this same way. Thieves, for example, transmit a "secretive, dishonest, sneaking disposition; and the child comes into the world ticketed for the

State prison by the nearest route." Thus nations fall. "In these disgusting facts we find one of the most potent agents in effecting the downfall of the nations. Licentiousness sapped their vitality and weakened their prowess. Empires fall victim to their lusts and are then succeeded by more virtuous ones" (114–15, 146, 149–50, 175, 203).

Kellogg presents the "Juke" family as a case in point. We begin with five sisters. Several of them were illegitimate, and three of them were unchaste. They later married men sired by a licentious, drinking, lazy father. Among their 709 offspring that can be accounted for, 280 were paupers, 140 were criminals, 60 were thieves, 7 were murderers, and 165 were prostitutes and adulteresses. They also spawned almost a hundred illegitimate children, and over four hundred descendants later afflicted with syphilis. In Kellogg's mind, as go the Jukes, so goes America (447).

Since the fate of nations is at issue, Kellogg calls for decisive action. His book raises the hue and cry. The remedies for masturbation, seemingly the root of evil, provide an example. Masturbation, in Kellogg's view, presents a serious medical condition. The treatment depends on the age of the patient. Like Hanchett, he recommends that children not be left alone and that they be occupied with tasks that tire them. "It is best to place such a child under the care of a faithful person of older years, whose special duty it shall be to watch him night and day until the habit is thoroughly overcome." In younger children bandaging the parts, tying the hands, and covering the organs with a cage have met with success. Circumcision almost always works. It should be done without anesthetic so that the child associates pain with the penis; the resulting soreness certainly will cause a cessation of the evil practice. For adults, a physician can explain the drastic consequences for the mind and body of the "secret vice." Citing the practice of a superintendent of the Iowa Asylum for Feeble-Minded Children, Kellogg endorses the use of sutures through the prepuce (foreskin) for "refractory cases." Erection thus becomes impossible and the "slight irritation" will help to overcome the disposition to masturbate. For women, Kellogg recommends the use of carbolic acid on the clitoris. Other treatments include sitz baths, hot and cold applications to the spine, vaginal douches, and saline sponge baths. The local application of electrical current works for some men, while the same treatment can be used for sexual apathy in women (294–95, 269, 318–21).

Castration, according to Kellogg, is an efficient but not justifiable remedy. "Even a father has no right thus to mutilate his own son, though we must confess that the lad's chances for becoming a useful man are fully as good as they would have been had he continued his course of sin." In one specific case, a father brought his ten-year-old daughter to the good doctor. She had acquired the habit of self-abuse from a German servant girl. All the methods suggested by Kellogg had failed to cure her. "It finally became necessary to resort to a surgical operation by which it is hoped that she was permanently cured. . . . It was a severe remedy, and may seem a harsh one, but every other means utterly failed, and the father insisted upon the performance of the operation as a trial."[1] The father declared that he would abandon his daughter to die if she could not be cured and his other children spared. Thus, fathers have no justifiable right to castrate their sons, but can have clitoridectomies performed on their daughters. The fate of nations, races, and individuals sometimes requires genital pain and mutilation, especially for girls and also for boys trapped in midwestern asylums (363, 418–19). Hanchett, as previously remarked, does not teach that masturbation impacts the fate of nations and views it mainly as a personal problem.

Moral education serves as the counter to mutilation. Children, according to Kellogg, should be taught self-control and self-denial. Such education should not aim to make children merely efficient calculators of their self-interest. This only instills selfishness and not love for what is noble or right. Children should be taught to act for the good for its own sake. Giving children rewards also teaches selfishness. Even the hope of a future life in heaven falls into this category. Kellogg wants to "instill into the mind a love for right and truth, and purity, and virtue, and an abhorrence for their contraries." In this way, children can be raised to be free from the "assaults of passion, of vice, of lust." Thus the individual, the family, and the nation can be saved. The alternative is the Juke family with its physically and morally sick offspring.

Besides a reference to Alexander the Great as a sodomite and a mention of a patient who wished to masturbate another man, sodomites/homosexuals do not figure in the work. Hanchett makes no references at all. Kellogg does refer to the Scythians and the Pueblo Indians of New Mexico to demonstrate that men can become women. The opposite possibility receives no discussion. The Pueblo Indians, for example, select a strong man to become a "mujerado," a figure necessary for religious rituals. He is masturbated several times a day and rides bareback, which causes a great deal of stimulation. Seminal losses occur constantly and, as a consequence, his sexual organ begins to shrink. Over time, masculine eros itself disappears and is replaced by a desire for feminine things. The Scythians achieve the same result through "excessive equitation." So even though Kellogg seeks to instill a love of the good for itself through education, his rhetorical strategy threatens disease and damnation, insanity and impotence, and in extreme cases, transformation into a woman (138–39).

Much like Hanchett, Kellogg presents us with a unified Christian worldview and mainly a traditional view of the role of sexuality within the great scheme of divine creation. Following common Christian teaching, which itself draws from classical Greek philosophy, Kellogg dichotomizes human nature into an animal part and a spiritual one. Procreation, according to Kellogg, embodies humankind's participation in divine power. Though only God can create *ex nihilo* and by word, men and women participate through the reproductive function of marriage. A notion of the Fall suffuses Kellogg's work, and he regards illness as a typical consequence of sin. Besides a propensity to evil resulting from the Fall, modern living itself provides a myriad of near occasions of sin.

Like other late Victorians Kellogg postulates a spermatic political economy, what Fellman and Fellman term a mercantile conception, as the basis of sexual relations (Fellman and Fellman 1981, 75–77). The body uses sperm to repair and vitalize internal tissues, and it should not be wasted even within marriage. Wasting this élan vital can easily lead to "imbecility, insanity, idiocy, melancholy and suicide." Men must, of course, control their sexual urges. In fact, God stands ready to punish any transgressions of the moral code. If men maintain self-control and since women really do not have (or barely have) any sexual desires, there is no need for men to lose sperm except within marriage for the purpose of having children. Kellogg's book thus becomes an exhortation mainly addressed to men about the necessity of preserving sperm. His rhetorical strategy relies on references to the divine plan and reason, but if this fails Kellogg, unlike Hanchett, is ever willing to threaten "imbecility, insanity, idiocy, melancholy and suicide." A particular type of breakfast cereal might also help. Women, on the other hand, largely bereft as they are of sexual feelings, are mainly advised to fulfill their part of the divine plan. Eve is the prototype; the pain of childbirth awaits.

Modern readers can readily dismiss Kellogg's work as the rantings of a religiously deluded, possibly impotent medical doctor from those old times before medicine truly became scientific. On the other hand, we can take his work as an example of an earlier type of medical knowledge that fused religion, natural philosophy, and science. Kellogg certainly was not deluded. Part of the American tradition includes a view of a righteous God who punishes moral transgressions. In Kellogg's view, these transgressions are acts of treason against divine governance and, hence, call for decisive responses. Though his teaching about masturbation seems extreme, the act must be understood as rebellion against divine governance, an ostensibly minor event that can, if amplified, cause the destruction of nations. The issue is rebellion and its potential amplification. Thus Kellogg calls for remedies including circumcision without anesthetic to thwart wider rebellion.

Sexual pleasure is an incidental by-product of an act whose purpose is to bring children into the world according to the divine plan. Thus, sexual relations are about man's participation in God's fructifying power, and woman's eternal enactment of Eve's punishment. The act represents a couple's participation in and even renewal of the divine plan. Pleasure has little to do with it. The divine plan in fact calls for humankind to turn from pleasure to the transcendent good. Hanchett, relying on St. Paul, would add that marriage itself is a distraction from the splendor of the good. The Fall itself and the consequent tendency toward evil resulted from one such turn away from God, and couples are reminded of this by the pain of each childbirth.

More *Plain Talk* about Restraint

A Victorian consciousness also permeates Dr. Henry Guernsey's *Plain Talks on Avoided Subjects*. *Plain Talks* was first published in 1882 and was reprinted four times before a revised edition came out in 1915.[2] The first edition of *Plain Talks* was published at a time when patriarchal systems attempted to deny that women experienced sexual desire; at the most, some writers like Hanchett acknowledged that women felt some desire, but much less than men did. The marriage ceremony in this period typically included references to St. Paul's epistle demanding that women be subject to their husbands, and "giving away the bride" was a normative custom in which one man, the father, gave his daughter's hand to another man, the husband. No one, of course, gave men away. Though it is a marriage manual, *Plain Talks on Avoided Subjects* does not make any direct references to the mechanics of intercourse. Really plain talk, even that between gentlemen over cigars in a drawing room, invited social anarchy.

Henry Guernsey, M.D., seeks to expose the evils that seduce young people for lack of warning. Parents, unfortunately, often shirk their responsibility—a constant observation in this genre—and thus there is a need for a book that not only talks plainly, but also addresses the general public as well as the medical profession. Kellogg and Hanchett agree with the need to educate parents and their children. All three authors are terribly circumspect. Kellogg does not even deal with the sexual organs at all; he does, however, constantly preach about the evils of alcohol and tobacco (Kellogg 1888a).

Guernsey assumes a functional view of the human body and quickly asserts an Aristotelian approach. A thing (an organ like the kidneys, for example) is good when it performs its function properly: "everything was created for use." Happiness consists of following natural function to its God-given end, the fulfillment of its nature. Taking the classical view again, Guernsey asserts that the brain exists to "govern and rule all below. It is the first organ formed and in an orderly life should control all the others" (Guernsey 1882, 13–14, 23).

The major organization of the text follows the life cycle: from infancy to childhood to adolescence and then marriage. Infancy takes up only three pages, but reveals a major preoccupation of the good doctor. In "Embracing the First Year of the Child's Life," he warns that "particular care and the utmost solicitude should be bestowed upon the genital organs. No rubbing or handling of these parts should be permitted under any pretense whatsoever—beyond what may be absolutely necessary for cleanliness" (24). "Early impressions upon these animal passions . . . are very abiding" (24–25).[3]

To avoid "sexual precocity" in childhood, parents should maintain surveillance over play activities. One could inadvertently cause sexual impressions in young children by "allowing them to repose playfully on their belly, to slide down banisters, to go too long without urinating, constipation or straining at stool, cutaneous affections, and worms." Sliding down banisters is especially dangerous, since this can lead to "inveterate masturbation." Priapism (persistent, involuntary erections) in male children requires medical aid, since this indicates a functional problem and can also lead to masturbation. In some extreme cases, death has been known to result. As always, touching the genitals either by the child, by parents, or by nurses, must be minimized. Above all, parents must seek to avoid the *"secret vice of the worse kind"*: masturbation.

This act is repeated time after time until the degrading and destructive (morally and physically so) habit is confirmed. As a result, the boy grows thin, pale, morose and passionate; then weak, indolent and indifferent; his digestion becomes impaired, his sleep short, disturbed and broken; he sometimes becomes epileptic or falls into a state of marasmus [wasting]; in any case he is in great danger of being totally ruined forever.   (29–35)

Children should "banish all thoughts of a sexual nature," speak with their parents about their struggles, and pray for help. Guernsey also recommends running, reading "good, pure stories," and taking part in useful endeavors. In these ways, a boy can conquer any lascivious thoughts and "rise to the dignity of a true man." "All sexual emotions should be subjugated." Following classical philosophy once again, Guernsey emphasizes the importance of instilling good habits in children so as to help the rational faculty control the passions. Teaching good habits is so important that masturbation is *"a sin chargeable to the parent."* Parents should be vigilant and make confidants of their children "for there should be *chastity* above all things." Guernsey devotes most of his attention to boys and mentions girls only toward the end of the chapter. His admonitions, however, apply equally (27–41; italics in original).

In discussing male adolescence, Guernsey reiterates his view that reason and will , ennobled by the divine one, should govern passions, desires, and tastes. The more animal passions rule a man, the more he becomes like a beast. Evil approaches through the mind. "If this evil be masturbation, then they are on the direct road to ruin. . . . If it be the commission of sexual intercourse with women, their ruin is still more certain." Poisons such as syphilis and gonorrhea await, and millions die annually from them. Catastrophic moral corruption assuredly follows physical corruption. "He loses all respect for the truth and all regard for his word; no dependency of any kind can be placed upon him, and he will not pay his debts or fulfill any moral obligation." Men in such a condition no longer find any pleasure in life. They wish to die; often they become suicides. "A search in any insane asylum will show that a very large proportion of patients are made up from those who masturbate or have syphilis. Stamp out these two evils, or rather *curses* . . . and the supply that feeds our insane asylums, aye and our penitentiaries, too, will become vastly lessened" (50; italics in original). Purity manifests itself positively in a man's countenance, carriage, and deportment. Vice produces opposite effects. Lewd thoughts, of course, must be avoided. They have "a debasing and deteriorating effect upon that well-developed form, upon that conscience so free, and upon that countenance so open and bright." Loss of seminal fluid must always be avoided. Its retention is promoted by good habits, which, in turn, lead to a lessening of sexual feelings. Similarly, the more a young man indulges sexual feelings, the more they will reoccur. Some misguided physicians, but certainly not Kellogg or Hanchett, mistakenly urge sexual indulgence for the sake of health, but Guernsey considers this a great error. Abuse—not neglect—causes the sexual organs to atrophy. Abuse in Guernsey's construction means "any irregular or premature exercise of their [organs of generation] functions; any application of them which cannot have, as its result, the propagation of the species." Abuse manifests itself for all to see. Vice cannot remain secret.

> Look at the habitual masturbator! See how thin, pale and haggard he appears; how his eyes are sunken; how long and cadaverous is his cast of countenance; how irritable he is and how sluggish, mentally and physically; how afraid he is to meet the eye of his fellows; feel his damp and chilling hand, so characteristic of great vital exhaustion. Taken as a class, how terrible are their lost virility, their miserable night's sleep, their convulsions and their shrunken limbs. They keep by themselves, seeking charm in solitude and are fit companions for no one; they dare not read their bible, they cannot commune with good angels nor with the Lord, our Savior. Is this picture not deplorable? It is at the last end of the chain I admit, but it is reached link after link, one at a time. (61)

Semen must be saved! Guernsey and Kellogg agree on this. Its waste, like the mark of Cain, clearly manifests itself. Semen, according to Guernsey, exists in a bank account that permits only withdrawals. Atrophy, moral bankruptcy, and ruin await spendthrifts.

> Man in a healthy state need not and should not lose one drop of seminal fluid by his own hand, by nightly emissions or pollutions, or in any way, until he becomes conjoined to a wife of his choice in the holy bonds of matrimony. Every time the seed of his body is lost in a disorderly or unnatural way, he injures the finest textures of his brain correspondingly, as well as the finest and most exalted condition of his mind and soul, because the act proceeds in its incipiency from a willful prostitution of these higher powers. (61)

When temptation comes, read an interesting book, exercise to exhaustion, plunge your arm into very cold water, or take a rapid walk. Nocturnal emissions and other abnormalities result from mistakes in diet and the consumption of liquor. Seminal losses make men "weak, pale, and feeble in mind, while all that was manly and vigorous has gone out of them" (42–67).

In adolescence, women undergo more change than men and, accordingly, should not be expected to have as much "power left for the tasks of school." Menstruation is a privilege and a "blessing from Heaven." It lends "loveliness to . . . [a woman's] character, beauty to her expression, music to her voice, and gracefulness to her form and movements." The monthly flow must not be suppressed, and injections to clean the vaginal canal should be avoided. Besides, such cleansing can often "excite sensations in the parts to which they are applied, that should remain perfectly dormant in the unmarried state." Daily external washings, however, are acceptable. As a girl grows into womanhood, she also develops the feminine mental state: "She must not allow herself to bear malice towards anyone, must not plot evil or attempt to 'pay off others in their own coin,' as it is called, or seek revenge in any way; but she must ever cultivate a forgiving disposition, good thoughts and good feelings towards everyone" (75–76). A pure mind embracing Christian virtue "lends enchantment to the eye, sweetness of expression to the face, music to the voice, and gracefulness of carriage." Men should be kept at a distance. "Do not allow any approach or touch beyond what is customary in the best of society at social gatherings." No kissing! After betrothal, a woman can accept affection from her intended as if it were from a father or brother. If a young woman has been properly educated, she has not "as a rule, any sexual propensity, or amorous thoughts or feelings." The laws of creation require that a woman sacrifice her feelings upon marriage and submit sexually to her husband. To act to the contrary subverts the laws of nature and could cause her husband's health to suffer.

Women, however, can inherit morbid conditions. As in the case of men, impure thoughts seem to reflect physical realities. Nymphomania—apparently understood as any sexual desire at all in a woman—can be cured through treatment of the constitutional symptoms. Sometimes women err and resort to "self-abuse" or turn to the opposite sex. Then they are ruined forever. The effect of "self-indulgence" is comparable to the damage done to men.

Since women really have no sexual feelings, why should they marry? Hanchett, as previously noted, poses the same question. According to Guernsey, women "have an innate principle of love for the male sex; and this love is drawn from the Lord above." In this assertion, Guernsey shares a rhetorical strategy with both Hanchett and Kellogg. Women, in his view, represent "good," while men embody "truth." Marriage thus conjoins goodness and truth. The physical manifestation of this truth in sexual intercourse has less importance than its spiritual reality. Sexuality in this view forms part of the order of creation and is *"never"* intended for mere pleasure. Carnal pleasures are profanations and perversions. Guernsey goes on to link love of God, conjugal love, and the love of infants. Women who do not yield willingly to their husbands are insubordinate. They disgrace their families and scandalize their friends. Worse yet, they sin against God. Children function as a gift from God, future angels in heaven, and should be welcomed. Guernsey advises against avoiding pregnancy and suggests that this brings physical miseries. Since pregnancy, in Guernsey's view, causes the mingling of the blood of the father—truth—and mother—goodness—by way of the embryo, pregnancy also transforms women spiritually, and they can transmit this enhanced being—truth conjoined with goodness—to their children. Marriage thus offers women a "new order of life" through a spiritual transformation; this understanding is foreign to both Kellogg and Hanchett (84–89, 90–99; italics in original).

Guernsey also presents the normative image of an economically privileged, white housewife of the time.

> How much it consoles, encourages, lifts up, and rests a man to return to his home after the trying scenes of a day busily spent in providing for the support of his family are over, to find his wife affectionate and serene, and all about the house brilliant with contentment. Such a wife if she has troubles, . . . and wishes to call the attention of her husband to them, will do it at a proper time, when she knows it will annoy him the least, and when he will be able to give her the most assistance. She will never try to annoy him; but endeavoring to be a true help-meet will seek in a proper and loving way to get him to be the same to her. (107)

In moving toward his conclusion, Guernsey adds another admonitory chapter on masturbation. *Plain Talks* ends by briefly discussing the purpose of intercourse once again. In sexual congress, an individual man's power becomes conjoined with the "Divine power," which then infuses a soul into the fetus and creates life. The womb thus becomes a sacred vessel filled with the results of male action, both divine and human.

Young women, as a consequence of biological necessity, do not do as well in school as young men. Besides natural educational deficiencies, the feminine character itself—understood mainly as niceness (see Brownmiller 1984, 13–19 as modified by Wolf 1991)—would preclude an active life in a laissez-faire public realm. Though women embody goodness, it seems to have no use except for self-beatification and the benefit of future generations. Uncorrupted women do not experience any sexual desire, and Guernsey seems to reserve the term "nymphomania" for any women that do. Given this assertion, Guernsey must then marshal reasons to convince women to fulfill their wifely duty: God commands it, nature requires it, and beatitude awaits. Men, unlike women, do have sexual inclinations, and masturbation is a constant preoccupation of Guernsey to an even greater extent than it is with Kellogg and certainly Hanchett.

Guernsey would subject children to a panoptic gaze so as to preclude abuse. Abuse, any stimulation of the genitals, is a serious matter. It can lead to death and manifests itself for all the world to see. The results are destruction, disease, and death, if not prison and the insane asylum. Guernsey, like Kellogg and Hanchett, conflates theology, philosophy, and science; all three serve to enforce his Victorian virtue. Guernsey teaches that reason elevates man above the animals and that it should master sexual passion in men even in marriage. Married love has a divine dimension, and at conception God joins together with a man to infuse life into the womb. Wasting semen offends God's law, reason, and medical science. Its waste leads to atrophy of the testes, moral bankruptcy, and even death. Since sexual excitement causes the production of semen, sexually exciting situations should be avoided. Logically then, private morality needs to become public law. In making the private public, society should seek to eliminate occasions of sexual excitement to protect future generations, the beatitude of women, and the virility of men, and to reduce the populations of prisons and insane asylums. Since all the world can see moral corruption in even the gait of a person, vice already manifests itself publicly.

Men represent truth, and in Guernsey's view truth and goodness mix in the womb. This mingling of truth and goodness enhances the being of the mother and is transmissible to children. Thus women, unlike men, can embody both truth and goodness. In fact, the greater this mixing through pregnancy, the more substantial the beatitude for the wife and the children. Nature, divine law, and beatitude bring women to marriage and motherhood.

Victorian Virtue

Guernsey and Kellogg sketch gender roles for economically privileged white men and women. They write for people who have learned through good habits to subordinate appetite to reason. Lower classes and recent immigrant groups around 1880, presumably, propagate mainly animal qualities and will keep prisons and insane asylums full. Anxiety marks the works of these authors. "They published . . . to reassure others and themselves; they constantly referred to laws in nature which they could not easily find replicated in the human world: all their calls echoed their fears of a lawlessness, of uncertainty, of a chaos beneath" (Fellman and Fellman 1981, 21).

Guernsey's conjoining of medical science, philosophy, and theology, combined with a dash of Lamarckian genetics, implicitly calls for the generation of social movements that would uplift lower classes, Americanize them, and bring them within the Victorian sexual regime of male self-restraint and female subordination. Guernsey's view also implicitly supports colonialism and eugenics. Kellogg mainly shares Guernsey's beliefs, while Hanchett restricts his focus to individuals and couples. Though Hanchett writes that women do experience some sexual desire, his praise of the chaste, single life as well as his general reliance on Christian theology puts him in the same league as his medical colleagues. According to Kellogg, modern living also serves as an impediment to chastity, and he is reacting to social forces such as urbanization and immigration. Lower-class dating patterns (dating itself being a relatively recent innovation) allowed and even fostered a loosening of sexual morals, which, of course, invited the degeneration of the race as well as the wrath of God (see, for example, Polsky 1991; D'Emilio and Freedman 1988, 203).

Since in this view women do not really experience sexual desire or have much less than men do, they cannot actually challenge the sexual regime except by refusing to breed. Men, on the other hand, can threaten the sexual regime (see Gordon 1978, 62). Male desire can not only subvert the regime, it can also challenge an economic system built on delayed gratification. The seemingly simple act of masturbation presents a microcosm of the problem. This act, taken symbolically, represents a turning away from God and nature's plan for the sake of selfish pleasure. If amplified, it could undermine the self-restraint built into both the marriage and economic systems. The rhetorical goal of these authors is to reinforce self-restraint among men of privileged classes, to get the message of self-restraint to the middle and lower classes, and to bring immigrant groups within the sexual regime, which assumes that middle- and lower-class males as well as immigrant ones should be brought to understand the spermatic economy. In fact, variations of this belief exist in the literature until the revised edition of Van de Velde's *Ideal Marriage* in 1965.

If Kellogg and Guernsey fail in their rhetorical project, with all their threats of insanity and God's wrath, immigrant groups and the lower classes could potentially bring down the nation by creating generations of imbeciles. Men must be educated to ignore the call of sirens; Guernsey and Kellogg are, in effect, supplying wax for their ears. National survival is at stake, and the first turn from self-restraint to gratification heralds ruin. Thus, some of our late Victorians are indeed fixated on masturbation, but mostly for its symbolic importance as rebellion against God and nature's plan. Semen must be spent only in marriage for the purpose of procreation. Men want children in order to demonstrate their virility, potency, and power. Children are trophies of male power (both human and divine). Guernsey suggests that large families help move humankind toward a better race.

Lystra in *Searching the Heart* classifies both Kellogg and Guernsey as restrictionists. They preach restraint and self-control and try to intimidate readers with visions of death and damnation (Lystra 1989, 108–9, 111). Kellogg and Guernsey, however, share many of the premises of more moderate late Victorians like Hanchett. All of them agree that men need to restrain their animal passions, and most of their admonitions, if not threats, are directed at men. The measure of manliness, in other words, resides in self-control. Hanchett merely adds a stronger admonition for women, since in his view they do experience some sexual desire. Hanchett unlike his colleagues does attack prudery. All these medical doctors agree on the evils of prostitution. It saps strength, health, wealth, and self-respect and strikes at the family itself. Kellogg and Guernsey, of course, stress all the horrible consequences in great detail. They all view marriage as a divinely ordained institution.

Kellogg and Guernsey stress continence, but Hanchett does not differ radically. Hanchett employs a hydraulic metaphor for male sexuality, while Kellogg and Guernsey adopt that of a bank account with limited withdrawals. Hanchett's metaphor leads him to write that discharges such as nocturnal emissions are inevitable when pressures mount and that this does not necessarily lead to damnation or disease. He even endorses intercourse every three or four days. The bank account metaphor, on the other hand, leads both Kellogg and Guernsey to view any withdrawals as a serious matter. Kellogg, for example, recommends intercourse on a monthly basis. All of them agree that the vital fluid is difficult to produce and exhausts male vitality. Kellogg and Guernsey go further in viewing it as having restorative powers. The view they share, however, reflects more than common medical beliefs and includes more than a horror of modernity, as Lystra would have it (1989, 110).

Hanchett's assertion that women do have some erotic desires and can experience sexual pleasure makes him appear moderate when compared to severe restrictionists, but Hanchett does share their Christian worldview. The purpose of marriage, according to Hanchett, does not lie in sex or even reproduction, but rather in the development of character. This combined with his fondness for Pauline theology leads him to regard the chaste, single life as ideal. The celibate life leads to health, happiness, and usefulness and allows individuals to focus on the "Lord's affairs." Marriage, though appropriate for most people, is second best and fills one's life with distractions. Kellogg and Guernsey urge continence for the sake of male health and vitality as well as the future of the nation, while Hanchett endorses chastity as the highest expression of Christian love. None of them accept sexuality as a secular religion, which Lystra argues actually defined the period (1989, 249–50). In fact, all of them are reacting to this development as well as changes brought about by industrialization and urbanization. Guernsey and Kellogg dream of Arcadian times and in some ways are Luddites as they call for continence in the face of the early stirrings of modernity. Hanchett's praise of the chaste, single life puts him in the same category as those arguing for continence and calls attention to Manichean influences that underpin their shared theology. All of them neglect a specific teaching of Genesis: "For God created humankind in His own image, . . . And all that God created was good." Guernsey and Kellogg demur when it comes to sexuality, while Hanchett prefers St. Paul (Jaeger 1961; Jonas 1958; Cochrane 1968; Voegelin 1968).

Though a Luddite and a Manichean in some ways, Kellogg also suggests a glimmer of a more modern truth: sex and gender categories are not immutable. Kellogg presents this in his example of the "mujerado" among the Pueblo Indians of New Mexico. Men, in his view, can change gender and become women in that they desire feminine things. These "mujerados" can also change sex. Kellogg thinks this results from excessive masturbation, which causes the penis to atrophy. Of course, he probably considered this the ultimate threat to men of his time. Loss of self-control could make them women. This can also be read as an explanation for the existence of gay men. On the other hand, Kellogg does not suggest that women can become men. About ninety years later, Alex Comfort's *Joy of Sex* debunks all that Hanchett, Kellogg, and Guernsey hold dear, and twenty years after the *Joy of Sex* we find RuPaul, an African American cross-dresser, as a cultural icon.

Both Kellogg and Guernsey argue that God's plan works itself out in nature. This leads both of them to discuss grace as a divine beneficence that helps people overcome temptation and evil. Both find it inadequate. Hanchett also writes about grace, but he does not dwell on the theological issues besides noting that it proves adequate in rejecting temptation. Both Kellogg and Guernsey, on the other hand, find all God's stratagems that call humankind to salvation inadequate. Implicitly, Kellogg and Guernsey seek to amend the divine plan to make it work better. In their own religious terms, this is truly sacrilegious. They themselves are in rebellion against God—in Dostoyevsky's sense—and seek to improve on the grand salvific design written into the nature of things. As Grand Inquisitors, they substitute their judgment for that of God and become in the very act cocreators. They are more than angry prophets, as Lystra would have it; their books function as new gospels that call humankind back to the Way, the Truth, and the Life (Dostoyevsky 1957, 218–44). (For a similar argument, see Goerner 1965, 55–56.)

Folklore Dissents

Less privileged economic groups in America as well as the upper class had access to other books that rejected the prevailing Victorian sexual regime. *Aristotle's Masterpiece* by [Pseudo] Aristotle presents a case in point. J. How first published the book in London in 1684, and it went through more than 150 editions over the next two hundred years. The British editions circulated in America; the first American edition was probably printed in 1766. American publishers printed the early editions as "pack books" that were probably sold by peddlers. The text was widely available in eighteenth-century America and informed popular knowledge and attitudes. By the time of Hanchett, Guernsey, and Kellogg there had been at least fifty American editions (Lee-Riffe 1992, 29, 38; Beall 1963, 208, 219).

[Pseudo] Aristotle, the author of the work, postulates different premises for understanding sexuality and demonstrates some of the threat that motivated Hanchett, Kellogg, and Guernsey to take pen in hand. Unlike them, [Pseudo] Aristotle uses religion as a smokescreen to disguise his intent, and the anonymity of the author offers even more protection from legal charges.

According to *Aristotle's Masterpiece*, sex is pleasurable to both parties, and women can even "have greater pleasure and receive more content than a man." The text teaches that the primary purpose of marriage is procreation, but also adds that a lack of sex for women causes ill health. Mutual orgasm, according to the text, is necessary for conception to take place. Articulating a piece of folklore, [Pseudo] Aristotle also teaches that pregnant women have the power to "mark" their fetuses by some "telepathic or extrasensory operation." Guernsey much later gives this piece of folklore a basis in medicine by holding that goodness and truth mix together in the womb (Beall 1963, 213 for the citations; Lee-Riffe 1992, 32, 34; Fellman and Fellman 1981, 9; Porter and Hall 1995, 48).

[Pseudo] Aristotle recognizes the clitoris as the locus of a woman's pleasure and compares it to a penis. The clitoris "stirs up lust and gives delight in copulation: for without this, the fair sex neither desire mutual embraces nor have pleasure in them, nor conceive by them." It is called "the sweetness of love, and the fury of venery." Hanchett, on the other hand, does not refer to the clitoris at all ([Pseudo] Aristotle 1796, 14, 16, with modernized spelling; Lee-Riffe 1992, 33).

[Pseudo] Aristotle is aware of what will later be termed "gender inversion." He thinks that effeminate men and masculine women result from male and female embryos attaching to the wrong side of the uterus. In his view, the different sides of the uterus are gendered: the right side is male, the left female. Gender inversion, thus, reflects biology (Lee-Riffe 1992, 33).

These old, probably well-thumbed little books with their archaic English also point us to another fundament of the sexual regime. [Pseudo] Aristotle uses the term "yard" for penis ([Pseudo] Aristotle 1796, 11, 12, 13, 14, 41, for example). According to the *Oxford English Dictionary*, as noted by Lee-Riffe, the archaic meaning of the term is penis, but it is also "associated" with its medieval usage as a "rod or staff carried as a symbol of office or authority" (Lee-Riffe 1992, 33; Porter and Hall 1995, 50; *Compact OED*, 3850). Kellogg and Guernsey implicitly accept this meaning. They instruct men to use their staffs of authority sparingly and only for conceiving children, and in the latter activity men share in the divine plan. Guernsey, as previously noted, allows women more of a role than Kellogg. [Pseudo] Aristotle teaches that the clitoris is like a penis and that it produces pleasure, but it is still not a yard in the full sense of the term. Women, in other words, lack authority, and only [Pseudo] Aristotle and Hanchett, among our authors, grant that they can have any sexual desire. All men have authority and its symbol at birth; all women, simply put, lack it. A century later, theorists like Judith Butler will distinguish between the penis as an organ and the phallus as a social structure (1990, 1993).

The Victorians and Their Virtues

Victorian virtue envisions a combination of the Christian gentleman and the robust self-made man. Women, passionless creatures in themselves or certainly having less desire than men do, helped tame masculine assertion, and silence about sexuality in the home, church, and press enforced the code. If necessary, working-class women were available for sexual gratification, though this was never to be talked about. Thus the Victorian system acknowledged that sometimes robust masculinity would triumph over reason and religion and that some men would seek sexual release. Of course, this creates a double standard from a contemporary viewpoint, but assuming that Victorians, both women and men, really believed that uncorrupted women remained strangers to sexual passion or experienced much less of it, then in their view what we see as a double standard would be a realistic adjustment to the natural world or God's plan. The major challenge in this sexual regime is to channel and control male sexuality. Though Hanchett is the only one of the medical authors who acknowledges that women do experience sexual desire, Victorian women undoubtedly did experience orgasm. How, one wonders, did they understand this synaptic hurricane? How does a woman experience and understand intimate pleasures in a sexual regime that barely grants its existence and offers only silence in the guise of *Plain Talk* or *Plain Facts*?

Supposedly Queen Victoria told her daughter on the eve of her wedding to "Lie still and think of the Empire." Though much of the advice literature propounds the view that women are mainly passionless creatures, married woman, as diaries and letters indicate, did take their sexual feelings as normal and did not consider themselves "freaks, deviants, or even strange for having sexual needs or expressing sexual interest to men *in private*." As Lystra argues, the ethic of romantic love sparked a mutuality in marital bedrooms as sex became a "sacrament of love" that bridged the gap between the ideology of the sexual regime with its emphasis on purity and the needs and experiences of married couples. Middle-class marriages became less patriarchal and more companionate, while men began to assert masculine privilege in the language of romantic love and sought to govern more by consent. Romantic love in some ways became a form of secular salvation as the ideology of the sexual regime and practice diverged (Lystra 1989, 58–60, 228, 235, 257; italics in original). Hanchett, Kellogg, and Guernsey, on the other hand, articulate the norms of the old regime and reject romantic love on medical, philosophical, and theological grounds.

Despite the norms of the old sexual regime, dating evolved as a social system and premarital intercourse increased. A new robust masculinity arrived center stage. These changes, combined with other factors such as urbanization, the gradual shift in the economy from production to consumption, and the newer understanding of Protestantism as a form of gentle deism, led to the triumph of the flapper in the 1920s. In large cities some men became bohemians or even flappers themselves. Chauncey's *Gay New York* persuasively demonstrates that these bohemians lived alongside fairies and gays. Thus America had its first sexual revolution of the twentieth century (see D'Emilio and Freedman 1988, 171–235; White 1993, 2–15, 189; Chauncey 1994).

2

"No Gods No Masters"
Margaret Sanger and America's Sexual Future

In addition to a general conservative reaction following the Civil War, empowered social groups, reacting to threats posed to the sexual regime by immigrant groups and recently freed slaves, joined together to enact obscenity statutes known as Comstock laws on both the state and federal levels. The federal statute, for example, prohibited the use of the mail for

> Every obscene, lewd, or lascivious, and every filthy book, pamphlet, picture, paper, letter, writing, print, or other publication of an indecent character, and every article or thing designed, adapted, or intended for preventing conception or producing abortion, or for any indecent or immoral use; and every article, instrument, substance, drug, medicine, or thing which is advertised or described in a manner calculated to lead another to use or apply it for preventing conception or producing abortion, or for any indecent or immoral purpose.　　　(Cited in Chesler 1992, 68)

Every state except New Mexico took some action, while twenty-four adopted legislation congruent with the national statute. Though birth control devices were still mailed and medical textbooks still contained some information, Anthony Comstock and his laws effectively ended any open discussion. Comstock considered nonprocreative sexual expression even within marriage "bestial and base." In his zeal to enforce repressive norms, Comstock created his own excesses. For example, store owners who left naked dummies in their display windows were arrested (Chesler 1992, 66–70; Halberstam 1993, 284).

Prior to the Comstock laws, midcentury newspaper advertisements announced the availability of "female syringes" and other birth control devices. In 1861 the *New York Times*, for example, carried an advertisement stating that "Dr. Power's French Preventives (condoms) sold for five dollars per dozen." In fact, prices were declining so that "most couples could afford to purchase condoms for six to twelve cents, diaphragms for a dollar, or syringes for forty cents" (D'Emilio and Freedman 1988, 60). Abortionists began advertising around 1830, and by the 1880s about one in every five or six pregnancies ended in abortion. In the 1860s, for example, "over twenty-five different chemical abortifacients . . . could be located through newspaper ads, postal circulars, and pharmacies." According to the commonly accepted notion of "quickening," human life did not begin until a woman felt the fetus move inside her; thus abortion posed no moral dilemma for many (Chesler 1992, 63; D'Emilio and Freedman 1988, 63, 64).

Despite Comstockery, birthrates fell among the privileged. Building on the original fears that led to the obscenity statutes in the first place rose newly augmented concerns about race suicide. The late Victorian fear that imbeciles and moral defectives would overwhelm the country blended with a horror of areas like New York's Lower East Side—a vision of naked, unwashed immigrant children pouring into the streets in endless numbers, their genitalia soon enough ready to spawn countless more. Lower classes and immigrant groups often had scant knowledge of birth control devices, and even if they did, they had little money to purchase them. Religious beliefs often condemned their use. So they spawned while the privileged acted otherwise and pondered their fate as reflected in census statistics.

Into this maelstrom came Margaret Sanger. She remains pilloried today in some circles as a *bête noire*. Some aspects of the birth control movement—sexual education in schools, for example—remain controversial and still inflame passions. Today's controversies, however, swirl mainly around abortion, a practice that Sanger always opposed. Sanger thought her dreams accomplished with the development of the birth control pill toward the end of her life, and she played a central role in its development.

Sanger's autobiographies are inadequate. She cooked the books, so to speak (Chesler 1992, 16–18). Her more recent biographers, with one major exception, neglect archival material and conclude, for example, that "persistent emotionalism compromised her effectiveness" (cited in Chesler 1992, 17). Ellen Chesler's well-known 1992 work, *Woman of Valor: Margaret Sanger and the Birth Control Movement in America*, consults the full range of sources and is usually judicious in drawing conclusions. Yet even Chesler, whose work is destined to define the issues for a while, finds Sanger inconsistent and sometimes befuddling. As Chesler puts it, Sanger was always a pragmatist, "perhaps at times even an opportunist." On a more general level, she views Sanger's later career as an attempt to distance herself from her own radical past to fit a conservative mold. Chesler sees this as an attempt to disassociate birth control—a phrase coined by Sanger—from any taint of radicalism. D'Emilio and Freedman, on the other hand, maintain that Sanger adapted to the times (D'Emilio and Freedman 1988, 243). Chesler's book, however, records glaring instances of consistency, not opportunism, when it comes to some controversial issues. In 1950 Sanger wrote an acceptance speech for an award from Planned Parenthood in which, according to Chesler, she derided "costly government welfare programs for their failure to weed out the 'feebleminded and unfit,' terms that were very much out of fashion [*sic*] following the tragic revelations of a decade of Nazi-inspired eugenic terror." Despite Sanger's perceived insensitivity to the horrors of the Holocaust, Sanger spoke favorably about limiting the birthrate of the unfit from her earliest activist days to her last ones. On the eve of World War II Sanger also renewed her membership in Jane Addams's International League for Peace and Freedom, even though she knew war was inevitable. She restated her major themes in the decade following the publication of her major works. At the Century of Progress exposition in Chicago in 1934, Sanger noted that progress consisted of "masculine psychology" or "male supremacy." Plans for world improvement would fail until women could control their own fertility. "*Free Woman* shall guide us into a future created by all embracing love through the consciousness of birth control" (Chesler 1992, 14, 16, 125, 367, 370, 417; italics in original). We cannot, of course, expect of Sanger the consistency of a Harvard undergraduate trained in logic, and we must also note the effects of persecution on her writing. Like many of today's feminist activists, Sanger often is more concerned with toppling patriarchal domination than abiding by the rules of its dominant discourse. Even though she was economically privileged by her second marriage, Sanger consistently denounced oppression, and even her views on eugenics, not at all uncommon at the time, were crucially qualified in several works.

In the 1950s Leo Strauss, a seminal philosopher at the University of Chicago, argued for a new approach to understanding the classics of Western thought. He postulated that both ancient and early modern philosophers wrote under persecution and must be read in a new way: "For the influence of persecution on literature is precisely that it compels all writers who hold heterodox views to develop a peculiar technique of writing, the technique which we have in mind when speaking of writing between the lines." Both ancient and early modern writers sought to address only "trustworthy and intelligent readers" in a way that had the advantages of private communications without its greatest disadvantage, that of reaching only a small audience. Strauss postulated a special type of writing that reached a wide audience while reserving an esoteric teaching for the few. This strategy avoided problems of political retribution. In this "writing between the lines," intelligent readers should look for purposeful contradictions, like those employed by John Locke, as well as the artful use of irony as a rhetorical device. As Strauss put it, "If a master of the art of writing commits such blunders as would shame an intelligent high school boy, it is reasonable to assume that they are intentional, especially if the author discusses, however incidentally, the possibility of intentional blunders in writing" (Strauss 1952, 24–25, 30).

Margaret Sanger was trained as a nurse and did not study at a great university like the one at Chicago. She most certainly, however, wrote under persecution. Examples abound. Early in the century, Sanger agitated for labor causes as well as birth control. Her activity in the latter actually grew from the former. Following the shooting of strikers in Ludlow, Colorado, and the subsequent surrender of the survivors to the Rockefeller interests, Sanger wrote in *The Woman Rebel* that the Ludlow victims provided examples of "courage, determination, conviction, [and] a spirit of defiance." She went on to add that "the greater tragedy for the revolutionary movement . . . was the 'cowardice and the poisonous respectability' of those leaders who apologized for the incident" (cited in Chesler 1992, 102). Previously Sanger had written about birth control for the same publication. Shortly thereafter she was arrested on four charges. Three of the charges alleged violation of the Comstock statute for her writings about birth control. The fourth listed her use of the mails to incite murder and assassination. She did write once that "agitation through violation of the law was the key to the public" (cited in D'Emilio and Freedman 1988, 243). After being charged she wrote *Family Limitation* and then fled to Europe. Looking back from a contemporary perspective, some commentators take Sanger's flight to indicate irresponsibility as well as desertion of her children, but after the Ludlow massacre her odyssey can also be taken as an act of prudence. The times were marked by revolutionary rhetoric and officially sanctioned violence against subversives. During World War I, federal and state security agencies tracked Sanger, which Chesler says might explain why later editions of *Family Limitation* dropped references to birth control as a means of liberation (Chesler 1992, 161). During a speaking tour in 1916, Sanger found the auditorium in Saint Louis locked. The authorities arrested her in Portland, Oregon. Boston officials threatened to break up any meeting at which she spoke. Being well attuned to the use of symbolism to make a point, she merely stood gagged on a Boston stage while Arthur Schlesinger, Sr., delivered her remarks (Halberstam 1993, 285). In 1921 after the Great War, Sanger organized the First American Birth Control Conference at New York City's Plaza Hotel. The conference was scheduled to conclude with a mass rally on a Sunday at Town Hall. Police, acting under the direction of New York's Roman Catholic archbishop, broke up the assembly (Chesler 1992, 161).

Persecuted she certainly was, and she did spend time in jail. So Sanger in her writings tends to draw back from her most radical conclusions and lets them lie implicit in her work. One of her early works, *What Every Mother Should Know, or How Six Little Children Were Taught the Truth*, published in 1916, demonstrates her careful writing method. In the introduction she lauds nature: "In order to perpetuate the species nature had endowed all animals with sexual instinct, and man is the only animal who is ashamed of this instinct. Man is the only animal with the intelligence to exercise the privilege of limiting his offspring, though he continues in his sexual relation." Even though the text is a guide to instruct children, Sanger makes constant references to the struggle for existence, with the corollary that only the strong survive. In a more traditional vein, she uses the example of birds to support the contemporary family structure and points out the necessity of protecting and caring for offspring. Besides the explicit reference to birth control in the introduction, the text appears commonplace and, indeed, suitable as a guide for children. On a more esoteric level, however, Sanger includes a teaching about the survival of the fittest as well as one reference to Darwin. She neglects to mention God (Sanger 1916, 5, 21, 37–43). In 1917 Sanger edited a volume entitled *The Case for Birth Control*. Probably because of the Comstock laws, the book lists no publisher. Some librarian at another university, probably a long time ago, stamped the contents page "restricted shelf."

Sanger's *Motherhood in Bondage*, published in 1928, consists of an edited collection of letters to her. In her introduction, she fulfills Strauss's dictate by making references to the "intelligent reader" and to those who have the "patience to read attentively." She concludes by "presenting this testimony to the jury of the intelligent American public" (Sanger 1928, xii, xvi, xix). The jury has decided for the most part on birth control, and the 1960s bear witness to the liberation of eros that Sanger foresaw.

In her later years, as the movement she sparked gained acceptance, she presented a persona acceptable to the guardians of social mores so as to foster liberation, which remained her ultimate aim. Her writing lacks the philosophical sophistication, the very artful contradiction appreciated by Strauss, but she was no fool. Overall, Sanger sought to communicate her message to a mass audience, especially the less economically privileged, while she also tried to avoid jail. As Florence Kelly put it in her *New York Times* book review of *My Fight for Birth Control* in 1931, "from that time on there has rarely been an hour of Margaret Sanger's life that lacked excitement, suspense, the peril of arrest, the threat of prison" (Kelly 1931b).

Hounded by the authorities, Sanger often lapses into silence, as she did in *Family Limitation*. Since later editions of the work dropped references to birth control, she could not be accused of violating the Comstock laws. *What Every Mother Should Know, or How Six Little Children Were Taught the Truth* demonstrates another way Sanger uses silence to instruct her "intelligent readers." In this work she emphasizes the role of evolution in nature, as she places her observations within the context of social Darwinism. She neglects to mention God. On the more esoteric level, Sanger suggests that she does not take religious belief systems seriously and in reality she aims to replace Christianity with a new religion of sexual rapture, which offers grace in the form of psychic integration. Almost like a pagan, Sanger embraces and celebrates passion. In doing this she undermines the notion of self-restraint built into the Victorian sexual regime. Sanger, of course, had immense difficulties dealing with the political power of organized religion and probably did not want to compound her problems by making it easier for clergy to brand her an immoral atheist from pulpits across the land. Her equivocations on eugenics point to another esoteric level to her writings. At critical points in her discussions, when it comes time to distinguish between the fit and unfit, Sanger almost always equivocates. With one exception she never makes the distinction. Without such a definition, any public policy discussion remains abstract and cannot be implemented. This points to a more subtle level of interpretation. Her equivocations suggest that she adopted eugenic principles in general terms, but mainly used this rhetoric for strategic purposes. She knew that a desire for increased living standards would lead Americans to practice birth control. In her political battle with the authorities and churches she desperately needed allies, thus she sought to co-opt the eugenic movement to her own purpose. Birth control, as she well knew, made eugenics irrelevant. She adopted the rhetoric of her times. Later in life she repeated her refrain, much as a politician automatically launches into a stump speech. She also never develops the political implications of her attack on social systems such as the family as embodying "masculine reasoning." She might well have thought that a multi-front war with the authorities and religious leaders was too much for one lifetime. Besides, she knew that birth control would spark the fundamental changes that would flow from free womanhood. She especially neglects to apply her understanding to marriage. In her day, married women were little better than chattel. She herself chafed at marriage's limitations, but she let her critique of the institution lie latent in her works. Decades later, as Sanger approached the end of her life, radical feminists began to offer critiques of the institution that echoed Sanger's original insights into patriarchal social systems. Sanger focused on what she saw as the linchpin of social change: affordable birth control for the masses. The wisdom of her strategy can be seen in the fact that Americans today take birth control for granted, while many religious leaders still fulminate against it. This approach to understanding Sanger is as plausible as one that considers her inconsistent, befuddled, and opportunistic. It is also more in harmony with the view of D'Emilio and Freedman.

Sanger became politically active at the turn of the century, but wrote mainly in the 1920s. In *Women and the New Race*, published in 1920, Sanger seeks to remake the world. Free motherhood, which will result when women revolt against "sex servitude," is the instrumental force. Subservient motherhood, according to Sanger, fosters tyranny by spawning ever more ignorant progeny; nations wage wars of conquest to increase resources to feed their ever expanding populations. Famine and plague, as well as the need for asylums to house "defectives," also result from overpopulation. Overpopulation leads to low wages, sweatshops, and peonage. Children end up competing against their fathers for jobs. The person willing to work for the least wins the competition. Some women revolt against their condition and seek escape from "sex servitude" through infanticide and abortion, but these women act merely as individuals and do not seek out the real causes of their misery or fight back as a group. Like Marx instructing the proletariat about the real cause of their misery, Sanger seeks to awaken true consciousness and group identity in enslaved women. As she sees it, countless children are doomed to serve as nothing more than "commodities upon the labor market." Subjugation of the masses due to overpopulation, however, predates modern enterprise. Birth control is the means to freedom and a way to undo the evils spawned by overpopulation. The late Victorians' mythical Juke family embodies the nightmare. As Sanger recounts the well-known story, one feebleminded man's progeny cost taxpayers some $1.3 million over seventy-five years (Sanger 1920, 1, 3, 4–7, 78, 92, 145–46, 233).

Sanger, modifying her socialist premises, focuses on gender and sees liberation resulting not from a proletarian revolution but from the end of women's enslavement. With her focus on gender and her call for its elimination as well as her concern with informing individual consciousness to create group identity, Sanger gravitated toward radical feminism long before its acknowledged advent in the late 1960s (Echols 1989). Women, according to Sanger, must come to a true knowledge of themselves, and the first step in this process is birth control. Once women demand "voluntary motherhood," slavery of both women and the masses will cease. Then, when women come to understand the "intuitive forward urge[s] within" themselves, they will not be concerned with "patching up the world," but rather with remaking it. The motivation for this radical change lies in the "feminine spirit." Though frequently manifested in maternity, the feminine spirit is much greater than motherhood. "Woman herself, all that she is, all that she has ever been, all that she may be, is but the outworking of this inner spiritual urge. Given free play, the supreme law of her nature asserts itself in beneficent ways; interfered with, it becomes destructive." In other words, in either positive or negative ways, the feminine spirit seeks to liberate itself (Sanger 1920, 8, 10, 11).

Undesired pregnancy and unwanted children are the major obstacles to the feminine spirit, and mothers pass on their chains to the next generation. As Sanger puts it, "A free race cannot be born of slave mothers. A woman enchained cannot choose but give a measure of that bondage to her sons and daughters. No woman can call herself free who does not own and control her body. No woman can call herself free until she can choose consciously whether she will or will not be a mother" (94).

Men will also benefit when women follow their inner spirit and re-create the world. The flourishing of the feminine spirit will "free her mate from the bondage he wrought for himself when he wrought hers. Only thus can she restore to him that of which he robbed himself in restricting her." All of this depends on women developing their "love nature[s]" apart from their maternal ones. Women will then be free to develop a "holy" love with their spouses, and this sacrament will provide for more spiritual growth and will blossom with "desired" children. "Love is the greatest force of the universe; freed of its bonds of submission and unwanted progeny, it will formulate and compel of its own nature observance to standards of purity far beyond the highest conception of the average moralist. The feminine spirit . . . will make its own high tenets of morality." This new morality will address the physical and psychological needs of women. It will also meet children's needs in that they will be enveloped with love. Thus the liberated feminine spirit creates a "race that is morally and spiritually free" (28, 94, 99, 180–85).

Racial purity was a dominant fixation, from the time of the late Victorians to Sanger's day. During this period, for example, the United States excluded Chinese. Even if Asians resided legally in the country, they could not become citizens. California as well as other western states prohibited Japanese residents from owning land. The U.S. Supreme Court upheld all these laws. Many viewed eugenics as a means to ensure racial purity, and many states adopted laws requiring sterilization of "mental defectives." When the Virginia statute was challenged before the U.S. Supreme Court in 1927 the great Justice Holmes wrote the court's opinion.

> We have seen more than once that the public welfare may call upon the best citizens for their lives. It would be strange if it could not call upon those who already sap the strength of the state for these lesser sacrifices, often not felt to be such by those concerned in order to prevent our being swamped with incompetence. It is better for all the world, if instead of waiting to execute degenerate offspring for crime, or to let them starve for their imbecility, society can prevent those who are manifestly unfit from continuing their kind. The principle that sustains vaccination is broad enough to cover cutting the Fallopian tubes. . . . Three generations of imbeciles are enough.

Only Justice Butler dissented.

Sheldon Novick, one of Holmes's recent biographers, terms this his "most notorious opinion," and then provides a long footnote supplying the context, if not a mild justification, for Holmes's harsh words (Novick 1989, 351–52, 477 n. 65). Only in 1973 did the federal government ban forcible sterilizations. This followed Senate hearings that revealed that in

1972 sixteen thousand men and eight thousand women were forcibly sterilized under federal programs (Pfaff 1997, 23). Sanger, like Justice Holmes, absorbed the racial purity ideology of the times, and this led to her qualified support of eugenics as an abstract principle. Most often she undermines eugenics by professing some agreement while raising a multitude of objections about its application. She mainly sought to recruit its adherents to her own cause.

Sanger wrote that developing a new American race would require birth control, because the intellectual development of a people lags behind the birthrate. In this context, birth control would "save the precious metals of racial culture, fused into an amalgam of physical perfection, mental strength and spiritual progress." Sanger imagines that this new American race will combine the best of all "racial elements." Her view is inclusive, not exclusive. Drawing from the late Victorians as well as folklore, Sanger argues that women transmit "racial efficiency" to their children and thus provide for a strong race. This happens only when women have the opportunity to develop the "mate relationship." Through this relationship they can transmit a "high love impulse" that "attunes and perfects" the being of their children. "The race is but the amplification of its mother body, the multiplication of flesh habitations—beautified and perfected for souls akin to the mother soul." At least in her first major work, Sanger regards race suicide thinkers as masculine fanatics (Sanger 1920, 44, 46, 68, 228–29, 230, 233).

Sanger, moving further away from her socialist roots, sees birth control as the third and most important battle for American liberty. The American Revolution is the first such struggle. One hundred years later the fight for religious liberty against blasphemy laws is the second. Birth control will be the third and most decisive struggle in that it will free the feminine spirit and call forth a new humanity (188).

In her first major work Sanger calls attention to the limitations of Marxism in understanding the oppression of women. Though she has not completely broken free of Marxian analysis, she turns toward gender as her central analytical concept in this "man-made society." Mere reform of the economic system will not end women's enslavement, but she implicitly accepts some role for capitalist enterprise. Sex servitude defines the core of the problem, and only birth control can end it. She retains a Marxist conception of a metastatic transformation of nature through a revolution, but the climacteric is birth control, not a proletarian revolution of (male) workers. She understands this as the third most decisive struggle in American history, one equal to that of the Revolutionary War. By implication, then, her text can be read as a declaration of women's independence. Its premises threatened all patriarchs, even well-meaning Wobblies. Marriage, as she will constantly teach, has two distinct and independent functions: procreation and the development of the "love natures" of the partners. Many contemporary feminists like Catharine MacKinnon also ground their work in a critique of Marx and echo Sanger's turn to gender (MacKinnon 1989, 1–80). Sanger, like Marx, foresees a revolution, but the one she imagines will flow from the liberation of the feminine spirit. The energy released from this epoch-making event will then be transmitted to future generations.

The Pivot of Civilization, published in 1922, concludes Sanger's voyage from socialism toward radical feminism. She now completely replaces economic analysis and its emphasis on class warfare with a focus on gender; her spotlight is aimed at feminine slavery resulting from enforced motherhood. Though this drift is implicit in *Women and the New Race*, she makes it explicit in *The Pivot of Civilization*. As she notes in the latter work, economic interests serve as one element in life, not the whole of it. According to Sanger, Marx neglected to give sex its proper role in human affairs. He merely wrote an "unconscious dramatization of a superficial aspect of capitalist regime[s]." He failed to note the "deeper unity" of the proletarians and capitalists and failed to "recognize the interplay of human instincts in the world of industry. Marx embodied all virtues in his beloved proletariat; all the villanies in capitalists." Though Marx granted that predatory capitalism sprang from overpopulation, he failed to follow through on his assessment. Marxism, according to Sanger, has become merely another dogmatic religion, and she now regards revolutionary socialism as "purely masculine reasoning." Birth control, on the other hand, provides the means to create a really new world and civilization, and Sanger now identifies herself with the victims of the witch hunts of Salem (Sanger 1922a, 8, 11, 14, 137–40, 154).

Sanger speaks more directly to eugenics in this book, but she remains skeptical. She launches into the subject by way of a critique of charities. The problem, as she envisions it, resides in the lack of balance between the birthrates of the fit and unfit. The answer does not lie in "cradle competition" as some claim, but rather in discouraging the rampant fertility of the physically and mentally defective. Since charities aid the survival of the unfit, they only compound the problem. Sanger uses draft statistics from the Great War to buttress her case. Draft boards rejected about 25 percent of inductees due to bad health or other defects. Twenty-five percent were illiterate. Later in the text she details the situation in Oregon, where some 10 percent of the population consists of "dependents, feebleminded, or delinquents." Over time, charities tend to make the unfit dominant by abetting their survival; different birthrates take care of the rest. In her final analysis, Sanger concludes that charitable work causes graver social problems than the social injustices sparked by the gap between rich and poor (25, 48, 55–56, 108, 112–13, 117–19).

Instinctive needs such as hunger and sex now define Sanger's vision. Given her seemingly empirical view that mental and physical defectives stand poised to take over the country, eugenics logically becomes a policy choice. She understands eugenics as "the study of agencies under social control that may improve or impair the racial qualities of future generations, either mentally or physically." She takes eugenics as the antithesis of socialism and understands it as an attempt to solve the "racial qualities" problem from a biological and evolutionary perspective. She argues that eugenic principles must be carefully developed by further study. Then these principles must be worked into the core values of a nation if they are to lead to practical effects. After making this qualified endorsement, she equivocates and raises substantial problems. Overall, Sanger believes that eugenics offers little more than renewed cradle competition. Democracy, where both the fit and unfit each have one vote, compounds this problem. Eugenists, according to Sanger, fail to recognize that birth limitation follows from attempts to increase living standards. Sanger also raises basic questions about the determination of fit and unfit, and she recognizes that middle-class biases permeate current understandings. Citing H. G. Wells, she notes that breeding for uniformity would exclude variety and forestall the emergence of geniuses. Eugenic legislation also ignores the influence of environmental factors. She continues to demur when it comes to sterilizing criminals. As Sanger puts it, "not merely must we know more of heredity and genetics in general, but also acquire more certainty of the justice of our laws and the honesty of their administration before we can make rulings of fitness or unfitness merely upon the basis of a respect for law." In another part of her text, however, she does endorse segregation for women of the moron class during their reproductive period and sterilization for feebleminded males. In an appendix, she recommends sterilization for the insane and encourages the procedure for those with inherited or transmissible diseases. Sanger defends this position on the grounds that sterilization does not preclude sexual expression. It merely guarantees that no offspring result. She draws her argument about eugenics to a conclusion by citing her mentor, Havelock Ellis: "If those persons who raise the cry of 'race-suicide' in face of the declining of the birth-rate really had the knowledge and the intelligence to realize the manifold evils which they are invoking, they would deserve to be treated as criminals." Though eugenics directs our attention to the biological nature of humankind, it proves mainly useful in its negative sense. Negative eugenics, as Sanger argues, shows how undesirable qualities spread throughout a nation. Sanger argues that birth control provides the most useful eugenic method and, thus, attempts to co-opt the debate over race suicide. At most, Sanger favors segregation and sterilization of the feebleminded and insane, while she demurs on criminals, perhaps because she was one herself (101, 104, 126–54, 170–72, 175, 177, 180–84,186–89, 282).

A good part of *The Pivot of Civilization* consists of a harangue against the Roman Catholic Church. In general Sanger argues against the church's attempt to legislate for non-Catholics. Her real argument with Rome, however, focuses on the meaning of the term "natural" as well as "feminine nature." Current morality, as Sanger sees it, poses a choice between concealing gratification and suppressing desire. This creates an inner conflict that breeds neuroses and hysteria. Following the dictates of psychologists like Ellis, Sanger proposes to create a liberated world without any conflict between behavior and desire. In its teachings about sexuality, the Roman Catholic Church gains power over men and reduces women to slavery. It teaches women to resist natural impulses and, accordingly, causes psychological harm. Later Sanger suggests that patriarchs invented the old morality to reduce women to "passive machines." In an angry complaint later repeated in the 1960s, she says, "We are not to be lectured, guided and molded this way or that. We are alive and intelligent, we women, no less than men, and we must awaken to the essential realization that we are living beings, endowed with will, choice, comprehension, and that every step in life must be taken at our own initiative" (210). When women are freed from traditional morality—really, traditional slavery—humankind will experience a new freedom. Reflecting once again the teachings of the new psychology, Sanger holds that the road to human development is found neither in heaven nor in the acquisition of wealth; rather, it lies inside each of us (197, 200, 205, 209–12, 218–19).

In *The Pivot of Civilization* Sanger elevates the new psychology as represented by Havelock Ellis to the rank of a master science. Just as humankind has progressed by gaining control over the forces of nature, the new psychology offers the conquest of forces within the psyche. The most elemental of these forces are sex and hunger. Birth control in her view deals with both issues simultaneously. She also calls for eradicating sexual constraints and prohibitions. In this sense, as will become fully clear in *The Joy of Sex* in 1972, birth control becomes the "instrument of liberation and human development." She distinguishes between sexual experience that is integrated and assimilated within the psyche and the extremes of asceticism and libertinage.

Sexuality can create a world of beauty and joy. This force will transform the world and show the way to an "earthly paradise." Women, of course, occupy a pivotal position and must first realize their strength, courage, and vigor. Self-realization for women, one that can be transmitted to children, will lead to a deeper love for humankind. "For in attaining a true individuality of her own she will understand that we are all individuals, that each human being is essentially implicated in every question or problem which involves the well-being of the humblest of us." Sanger then raises a discordant note. "Every single case of inherited defect, every malformed child, every congenitally tainted human being brought into this world is of infinite importance to that poor individual; but it is of scarcely less importance to the rest of us and to all our children who must pay in one way or another for these biological and racial mistakes" (274). In the context of this argument children are necessary for the psychological development of the parents as well as the perpetuation of the race. "Close at hand is our paradise, our everlasting abode, our Heaven and our eternity" (225–29, 232, 239, 271–76).

In this work Sanger postulates a fundamental unity between owners and workers, while Marx saw only conflict and warfare. This unifying force is patriarchy, though Sanger never explicitly names it. She also smashes her socialist ideological blinders and discovers that current social structures reflect "purely masculine reasoning." She now recognizes the old morality as a patriarchal trap for women. Though she understands that false consciousness caused by a patriarchal ideology keeps women in chains, she does not fully realize that the road to freedom lies in exploring consciousness, as other theorists argue six decades later (see, for example, MacKinnon 1989, 83–105). She finds the way out, rather, in birth control, though she suggests that the fundamental problem lies much deeper within the social structure. Her argument with the Roman Catholic Church centers on feminine nature. She disputes a unifocal purpose of marriage, and contrasts the new psychology with the traditional Roman Catholic teaching. In this view, repressed sexuality leads to human misery. As Sanger anticipated, psychology eventually comes to define the meaning of intimate behavior, and the old teachings, rooted in theology and natural philosophy, fade in importance.

Eugenics, especially after the Holocaust, clouds Sanger's reputation to this day. From her earliest writings to her last speeches, she consistently preached against unfit people spawning offspring. Though consistent in her stump speeches, she equivocated on eugenics and largely tried to co-opt the movement as allies in her struggle to make birth control available to the masses. Though perfectly willing to make speeches lamenting the birthrate of the unfit, she remained skeptical of most practical proposals. She was well aware that class biases permeated the very understanding of fit and unfit, and she declined to apply eugenics to criminals. On the other hand, she did accept sterilization or segregation for the insane and those with transmissible diseases. Birth control provided a much better solution. As Sanger knew, privileged classes limited births to increase their living standards. Though she did not make this explicit, lower classes could be lured to use birth control by the same economic appeal. Per capita income within a family, after all, is higher if there are fewer children. On eugenics, Sanger went no further than Justice Holmes, and both of them reflected their times. Sanger's equivocation on eugenics could also reflect the fact that she as well as her mother had tuberculosis. In some formulations, both were unfit to have any children at all. Sanger's mother died at age forty-nine after delivering eleven babies and surviving seven miscarriages (Chesler 1992, 47).

Sanger roots her work in the new psychology, Ellis much more than Freud, and argues that integrated and assimilated sexual experience can provide the road to happiness. Increased psychic integration for women can be transmitted to children and, thus, liberation can lead to a new age. Though Sanger broke with Marx, she always retained his vision of new heaven and a new earth: "Close at hand is our paradise, our everlasting abode, our Heaven and our eternity."

In 1926 Sanger published *Happiness in Marriage*. This text comes closest to contemporary marriage manuals and finds an echo in Van de Velde's *Ideal Marriage* in the 1930s and Comfort's *Joy of Sex* series in the

1970s. She opens with a lament about sexual ignorance, a standard trope in this genre. As Sanger sees it, males tend to have sexual experience without real knowledge, while women remain ignorant and lack experience as well. This, of course, causes marriages to fail, and her book attempts to address the resulting problems. Sanger calls for marriage to embody the "complete union of body and mind." She asserts that sexual intimacy has three functions. In a sharp break with many of her late Victorian predecessors, she postulates that the first consists of physical relief. Next she details the obvious purpose of procreation. Last, she asserts that sexual intimacy expresses the communion between husband and wife and that this rapture has the most to do with the art of love. Her book, then, becomes a paean to sexual rapture, later to be taken by Alex Comfort in his *Joy of Sex* series as a peak experience (Sanger 1926b, 6, 14–17).

Intimate behavior, as Sanger puts it, turns passion into poetry. "Sex expression . . . is the consummation of love, its completion and its consecration. Sex expression is an art." This gift brings men and women to experience the beauty of life. A willingness to embrace passion drives Sanger's vision. Its denial sets loose destructive forces and cuts people off from life's poetry. In an echo of the late Victorians, Sanger believes that individuals should store "vital Power" for the first twenty some years of life and not deplete their "bank account[s]." Passion measures the extent of one's reserves. Sexual intercourse, however, does not deplete one's bank account as some of the late Victorians thought. Rather, it energizes the body and psyche.

> For love stimulates the whole glandular system, releases into the body a fresh supply of energy, breaks through the old inhibiting and hindering fears, sweeps aside narrow, prim and priggish ideas of life's values, brings new spring to the step, fresh color to the cheeks, depth and spark to the eye. Love taps an unsuspected and inexhaustible supply of energy which the young lover may convert into ambition and achievement. This is why all the world loves a lover and that is why men and women must learn to remain in love, even though married. (19–22, 32–34, 48, 153)

Men must learn to concentrate on their mates and not merely their own desires. They should avoid haste and violence, and should seek to calm fears and apprehensions in their partners. Sanger, like Van de Velde in the 1930s and Chesser in the 1940s, charges men with responsibility for awakening passion in their wives. With "aggressive gentleness" men need to rouse latent desire so that partners can discover together the "chain of ecstasy." Men thus become gods for their wives. "In leading her successfully, nay triumphantly, through this mysterious initiation, he becomes for her a veritable god—worthy of her profoundest worship. He is sharing with her the greatest and most unforgettable adventure of her life. This experience is the true marriage." As men become gods by awakening dormant passion, their spouses drop the guises of girlhood and become "fairy princesses" (123–26, 130).

If a husband can blend his desires with those of his wife, they can experience rapture simultaneously. Though women have been taught to be passive, they should "abandon . . . [themselves] to it [rapture] utterly." These guidelines mark the path to mutual fulfillment and lead to a spiritual union of souls, not merely that of bodies. "Make the love you have found and which means so much to both of you *your religion*" (140–42, 170, 225; italics in original).

Some of the late Victorians tended to view withdrawals from the spermatic bank account—even within marriage—as steps on the road to ruin. Though Sanger accepts the bank account metaphor, she sees withdrawals leading to happiness and fulfillment, and rapture makes new deposits on account. Though she breaks with the prevailing sexual ideology on this issue, she reinforces the old view that sexual rapture changes one's visage, while she also reinforces existing gender roles with her references to gods and fairy princesses.

In her view men are aggressive, while women play the role of Cinderella. Women should keep men guessing, be elusive and hard to catch. "The love of the majority of men is deepened and strengthened by resistance. It puts them on their mettle, gives them the necessary obstacles to overcome, and puts them to the test." Later in the text Sanger uses victory and conquest rhetoric to define relationships. Unlike the late Victorians, Sanger believes that sex, not restraint, correlates with success in the tasks of life. Even a married woman's countenance reflects her husband's skill as a lover. Jewels and the latest fashions, on the other hand, merely display monetary success. Wives, according to Sanger, desire beauty and youth to court favor with their husbands. This expresses their love, and men must help their wives to keep their "charming" qualities (40–43, 60–61, 90, 119, 226–27).

Newly married couples need two years to cement their relationship. Sanger recommends birth control during this period so that couples can become spiritually and economically prepared for children. In this prelude couples should try to discover passionate love as well as spiritual growth. After outlining available birth control techniques, Sanger once again explicitly rejects abortion as harmful. She also opposes trial marriages (69–70, 195–97, 214).

In her marriage manual Sanger proposes three purposes for sex: physical relief, reproduction, and communion between husband and wife. The book sings of love's consummation. By now Sanger can write confidently within the framework of the new psychology and explicitly seeks to liberate passion. She challenges readers to engage in the poetry of life and discover its "chain of ecstasy." She does not, however, break completely free of patriarchal thinking. She declares that men can become gods and women fairy princesses. Gods and fairy princesses, however, occupy different rungs on the great chain of being. She also continues to embrace traditional sex roles and quite easily adopts the conventional rhetoric of sexual conquest. Though Sanger had broken from Marxism and glimpses radical feminism, she remains enraptured by the new psychology, which she does not see as patriarchy in a different guise.

Sanger's other writings deploy many of the same themes elaborated on in her major works. In *The Case for Birth Control*, a restricted shelf book, she views the population problem in terms of class. Classes embedded in poverty and misery spawn hosts of descendants, while the wealthy have few children. Knowledge also has a class base. The wealthy have it, the poor do not. The laws, of course, prohibit teaching the poor about birth control and thus force them to seek abortions. As Sanger puts it, "Our lawmakers close their virtuous eyes." According to Sanger, three hundred thousand babies die every year from ignorance and neglect. "Solicitude for woman's morals has ever been the cloak authority has worn in its age-long conspiracy to keep women in bondage." The solution, of course, resides in birth control for the masses, and she calls for a free clinic (Sanger 1917, 5–11).

Her *Debate on Birth Control*, the text of an actual debate, was published in 1921. Once more Sanger argues that women must be free to choose motherhood. As in all her writings, "large families and poverty and misery go hand in hand." Marriage has two equally moral but independent functions: love and parenthood. In her continuing attempt to co-opt the race betterment movement, she also argues that birth control will improve the quality of the race (Sanger 1921a, 14, 18, 25, 28, 48, 54).

As previously remarked, the New York City police stopped Sanger from speaking at the close of the First American Birth Control Conference. She spoke several days later, and the American Birth Control League published her remarks as *The Morality of Birth Control*. In this address she links morality with brain development and holds that irresponsible and reckless behavior, is immoral. She never provides a definition of irresponsible or reckless behavior, much as she never defines fit or unfit. After reiterating that women must have the right to control their own bodies, she notes that children, in turn, have a right to be desired, be conceived in love, and inherit sound health. It is immoral and uncivilized to disregard the "suffering of lives that will come." Though nature uses disease and famine to reduce population, the better and more civilized method is birth control. Birth control also exhibits forethought for others and a recognition of the value of life. As Sanger sees it, upper classes, respectable and moral members of the community, have knowledge of birth control and make use of it. The middle classes are equally intelligent and responsible, but lack knowledge of birth control. The irresponsible and reckless, by implication the lower classes, pay no attention to the consequences of their actions or have religious beliefs that preclude them from controlling their numbers. Many among them are feebleminded, diseased, and poor. Since they cannot support themselves, they should not be allowed to have children that others will have to support. "We do not believe that filling the earth with misery, poverty and disease is moral." The Roman Catholic Church, as previously remarked, opposed birth control and ferociously fought Sanger. In this angry formulation, Roman Catholic immigrants with their large families are by definition irresponsible and reckless and should not be allowed to have progeny. Rhetorical revenge indeed (Sanger 1921b).

In *Women, Morality and Birth Control*, Sanger once again states her case forcefully, if not simplistically: "All our problems are the result of over breeding among the working classes." Morality she again defines in terms of what uplifts and aids the survival of the race. Birth control will lead to "higher individuality" and a "cleaner race" and, thus, is moral. No one has a right to have defective children. Similarly, couples have no right to have a child when they do not have the resources to care for it. Since a mother's strong emotions from the time of conception may affect the child, fear of pregnancy can have an undesirable influence on offspring (Sanger 1922b, 10, 15, 54–55).

In "The Children's Era," published in her edited work *Religious and Ethical Aspects of Birth Control*, Sanger speaks through a plethora of mixed metaphors. She identifies the unfit with weeds in a garden, and the poor with those who arrive at a train station without baggage. This short piece, however, is mainly important because of an idea she rejects. "I would like to suggest Civil Service examinations for parenthood! Prospective parents after such an examination would be given a parenthood license, providing that they are physically and mentally fit to be the fathers and mothers of the next generation." Then she demurs, as is her style on this issue. "This is an interesting idea—but then arises the questions 'Who is to decide?'" (Sanger 1926a, 56).

Other works also reinforce themes elaborated on in her trilogy (*Women and the New Race* [1920], *The Pivot of Civilization* [1922], and *Happiness in Marriage* [1926]). *Woman of the Future*, published in 1936, an ominous time in European affairs, begins with eugenics but quickly launches into an attack on the failure of science to get "humanity out of the muddle in which we find ourselves today." Humanity can be redeemed only by woman's creative energies, which will be liberated by reproductive mastery. According to Sanger, ever growing populations only serve the needs of militarists. Women indiscriminately breed babies for slaughter (Sanger 1936, 22, 24, 27, 29, 30).

Chesler, Sanger's most scholarly and sympathetic biographer, suggests that later in her life she became an opportunist by muting her radical teachings to curry favor with the privileged. Such a charge could be leveled against many activists seeking social change. There are other ways to understand Sanger, however. Even in her first work, Sanger implicitly accepts some elements of capitalism. Sanger always emphasized that the upper classes' desire for higher living standards led them to use birth control. We can surmise that a similar force would work for the lower classes if knowledge of birth control became available and economic advancement a reality. Sanger, of course, provided the knowledge. Birth control, as is clear in all of her writings, would liberate the feminine spirit and lead to a new world. She always wrote of this effect as a natural consequence. Later in her life, when she sought to make her crusade effective and courted philanthropists like Rockefeller, she could easily mute her radical views about the liberation of women and the evolution of a new humanity, because she believed that the effect would follow automatically. Much as Marx thought that the revolution was inevitable so did Sanger. One key to the process would be the lower classes' understanding that their living standards would rise when they limited their families.

Sanger provided the means, and awaited what she believed was inevitable. Sanger lived till 1966 and witnessed the beginnings of the media age. She never wrote about the effects of television advertising and the evolution of a consumer society on her movement, but they both undoubtedly affected the aspirations of lower classes for material things.

Sanger comes close to inventing radical feminism, much before its eruption in the late 1960s and early 1970s. Emma Goldman was also part of this breakthrough, and Sanger, as Chesler notes, borrowed many insights from her. Goldman never muted her radical views and was deported in 1919—an event probably not lost on her compatriot. Sanger never acknowledged her debt to Goldman; in fact she criticized her and dissembled about their early association (Chesler 1992, 86–87). Both women took the readily available socialist ideology rooted in the labor movement and adapted it to reflect the experience of women. Sanger, for example, began to focus on gender rather than class and transmutes the proletarian revolution into a revitalized world created by the feminine spirit. But Sanger's fundamental insights that gender means slavery for women and that masculine reasoning (patriarchy) defines social structure fade away with her turn to the new psychology as propounded by Ellis, which ensnared her thinking. In her marriage manual she writes that women are fairy princesses and men are gods and discusses intimacy in terms of pursuit and capture. Sanger thus ends up reinforcing traditional norms. She does, however, make a case for passion and rapture and reinterprets the bank account metaphor in such a way as to reverse its implications. In her view, withdrawals lead to new deposits. Though she never reconciles her views on the matter, the revolution sparked by the feminine spirit gets transformed into sexual ecstasy as a religion. Sexual rapture as a religion, a peak experience, will be taken up by Alex Comfort in his *Joy of Sex* series in the 1970s (Echols 1989).

Sanger's writings, prudent as they are in many ways, still got her arrested, and her clinic activities put her in jail. If we look to her personal life, how she actually conducted herself, we find elements of a more radical teaching that could be taken to challenge marriage itself. In all her writings, Sanger argues that birth control should be made available to married couples, and she condemns libertinage consistently. On the other hand, she acted herself on the basis of free love.

Sanger began as an activist in the early 1900s in New York City's Greenwich Village, which was then at a peak of radical fervor. As Chesler describes it,

The Village crowd was, of course, even more notorious for flaunting conventional marital and domestic arrangements than for advancing economic radicalism. Its apparent contempt for the moral constraints of bourgeois life was so intense that Max Eastman, intemperate editor of *The Masses*, the fashionable intellectual journal of the left, used to refer to those years as the "adolescence" of the new century. (Chesler 1992, 80)

Though Sanger never attacked marriage in print (this assault would come later in the 1960s and 1970s from Weathermen/women, radical feminists, and new lesbian and gay activists), she engaged in a multitude of liaisons, including one with Ellis himself as well as H. G. Wells.

A writers' retreat at Wantley in England provides a glimpse of a new world. Hugh de Selincourt, the owner of the estate, sought to create a "morally unconstrained universe." Based on theories propounded by Ellis, residents at the estate sought "sensuous living." Besides music and poetry, this included "an unfettered expression of physical love as a dimension of friendships formed within the group." Sanger later wrote that Wantley would always "radiate beauty, stimulate mental and spiritual growth, utter kindness, unselfishness, and entirely do away with the pettiness of jealousy, which so often occurs in the regular marriage." She visited Wantley twice in 1920 and tried to return whenever she visited England. Sanger never explicitly attacked marriage and usually wrote in its defense, but her incipient feminist principles could easily have led her to such a critique. Social institutions, as she wrote, reflected male power. She neglected to mention that marriage was one of these institutions. She knew and experienced other possibilities. Sandstone in the late 1960s helped to re-create some of Wantley's possibilities, though on a nonelite, more democratic level (Chesler 1992, 183–84; D'Emilio and Freedman 1988, 326; Talese 1980).

By the 1950s Sanger's views on birth control gained popular acceptance. Even *Reader's Digest* mentioned her. In 1950 Sanger began an association with Gregory Pincus, a research scientist, and asked him whether a drug could be developed that would stop ovulation. Out of this encounter came a grant from Planned Parenthood, and Sanger later arranged generous funding. Pincus "envisioned a pill that would prevent contraception by mimicking the hormonal condition of pregnancy, when the body blocked ovulation of its own natural instincts. If you could suppress ovulation, he believed, you could suppress fertilization." Sanger's dream came true in 1960, when the Food and Drug Administration approved Enovid. By 1963 over two million women used the pill, and a sexual awakening was soon to occur (Halberstam 1993, 288–93 and 604–6).

Even with John Kennedy, a Roman Catholic, in the White House in 1960, Sanger quite rightly felt her mission fulfilled—though she did have doubts about Kennedy. Whether or not she still awaited a revolution or foresaw the end of marriage, she had at least fulfilled her goal of making birth control widely available. Yet problems remained. The pill required expensive visits to doctors' offices and remained beyond the resources of less privileged women. Ignorance about sexuality, even in the hip 1960s, abounded. Within two decades the battleground shifted to sex education in the schools and abortion. The advent of acquired immune deficiency syndrome in the late 1970s inflamed the debate on sex education.

Should school authorities seek to provide fairly explicit information to protect sexually active teenagers from AIDS? Or at the other extreme, should authorities tell their students to "just say no"? In New York City, certainly one of the world's most sophisticated cities, the new schools chancellor, Rudolph Crew, who was appointed in 1995, approved an AIDS curriculum submitted by an advisory council. The council's report lists "honoring my commitment to God" as a reason for chastity and tells students that state law prohibits anyone under seventeen from having sexual relations. The council changed an earlier plan that called for demonstrating the proper use of condoms in classrooms; the revised plan allowed private instruction upon request (Friedman 1995, 41–42). Public policy disputes about sex education reflect America's ambivalent attitudes about sexuality. Margaret Sanger did a great deal to shift the course of the zeitgeist. The awakening of the feminine spirit continues.

3

The 1920s and America's First Sexual Eruption

As Sanger well knew, well-educated, privileged couples had already taken control over the size of their families. In 1890 less than 25 percent of families in which the husband worked as a businessman or a professional had five or more children, while 40 percent of farmers and unskilled workers still had five or more. In fact, the gap in these birthrates, presumably one between the fit and unfit, produced the concern with race suicide in the first place (Fass 1977, 60). Despite Comstock laws, contraceptive information and devices remained available to the privileged. Once contraception became widely available, the emphasis in marriage slowly moved away from procreation and shifted to the relationship between the partners. Sex as an expression of love between partners became coequal with procreation. Havelock Ellis, for one, taught that through sex a person found the real self stripped bare of social conventions. Freud would not disagree. Much later in the 1920s procreation hardly figures at all in some of the advice literature. Among the new psychological ideas just starting to permeate the culture was the belief that the early development of children was crucial to their later success in life; as a result, the emphasis in child rearing shifted from quantity to quality (D'Emilio and Freedman 1988, 225, 226).

Showered with love and affection and raised in an era that fervently accepted Mary Baker Eddy's cheerfully positive "Mind-Cure" thinking in Christian Science, young people reared in this dawning age of depth psychology had more awareness of their unconscious, but in many ways they lacked an understanding of the darker realities of life. Poorly adapted to endure a massive social crisis such as the Great War, young Americans who emerged from these modern family environments later rejected the optimistic worldview that they had been force-fed as children. Disillusioned and resentful of the older generation, which they felt had been disloyal, America's youth sought to challenge the existing order while remaining reluctant to provide any answers of their own.

The Great War, the one to end all others, defined the era, much as Vietnam would shatter American complacency in the 1960s. Slaughter in the tens of thousands battered consciousness. The Battle of the Somme is an example of the wanton carnage in all its hideousness. The battlefield selected by the Allied generals allowed for simultaneous assault by many divisions. According to the plan, more than thirty divisions marching side by side would assault the German trenches about a mile or so away. In preparation the artillery stockpiled almost three million rounds of ammunition. The Allied plan took into account the inexperience of many of the British divisions. Only a few of them had many long-serving volunteers. Most of the British units consisted of one-thousand-man battalions raised for the war; these troops, called the "New Army," had little equipment during training. As John Keegan puts it, they wore "civilian tweed" during training and later they were given "postman's serge." Many of the "New Army" divisions received their first rifles just before embarking for France. Taking the lack of training into consideration, the planners relied heavily on artillery to prepare the assault. As the planners envisioned it, heavy artillery fire would cut the German barbed wire, collapse their trenches, and bury them alive in their more deeply fortified positions. The plan called for the untested soldiers merely to walk behind the artillery barrage to the German trenches. The plan then called for the barrage to move forward, and the soldiers were then to assault the second line of trenches.

The artillery began its bloody work on June 24, 1916, and the barrage lasted a week. On June 24, 138,000 rounds were fired toward the German positions, while on June 30 some 375,000 shells exploded among the German lines. Unforeseen by the British planners, more than half the German defenders survived the barrage in their deep fortifications. They raced for their own trenches and then began to fire on the advancing British troops. In many places the artillery failed to cut the wire and German machine guns raked the troops at will.

The British soldiers, dutiful to their orders, climbed from their own trenches and marched forward in waves separated by fifty to one hundred yards, with the men walking two to three yards apart. The First Royal Inniskilling Fusiliers suffered 568 casualties in the first couple of minutes, 246 of them dead. The First Newfoundland Regiment in what seemed an instant had 710 killed, wounded, and missing. Out of sixty battalions committed to the first wave of the attack, German machine guns quickly butchered twenty of them in no-man's-land. On the first day, the British lost sixty thousand soldiers; twenty-one thousand were killed, the rest wounded or missing. Most of the carnage took place in the first hour, if not the first few minutes. As one British officer said, "God, God, where's the rest of the boys?" The battle for the Somme dragged on until November 18. The British had 419,654 men killed, wounded, and missing, the French about 200,000. British newspapers were filled with endless pages of casualty lists, and to some it seemed that British manhood had died at the Somme. Later, during World War II, when General Marshall visited England to urge an early attack on the continent, he was cut short by Lord Cherwell: "It's no use—you are arguing against the casualties of the Somme" (Keegan 1976, 207–89). The war's wanton carnage particularly challenged the consciousness of the younger generation. Many lost faith in God as well as Enlightenment ideals such as progress and reason. Hemingway later replaced "heaven" with "nada" in one short story: "Our Father who art in Nada."

American entry into the war created tremendous social dislocations. Many women, at least for a short time, were welcomed into the labor force and found some freedom from parental control. They also achieved a modicum of financial independence. Millions of men, many from small towns, were herded together into training camps far from parental oversight. Military authorities at first tried to enforce traditional norms. President Wilson, ever the proponent of Christian Mind-Cure, said that he sought "to surround our troops with a healthy and cheerful environment." He pledged to not only make the sons of America more virile, but also enhance their "spiritual values which come from a full life lived well and wholesomely" (Allen 1918, preface). Empowered by new repressive laws and aided by vice crusaders and social hygienists, the federal government forced cities to close their red-light districts and prohibited alcohol near bases. "The military suspended writs of habeas corpus, arrested women en masse, and forcibly held more than fifteen thousand in detention centers averaging ten weeks" (D'Emilio and Freedman 1988, 212). Contrary to the hopes of moral reformers, closing red-light districts had no measurable effect on venereal disease rates, which remained at 13 percent in 1918. Military doctors soon discovered that old infections acquired before military service posed the greatest problem. Some reports held that 25 percent of inductees had venereal disease (Brandt 1985, 77). The secretary of war appointed a Committee on Training Camp Activities to enforce the military's moral code. As one of its members said, "Sex organs do not have to be exercised or indulged in, in order to develop them or preserve virility." "Forget them, don't think about them, or dwell upon them. Live a good vigorous life and they will take care of themselves" (cited in D'Emilio and Freedman 1988, 211, 212). But the soldiers did think about them. After a 500 percent increase in venereal disease rates among American soldiers near St.-Nazaire, General Pershing stationed military police around brothels and saloons at debarkation points. Eventually the army gave up its offensive on moral prophylaxis and started giving condoms to the troops. Reformers considered this a surrender to immorality (212, 213).

Loss of faith in old ideals, combined with a growing acceptance of the new psychology, led to intense introspection, what Ann Douglas terms "terrible honesty," and a narrow narcissism (Douglas 1995). Consumerism and mass advertising techniques fed the new mood for instant gratification. Sex, as Sanger argued, became a means of self-expression and growth, a good in itself. Radical communities, like the one in New York City's Greenwich Village, soon challenged monogamy and Victorian purity.

New York's radicals also participated in the public flowering of African American arts in Harlem. The availability of work in northern factories during the war caused an exodus of African Americans to northern cities. As a consequence of this migration, jazz and the blues entered the mainstream, though white audiences demanded white performers. Blackface was acceptable, but not blacks in whiteface. Though African Americans tended to be Christians of one sort or another, many did not accept the harsh strictures of Victorian morality or America's Puritan heritage. They had evolved marriage institutions that reflected the reality of slavery and maintained some of their indigenous conceptions of sexuality. For their new white admirers, they came to represent the primitive, the erotic itself, and the id of Freud's formulation (Douglas 1995, 98; D'Emilio and Freedman 1988, 187).

All the while, lower-class dating patterns evolved through the use of public spaces such as New York City's Central Park for courtship, and later this immigrant pattern became the norm. Tenement living, after all, provided little private space. "Popular amusements created not only a heterosocial environment charged with youthful sexual energy, but also a commercial relationship between male and female that mirrored the larger social context." Since men mainly had access to money, dating became a system of treating that included "expectations of sexual exchange—what would a young woman give, sexually, in return for the favors of a man." Young men, no longer bound so rightly to the earlier masculine world of taverns, turned to the pleasures of "commercialized leisure" (D'Emilio and Freedman 1988, 197–99).

Eros came storming into popular culture. Young people were expected to pursue love, and it I came acceptable to mingle in commercial establishments. "Sex was something to be discussed and displayed, whether through popularizations of Freud, the true-confession magazines, or the romantic imagery of Hollywood films." The evolving consumer economy bound all this together. "An ethic that encouraged the purchase of consumer products also fostered an acceptance of pleasure, self-gratification and personal satisfaction, a perspective that easily translated to the province of sex" (234).

A Look at Love and Life

In the mid-1920s Joseph Collins, M.D., penned *A Doctor Looks at Love and Life*, which became one of the best-selling manuals of the decade. Collins despairs of grasping a universal truth of sex. "No one knows the whole truth, and if he did he would not be allowed to tell it. Church, convention and commerce do not want it and will not have it." In a break with Victorian tradition, Collins haltingly advocates an increase in some erotic gratifications. Masturbation before marriage, for example, now becomes a healthy activity. Despite this rupture with the tradition, Collins views sexual function in terms of procreation within marriage and like his medically trained predecessors provides no details for the mechanics of the "supreme embrace." Though Collins's work is notable due to its call for less repression and its rejection of religious norms in favor of scientific ones, the text also trumpets the arrival of homosexuals, inverts, and urnings into popular consciousness as well as their demonization as victims of a birth defect. In fact, Collins devotes a third of his book to the subject. Collins calls for toleration of natural inverts, but not for those who acquire the trait (White 1993, 68).

Collins's new scientific view holds that instinct motivates behavior and that reason can only modify the results. Repressed instincts demand some "payment." In Collins's view, sexual needs differ among men and women and occupy a continuum from 100 percent to zero; impotent men and frigid women are at the extremes. Some men, for example, have a 30 percent need, while others might have 90. Marital troubles arise when individuals have different needs; for example, when a man has 90 percent and a woman has 5. Embracing social Darwinism, Collins goes on to read genetics into social structure, which he understands as a natural succession of "ruling stocks." This concept is potentially inclusive and somewhat democratic as opposed to the notion of race suicide, which seeks to permanently place one racially identified group in a hegemonic position.

Collins also acknowledges the politics of the double standard, foresees a day when birth control will be readily available, and prophesies a new sexual morality that will reflect women's growing equality and economic independence—a time when psychology and not theology will guide behavior. Western culture makes women either strumpets or slaves; this view of women affects their consciousness. Frigidity, for example, can reflect ignorance, a husband's selfishness, or resentment at being treated like property. Some women, it turns out, have absorbed the culture's lessons and are satisfied with their slavery, while men, on the other hand, will not acknowledge their privileged position as masters.

Beyond the production of spermatozoa and ova, Collins dismisses other sexual differences as "negligible." Such differences reflect only environmental factors. Gender, a learned thing, thus comes to eclipse sexual difference. (In contrast, Van de Velde's *Ideal Marriage* in 1930 builds on the recent discovery of hormones and reasserts essentialism as well as emphasizes sexual difference). Given the current divorce rate, Collins finds that marriage "is not a great success." Generally companionate marriage is his ideal. The religiously inclined, as he sees it, defeat all attempts to reform marriage. Collins also sees a need for religion to reconcile itself with science. Overall, Collins proves more of a hostile deist than an atheist (Collins 1926, 13, 17, 19, 22, 26, 31–32, 36–38, 42, 45, 51, 52, 53-54, 60, 102).

Collins, as previously remarked, recognizes the existence of inverts, homosexuals, and urnings. He does not, however, carefully distinguish these three character types. On the whole, he views homosexuality as a misplaced sexual endowment that marks three out of one hundred people, and his understanding most often coincides with the inverted gender approach. Though constant fear and suicide mark inverted lives, he has met many "well balanced" ones in his psychiatric practice. Collins contends that most inverts, especially men, are born this way. If they marry and propagate, they contribute to the increase of deviants, and in this sense inverts result from a genetically transmissible birth defect. When medical science understands more about the sympathetic nervous system and ductless glands, such natural deviants will disappear. If homosexuals limit themselves to emotional and intellectual fulfillment and are celibate, they are not degenerates but merely "victims of fate." Such people are "the most to be pitied of all nature's misfits." Though Collins rejects much of the new Freudian theory, he does accept its view that sexuality evolves from self-love through love of the same sex to love of the other one. In this sense, "misfits" have made an immature love object choice (66, 67, 68, 74, 87).

Bad habits, including kisses, embraces, tender intimacies, feeblemindedness, and evil companionship, create other degenerates, especially female ones. Lesbianism specifically "flows from idleness, boredom and loneliness, and its victims are as a rule under- or oversexed." The cure for acquired inversion lies in promoting good habits. Bad tendencies show up early in life; the doctor recommends organotherapy—treatment by extracts from animal organs—as a cure (101).

Collins's begrudging tolerance for natural inverts demands erotic quietism on the part of these "victims."

> If the opportunity offers itself, he should be encouraged to believe that . . . [ability and idealism] are compensations, and in return for them he must refrain from conduct which is beyond tolerance of normal man and which the state holds to be a crime. Fortunately the true homosexual has deep religious sentiment; he is moved by ceremony and intrigued by mysticism. He should be reminded that the troubled waters of spirituality may be calmed if the heart will say: "Thy will be done" and repeat it until it becomes automatic. (101)

"We should rid ourselves of the notion that we are the keepers of the natural homosexual, but we should hearten ourselves to prevent and cure those who accidentally or deliberately acquire vicious sexual habits" (92).

Wells of Loneliness

The Doctor Looks at Love and Life recognizes the primacy of gender over nature and suggests that patriarchal norms are ultimately enforced by false consciousness. In this sense, readers might take the text as an implicit call for dismantling sexual roles rooted in false, that is, unscientific conceptions of nature and enforced by religious prejudice. Progressive as the text might seem in its calls for tolerance for some "victims of fate," it also provides a recipe for their elimination. Recognition of inversion is linked to its elimination. Understood as a genetically transmissible birth defect, natural homosexuality can be eliminated if victims are encouraged not to marry and if medical science makes the necessary advances. The victims must acknowledge that they are mutants, doomed misfits. Psychoanalysts should encourage such misfits to think of their other gifts and seek nonsexual outlets for their love of ritual and mysticism. Good habits among the young, on the other hand, will reduce the number of acquired misfits. If the inversion is caught early, a medical regimen might work. Though the text does not become explicit on the point, Collins seems willing to suggest helpful laws that promote good habits.

When the doctor looks at love and life, he calls public attention to "misfits" and then recommends toleration of natural ones. He does this within a scientific framework that subtly promises their elimination. Toleration, in other words, will prove only a short-term necessity. All of this depends on the cooperation of misfits in that they do not marry and understand themselves as "victims." Psychiatry, as represented by Collins, names the phenomenon inversion/homosexuality and labels it either a birth defect or an acquired vice. As long as deviates internalize these norms, their cult of victimness helps lead to their own gradual elimination. The good doctor inculcates into consciousness a sense of self/identity that is suicidal/genocidal. Collins, as previously remarked, remains well aware of the role of consciousness in rationalizing repression. And thus, as Foucault notes, the homosexual became a species (1978, 43).

The doctor's look at love and life also encapsulates the emergence of psychiatry as a master discipline in opposition to religion. Earlier medical doctors like Hanchett, Kellogg, and Guernsey sought to provide a grand synthesis that conflated sexuality with theology and natural philosophy. Van de Velde will ostensibly return to this preoccupation in *Ideal Marriage*. Collins utilizes the new science of the mind to offer liberation to women and promise an end to misfits. The control and elimination of misfits displays the power of this scientific way of thinking, and part of Collins's purpose lies in convincing the public of the dangers such "victims" represent.

The doctor's elaborate celebration of robustness not only reflects the mindset of the 1920s, but also heralds a reconstruction of masculinity. In the Victorian period, masculinity combined somewhat contradictory images of the robust male and the Christian gentleman; the latter tempered the former. Over time, the cult of robustness eclipses that of the Christian gentleman and, as MacKinnon among many others notes, the culture came to eroticize masculine power as experienced/embodied in erections. The first requirement, as Collins well knows, consists of delegitimizing religion. "[Klanners and Fundamentalists] . . . are determined to put God in the Constitution, and more determined that science prejudicial to literal acceptation [*sic*] of the Old Testament shall not be taught in public schools and institutions of learning supported by State funds." What happens, however, if some misfits and women come to realize that they have internalized a false consciousness? (178; see MacKinnon 1989, 126–54, White 1993).

As psychiatry sought to become a discipline, it offered society a token of its panoptic power and potentially built a constituency in its call for the liberation of women from false consciousness as well as its promised control and elimination of misfits. This leads to issues of consciousness as well as the power to define female and inverted/homosexual experience. Not surprisingly then, homosexuality over time becomes a cathectic issue within psychiatry (see Bayer 1987).

Economically Emancipated Women and Marriage

The marital advice literature in this decade also reflects the new view of gender. *Marriage in the Modern Manner* by Ira Wile, M.D., and Mary Day Winn presents a case in point. Wile was trained as a psychiatrist, while Winn worked as a writer and journalist. According to these authors, lasting love results from a gradually developing relationship built on shared habits as well as admiration and sympathy. Love at first sight represents the contrary and mainly reflects the influence of romance literature. Sex is not the central aim of marriage. The intellectual, emotional, and social rewards are just as important. In their view, sex is a means, not an end, in marriage. They criticize the view of New York University students who, when they rank ordered the qualities they sought in a mate, listed health, beauty, and wealth (Wile and Winn 1929, 8, 13, 20).

Keeping with the changing direction of the sexual zeitgeist, Wile and Winn herald a new kind of woman: a companion, not merely a housekeeper. Women are now better educated, which is a "blow at masculine supremacy." They know more about the world and have much more sexual knowledge. In fact, women are now more likely to be sexually experienced. Wile and Winn go on to enumerate the marks of the new woman. She has more time due to the development of household appliances. She also has more emotional stability and can provide real companionship to her mate. Her strength and endurance have improved. The biggest change, however, lies in the economic realm. Marriage for many women is no longer an economic necessity. Since women now were in the labor force, the new woman had more opportunities and, consequently, experienced more independence and freedom. Wile and Winn view this as a positive change for men, since it relieves them of economic pressure to provide for their families (27, 28, 31–34).

In a chapter entitled "Sex Communion," Wile and Winn define marriage as a social institution where the partners have a responsibility to each other as well as the next generation and the rest of the world. Sex communion is the "consummation of mutual affection." It enacts a spiritual relationship marked by sharing. A vital factor in making a marriage work, sex communion requires an equalization in excitability, responsiveness, and nature. Sensual phases of sex communion, however, pale in comparison to the "esthetic and spiritual attributes that are far more significant" (53, 54, 57).

Married couples must choose either contraception or continence. America's falling birthrate demonstrates that procreation no longer serves as the only goal of marital union. In fact, reproduction must be brought under the control of reason. Contraception means a "refusal to create life, except at such times and under such circumstances as appear favorable for those creating it and for the child." They argue that abortion can be defended only when the life or welfare of the mother is at stake. Like Sanger they also know that about one-third of pregnancies end in induced abortions, which means that about one hundred thousand occurred every year. According to Wile and Winn, about six thousand women die every year from these abortions. From their point of view, it would be better to teach contraception in the schools and make it a required part of high school curricula. Religious education in Sunday schools has failed (59–62, 66).

Eight and a half million women work; of these, according to the authors, one-fourth are married. These women have the double role of homemaker and worker. As Wile and Winn point out, what often begins as an equal sharing of tasks in a marriage can easily become a 50 to 150 percent arrangement. The authors do not view household tasks as gendered. In their view, influenced as it is by the new psychology, everyone is part masculine and feminine. They advocate that men and women make full use of their personality, and live in harmony with both sides of their psyches. Whoever is better at a task should do it. Some women, in fact, should leave the raising of their children to others, even though biological mothers remain the ideal choice to rear children. Women are thus caught in a conflict of social roles. The old role dictated by tradition conflicts with the new one that offers freedom and self-expression. The actual roles of women in America measure the intensity of the conflict between these two conflicting and competing views (124–27, 130, 134, 138).

In former times women used to marry for physical protection, but according to Wile and Winn, this is less necessary now. Women now marry to enjoy companionship and love and to have children. They are less satisfied with "mere masculinity" understood as physical strength. The authors accept divorce as a reality and distinguish between biological roles such as male/female and social ones such as husband/wife. Given the divorce rate, they suggest that plural, consecutive marriages have become the American norm. "It is difficult to see how the public is greatly benefited by the preserving of an incurably unhappy marriage, especially if the couple, after divorce, can find other partners and build up two satisfactorily adjusted marriages in place of one that was unsatisfactory." Though no longer so stigmatized, divorce still leaves psychological scars. Parallel to their argument about contraception and education, they go on to say that high schools should require a course on marriage and parenthood. They conclude their discussion of divorce with a discussion of alimony, and wonder if it is really necessary any more (176–79, 213, 222, 247, 263–64).

Like Collins, Wile and Winn view gender as a social construction as the term is used today. Collins views gender as anchored in consciousness and, consequently, difficult to change. Wile and Winn, on the other hand, report that major changes have already taken place. According to them, economic forces such as access to jobs account for changes in women's status. These changes go hand in hand with technological developments that have lessened the burden of housework, allowing women more leisure time. Wile and Winn suggest that household tasks, previously thought of as gendered, should be assigned on the basis of ability. Otherwise, as they note, women can end up with both a job and all the housework. Collins's book reflects the new psychology, which includes its view of instinct and the penalties for harsh repression. While advocating some of the conclusions of the new psychology, Wile and Winn do not subscribe to any particular system such as those constructed by Freud and Ellis. Much more so than Collins they embrace companionate marriage.

Collins asserts that the purpose of sex lies in procreation within marriage. He does foresee a day when contraceptive information will be widely available, but he does not reflect on the consequences of this pending change. Wile and Winn, publishing three years after Collins in 1929, assume the availability of birth control and thus shift the focus of marital relations from procreation to the relationship between the partners. Companionship between spouses should include, among other things, shared habits, admiration, and sympathy.

Male power is a central issue in both works. Collins sees it rooted in a false consciousness that is imposed on women, while he also suggests that psychiatry provides a means to loosen at least some of these constraints. According to Wile and Winn, economic opportunities now afforded women have already ripped patriarchy's bonds asunder.

Modern marriage toward the end of the 1920s reflects the (partial) economic emancipation of women, their ability to enter marriage more as a choice rather than a necessity of survival, and their ability to choose procreation as an option. Though Collins recognizes that masculine power enforces gender roles, Wile and Winn celebrate the end of such constraints. Gender roles in their view are thoroughly variable and even child care might best be delegated. Dominance and power in marriage, formerly assigned to men as breadwinners, is now variable. Even women are dominant in some marriages, and if the husband does not resent it, these marriages are likely happy ones. Toward the end of the 1920s, the gender binary has been challenged, and masculine supremacy called into question (Wile and Winn 1929, 179).

Marriage as a Science

As part of the reassessment of marriage and gender roles, Robert Binkley and Frances Binkley in 1929 wrote *What Is Right with Marriage: An Outline of Domestic Theory*. Robert Binkley trained as a historian, served on the faculty of New York University and Western Reserve University. Frances Binkley, a librarian, was his wife. In it they search for an "excellence intrinsic to marriage." Though aware of empirical research such as the Lynds' study of Middletown, they search rather for universal, normative standards. Through an interplay of empirical and normative concepts, Binkley and Binkley seek to construct a science of marriage. They propose to deal with marriage in its natural state, not as a social institution, and in their project they expect to establish a new academic discipline. Drawing on concurrent changes in nursing, medicine, and psychiatry, among many other fields, they set the norms for a discipline in Foucault's sense (Binkley and Binkley 1929, vii–ix).

According to the authors, marriage consists of "a personal relationship between a man and a woman, involving sex intercourse between them, and having an aspect of permanence or duration." Permanence is the key element that distinguishes marriage from love affairs, and sexual intercourse remains an end in itself. The family, contrary to the old teaching, is not a mini-state with the father as sovereign. In nature the family has no faculty of choice, a will in the Christian sense, and much of family life takes place without "corporate decisions." Binkley and Binkley view family life in terms of cycles of tension and accommodation. The family is not a political, social, or economic unit and actually transcends such categories. Since the natural family is not political, they do not view it as patriarchal (42, 80, 85, 86, 88, 99–100).

Consonant with previous work, they regard children as a matter of choice, not a divine or natural necessity. Putting the case as strongly as Sanger, they state that

> There is a certain stultifying habit of mind by which merely potential children are thought of as having supreme claims upon us, as if they were already lying in their cribs and reaching up their hands. This way of regarding the potentialities of the womb is much in use among elderly sentimentalists who wage a war of propaganda against birth control.

If children are a matter of choice, the authors ask, how do they fit into families? Children serve as joint property, cherished objects, and competitors. The parents must balance and weigh these values in making their decision to have children. What is appropriate for one point in their lives might not be for another (167–69, 186).

Monogamy, termed by the authors the "sex monopoly," reflects religious values that demand virginity before marriage and prohibit adultery after. According to Binkley and Binkley, the contemporary revolt against marriage is a revolt against sex monopoly as currently understood. They propose to ask what is lost and gained by this linkage between marriage and monogamy. In evaluating aesthetic concerns, the issue of jealousy, and the risk of parenthood, Binkley and Binkley continue to stress the centrality of permanence and duration in marriage relationships. As they put it, "If a sex relationship is permanent, if its duration aspect is dominant, then it follows from the fundamental definitions of the principles of marriage that the union must be regarded as a marriage, and the persons as members of a natural family." If a married person has a permanent liaison with someone else, then it is a polygamous relationship. Easy divorce and free love differ in only one significant way: only in the first case is the community informed of the relationship. Binkley and Binkley posit two fundamental problems with the sex monopoly. Virginity is no longer regarded as necessary for either men or women, and absolute monogamy functions more as an ideal than a reality. Sex monopoly is not intrinsically good, while sexual liberty is not intrinsically bad. The challenge, as they articulate it, is to devise a system that supports sex monopoly (188–94).

In terms of domestic theory, Binkley and Binkley view divorce as both a symptom and a disease. It destroys the durational aspect of marriage and is an "absolute evil." And adultery and polygamy decrease domestic interaction. "Sex liberty does not pretend to contribute anything of positive value to the natural family. Sex monopoly, rather, is the norm of family life." Natural marriage includes sex monopoly as an ideal, but not a norm to be imposed. Problems arise when the sex monopoly is imposed on the family as a social institution. They suggest that couples settle the matter for themselves. As Binkley and Binkley see it, families in their time have lost their economic, political, and religious functions; as a result, more emphasis is being placed on sex. They end their discussion by recommending the sex monopoly as a means to protect domestic interaction and duration, key aspects of the marriage relationship (215–18).

Collins, Wile and Winn, and Binkley and Binkley all record fundamental changes in gender norms. Unlike the others, Binkley and Binkley take these changes for granted rather than detail their evolution. They assume, like the others, the availability of birth control information and devices, and they analyze the corresponding changes in the marriage system as part of their attempt to establish a domestic science. As noted by Wile and Winn, once children become merely one option in marriage, the understanding of the relationship must change to focus more on the relationship of the partners. Binkley and Binkley find the basis of marriage in the permanence of the relationship, and they fret over a system that allows easy divorce. In their view a system that allows easy divorce is really a polygynous one, and they cannot distinguish between marriage and a long-term liaison. Collins, as previously remarked, finds the gender system patriarchal and offers psychiatry as the only hope for women. Wile and Winn find that the system has changed to allow women more equality, and they celebrate the new roles open to them. Binkley and Binkley, on the other hand, do not think the system is patriarchal at all. Unlike the other authors, they take the recent changes in gender roles as a given and try to construct a new discipline of marriage that takes the changes into account.

The Collapse of Marriage

In *The Marriage Crisis* Ernest Groves paints a grimmer picture of the 1920s and the changes brought about in marriage. Groves, a sociologist, led the way in bringing courses on marriage and the family into collegiate education. According to Groves the "extreme collapse of matrimonial experience as recorded in the divorce statistics" illustrates the depth of unhappiness with marriage. Groves posits two solutions: we can return to the past with its strict divorce laws or make divorce a function of mutual consent. As Groves views the situation, birth control allows for companionate marriages, and advocates of this type of relationship understand their union as a purely personal matter and favor divorce by mutual consent. The author seeks to discover whether or not divorce by mutual consent will increase public happiness and proposes practical suggestions about the marriage crisis along the way (Groves 1928, vii–ix).

The confidence of the nation's youth in marriage has been "roughly shaken of late." Marriage, however, has important social benefits, and though many individual marriages fail, the standards for the institution cannot be based on the failure of individual marriages. As Groves sees it, marriage failures in the 1920s result from changed social conditions, and the nation's "moral and educational leadership" has failed to provide an appropriate education. The current laissez-faire policy will not work (6, 12–15).

Like the other authors, Groves tries to distinguish the essential characteristics of marriage: union (in the sense of togetherness), the fact that this union lasts for life, and the fact that it is publicly announced. He supports this trilogy with arguments about human nature and culture. As Groves surveys the late 1920s, he sees a "pleasure philosophy of life" changing marriage. The period is marked by less altruism or any sense of obligation. Social change reflects not merely this turn to pleasure, but also the reality that this change has spread to the masses. A "democracy of opportunity" marks pleasure's popular appearance. Marriage always entailed self-sacrifice and "moral endurance," but the newer view finds it to be a denial of personal satisfaction (30–33, 36–37).

Birth control also drives this process. Groves makes a prescient statement:

> These expressions of emotion at least reveal the revolutionary character of the discovery of more effective methods of limiting birth and warn us of the disturbance bound to follow if science finally discovers, as is not unreasonable to expect, absolutely dependable methods of birth control. If this happens, one of the most momentous inventions in the social history of mankind will have been brought about—one that will have large consequences, either for human good or ill.

Margaret Sanger, who will one day arrange research funding for the birth control pill, will be a major figure in bringing about such momentous changes. Groves sees birth control as "largely responsible" for the marriage crisis, since it makes marital stability more difficult to maintain, while it advances the pleasure philosophy. Three major interests protect marriage: property, sex, and affection. The family, however, no longer serves as an economic unit, and birth control, no longer confined to a social class, has changed the old standards and made sex a private matter. Thus affection becomes the glue that supports marriage, which then incorporates the economic and sex interests. Affection then makes the other two interests "allies" (38, 40, 46–50, 58, 60, 64).

The times made trial marriages a real possibility. Youth, as Groves says, now can have sexual intimacy without any responsibility. A young woman involved in such a relationship that Groves cites notes only the difficulty of finding landlords willing to rent furnished apartments. While birth control lessens restraint, society now accepts that women are legitimately entitled to a sexual life. Groves forecasts a separation of sex from intimacy and assigns the blame for this crisis to America's moral leaders. Education, public opinion, and social standards must be made to serve the family. Groves laments the effects of materialism on American values and argues that sociology, psychology, and psychiatry should be applied to the home. Sounding a new note, Groves suggests the creation of family counseling bureaus and recommends that divorce courts become counseling agencies employing experts trained to deal with social maladjustment (153, 159, 173, 182, 184, 192, 194, 197–99, 202, 208, 222–26).

Mothers, according to Groves, also need practical help. Childbirth should be made safer and less painful, and when new mothers leave the hospital they should have help to ease their burdens. Groves specifically cites the nursery school movement and notes the possibility of household visitors who would allow new mothers to take brief vacations. He rejects state subsidies for families based on the number of children, but rather advocates extending the concept of life insurance to cover accident, illness, loss of the income provider, and later educational assistance for growing children. Wide coverage would make such insurance affordable. The middle class, as Groves sees it, desires security, which he understands as "freedom from disaster" (227, 231–36).

Marriage and Its Difficulties

Marie Stopes's book, *Married Love: A New Contribution to the Solution of Sex Difficulties*, was in keeping with the new emphasis on eros, although the title indicates that all was not well with the transition. First published at the end of World War I, the book was printed and reprinted throughout the twenties and into the early thirties. Stopes was trained in botany and geology and lectured on ancient plants from the cretaceous period. Her interest in sexuality was sparked by an unhappy first marriage and a happy second one. For Stopes, love and sex are undeniable and universal. "Every heart desires a mate," and everyone dreams of happiness in marriage. Unfortunately, happiness proves elusive for many couples. Society recognizes this unhappy state, and some suggest that the bonds of marriage should be loosened and divorce be made easier. Like Binkley and Binkley and Groves, Stopes believes that easing divorce laws is not a good solution. For Stopes, like the writers of other marriage manuals, the chief reason for unhappiness in marriage is sexual ignorance. Changing partners will not necessarily cure ignorance (Stopes 1931, 1).

The centerpiece of Stopes's book is her theory about sexual receptivity in women, or what she terms a woman's "sex tides." The problem she attempts to deal with, presumably the sex difficulties of the title, is the difference in the frequency of desire for sexual congress between husbands and wives. She attributes woman's "contrariness" (her fluctuation in sexual responsiveness) to natural physiological rhythms and insists that women are "not essentially capricious" (25, 27).

Predating Kinsey in her approach, Stopes has come to her knowledge of female responsiveness by carefully and gently questioning a number of women about their sexual feelings. She urges readers to put aside absurd teachings from an earlier era that nice women do not feel desire or that women have no sexual instinct but must acquire it after marriage. Stopes points out the reasonableness of her approach and also notes that women and their experiences have been neglected for too long (37, 38).

Stopes defines the sexual desire of women as firmly rooted in their biological nature. As a scientist, Stopes tries to bring sexual behavior and science together to achieve greater understanding. According to her research, women have a Periodicity of Recurrence (36, uppercase in original), or more plainly put, times during which they are especially desirous of intercourse. According to the calendar she constructed based on data gathered from an unknown number of women, these periods occur either three or four days before menstruation or three or four days after, and then again fourteen or so days later. She illustrates this with graphs constructed from data obtained from a few representative cases. Some women, however, are aware of only one, or sometimes none of these periods of stimulation, while others "may be perpetually stimulated by her love and by his being and are thus, always ready for the 'uttermost union'" (52).

The problem in achieving sexual harmony is now clear. A man, who is always able to be aroused and who must work hard to suppress sexual feelings, is coupled with a sexual partner who may feel desire twice a month, if she feels it at all. Unless a man knows this, he is likely to feel rebuffed by a capricious wife, one who is sometimes ardent and sometimes rejecting. The solution to this problem is twofold. First, husbands must become aware of this periodicity and capitalize on it, realizing that this is the time when wooing will have the most success. Second, a husband should understand that intercourse is possible on some occasions other than during this period of recurrent desire. He will, however, have to go very slowly, wooing his wife and making sure that she is aroused properly. Her orgasm depends on his abilities, and orgasms are necessary for health.

Stopes has not totally given up the spermatic political economy of the late Victorians. Rather, she has modified her approach. Noting that seminal fluid is filled with substances precious to the body, she says, "It is therefore the greatest mistake to imagine that the semen is something to be got rid of *frequently*" (59–60; italics in original). She recommends that married couples have sex several times during a period of two or three days followed by ten days during which no unions occur. The sexually active days should, of course, coincide with the woman's Periodicity of Recurrence. Thus, two very different sexual natures will find harmony and satisfaction (61).

Stopes uses a chapter on sleep to talk about the importance of female orgasm. Failure of husbands to "effect orgasms for their wives must be a very common source of sleeplessness and nervous diseases of so many married women." In fact, physicians should always ask women who are "worn and sleepless" about their marital relations, although a number of physicians believe that female orgasms do not exist. Lying awake next to a peacefully sleeping, satisfied husband breeds all sorts of bitterness and bad feeling. If a marriage is to be truly happy, both parties must be sexually satisfied (81–82).

In the same vein as other marriage manuals of this decade, *Married Love* represents at least a partial break from the earlier views of Kellogg and Guernsey. In contrast to their restrictionist views, Stopes encourages couples to engage in sex. She does partially agree with Kellogg and Guernsey in that women do have periods during which they do not feel sexual desire. Stopes renames Kellogg's rut the Periodicity of Recurrence, and it occurs twice a month. She recognizes the existence of spontaneous female desire while Kellogg and Guernsey deny it. Stopes does not censure a more frequent sexual schedule if both parties desire it. Frequent sex according to Kellogg and Guernsey leads to the ruin of individuals and nations. Once Stopes adopts the Periodicity of Recurrence, she cannot then agree with the more liberal views of Hanchett, who recommends sexual congress every three or four days.

Stopes takes contraception as a given, but she also assumes that all married couples want children. Thus contraception does not serve to make children optional as it does for Binkley and Binkley and Groves, but rather it serves to help couples decide when they want children and how many. Stopes does not see the advent of the pleasure philosophy that so worries Groves. For her, erotic pleasure is confined to the marital relationship, where it should be nurtured carefully (112–14).

In contrast to Wile and Winn, who envision women as having multiple roles, Stopes does not see that women have been much emancipated from the home. While women are becoming more and more independent, all "too often, marriage puts an end to woman's intellectual life." She advocates that women develop their own powers, including occupational activities and interests, to make them more interesting partners for their husbands. Men are naturally rovers and will turn to others, even prostitutes, if their wives are not interesting. For those who can, Stopes even recommends separate bedrooms as a way of avoiding overfamiliarity and a consequent loss of pleasure in each other's company (100, 139, 148).

Males always initiate sex. While the husband should look for tiny cues from his wife that indicate she is open to sexual congress, these cues should not be too bold. The essential nature of the male is to hunt, and the chase is important. The female must not be sexually aggressive since this could cool her husband's desire. Her advice to wives is "Be always escaping." It is the man's job to woo his wife, and the woman's to make him want to woo her (99).

In *Married Love*, Stopes confines herself to a discussion of marriage. Like most of the works written during this period, actual details of sexual congress are absent. She does not broach subjects such as masturbation, divorce, or homosexuality. Neither does she deal with the social implications of contraception or expanded roles for women. Hers is a book intended to give advice about marriage to young couples of the time. Primarily Stopes's work seeks to legitimize sexual behavior and especially female erotic feelings. Striking a balance between what she considers to be too much sex and too little, she recommends fortnightly coitus because that coincides with her law of Periodicity of Recurrence of female desire. Sex, however, is not just for procreation, but also cements the marital bond. Good health also depends on good sex and orgasms for both partners. This is a marked departure from manuals like those of Kellogg and Guernsey, who deny female sexual feelings and advocate abstinence even in marriage. Perhaps more than any of the other writers discussed here, Stopes epitomizes the increased importance of eros in popular culture.

In the absence of cataclysm, sexual mores like family structure itself change slowly over time. The change in thinking about human relationships begins with the early modern philosophers such as Hobbes, Locke,

Rousseau, and Kant. Though they regard the family as pre-political, they quite purposefully discuss male interactions as rooted in self-interest. In other words, other men are to be considered as use objects at best, enemies at worst. They view human life as a struggle set against a state of nature; all norms are conventional and rest ultimately on force. As these norms came to inform Western culture they penetrated the (constructed) private sphere of the home. In this modern view, pleasure as Bentham and Mill well knew is one thing that most people will definitely seek. Inevitably, pleasure would come to define even intimate human relationships. Practice, probably reflecting religious constraints, lagged behind. The 1920s represent an American eruption of a raw eros, one that sought the forbidden even in Harlem. Similarly, the 1960s represent another such eruption, but this one was more widely enjoyed since it was amplified by the media. All along, pleasures once reserved for aristocrats become more widely known and experienced. Marriage and sex manuals in this sense chronicle the democratization of sexual pleasure.

Changing sexual mores, partially sparked by available and affordable birth control along with greater freedom for women, led social commentators in the 1920s to either redefine marriage or attempt to save it. Similarly, following the challenge to sexual orthodoxy in the 1960s, some of today's more vocal conservative commentators also seek to save marriage. Robert Bork is a case in point. In his jeremiad, *Slouching towards Gomorrah*, Bork posits that the "collapse" of marriage leads to children who are "less happy, less physically and mentally happy, less equipped to deal with life or produce at work, and more dangerous to themselves and others." No-fault divorce, part of a larger feminist conspiracy, contributes to the collapse of marriage (Bork 1996, 158, 204, 208). Other conservative polemicists and activists have supplied plans to revitalize marriage. In general, they advocate eliminating no-fault divorce or changing the laws to allow covenant marriages (Gallagher 1996; Johnson 1996). Other commentators of a more progressive bent advocate domestic partnerships as an alternative to traditional marriage. Such partnerships are inclusive and recognize alternative relationships. Many universities and corporations, Levi Strauss and Disney included, now offer domestic partner benefits to their employees. Domestic partnership offers an alternative to conventional marriage without sparking the political battle that would result from any attempt to modernize marriage statutes to reflect the reality of divorce rates.

4

Sexual Eruption and
Then Reaction
The Interwar Years

Theodore H. Van de Velde, a retired Dutch gynecologist, caught the attention of educated circles in London with his 1926 edition of *Ideal Marriage: Its Physiology and Technique*. This book, the first volume of a trilogy, proclaims that a critical goal of marriage consists of sexual pleasure shared by husband and wife. Sex, according to Van de Velde, is neither evil nor debased. Men, in fact, should even learn how to please their wives, who have different arousal patterns and responses. Van de Velde even supplies graphs to help his readers understand these differences. He also provides the basic physiology as well as the appropriate techniques, which he states in a manner reflecting the times. Being steeped in Victorian thought himself, he could speak to his post-Victorian readers without either alarming or scandalizing them. Though Van de Velde worked diligently to keep his text within the bounds of Roman Catholic theology, the church still placed his book on its *Index Librorum Prohibitorum* (index of prohibited books) in 1931. Van de Velde's extensive table of contents, organized for ease of reference, foreshadows the menu approach later used by Alex Comfort in his *Joy of Sex* series in the 1970s.

First published in London in 1926, *Ideal Marriage* became readily available in America in 1930. The original edition went through forty-two printings. Sales figures are not available before 1945, but after World War II the hardbound edition sold more than five hundred thousand copies. Because of the work's popularity, Random House published a revised edition in 1965, two years before the "Summer of Love" exploded in San Fransisco. In 1980 Greenwood Press finally ended the run by printing *Ideal Marriage* as an important antiquity. Van de Velde stayed in print in English from 1926 through at least 1965, a run not yet equaled by even the *Joy of Sex* series (Breecher 1969, 83, 84–85, 96).

An underlying, conservative purpose informs the work. If couples could achieve ideal marriage, then those who say that marriage is a failure and call for its abolition would be silenced. Van de Velde offers a seemingly new solution by granting women equal sexual pleasure and some power in terms of erotic role reversals, but he also argues implicitly and explicitly that birth control lessens a woman's being. The most he will sanction in *Ideal Marriage* is the rhythm method. Without birth control women would have more offspring, and insofar as children hold a marriage together, the institution would be strengthened. Van de Velde, then, must educate his readers, most certainly husbands and medical doctors, to reject the growing knowledge about birth control. He seeks to reinforce the reproductive matrix: the linkage between marriage, sex, and reproduction. In this sense Van de Velde represents a conservative reaction to early feminist thought as represented by Sanger as he attempts to limit growing reproductive choices. Dr. Ruth adopts a similar rhetorical strategy during the "Reagan revolution" in the 1980s.

The first printing of *Ideal Marriage* came with an insert after the title page: "The sale of this book is strictly limited to members of the medical profession, Psychoanalysts, Scholars and to such adults as may have a definite position in the field of Physiological, Psychological or Social Research." The tone of the work is academic: Latin and indirect expressions are used throughout. But Van de Velde, unlike the late Victorians, explicitly accepts pleasure as a part of the scheme of things, and he discusses physiological details and practices formerly deemed suitable only for bawdy houses. By 1930 Margaret Sanger had already spilled the birth control secret, but Anthony Comstock could still reach from the grave and enforce the hegemonic moral order; hence the prudent publisher's insert (Van de Velde 1930, n.p. [ii?]).

Van de Velde, as he puts it in his preface, seeks to reduce the embarrassment of patients in consultations with their medical doctors by answering some of their basic questions. He also aims to help couples who do not enjoy regular medical attention. This, of course, gives the lie to the publisher's insert. Seeking to increase people's happiness, he says he will also write in plain language—at least plain for the times. Van de Velde teaches that happiness in marriage includes ecstasy but also transcends physiology; it is not merely synapses and neurons in an electrical grid system (xxiv).

Van de Velde's personal introductory statement adds that he seeks to bring enlightenment to unspoken things, and as a consequence he expects discordant results. As he sees it, his retirement as a gynecologist in addition to his age have freed him from many constraints. He is now free to write what he considers necessary. In the world as Van de Velde beholds it, there is far too much suffering and not enough joy. His qualifications for leading us toward joyful marriage include his experience and age as well as his knowledge of medical theory and practice. Now in retirement at the age of fifty, he is detached and beyond the excesses of youth, but he still knows the pull of eros. Van de Velde rejects the use of a pseudonym and feels duty-bound to sign his work. Otherwise, it might lose some of its moral purpose (xxv–xxvi).

Van de Velde opens his text by stating that when marriages fail they can be hell. In his view, marriage should be merely purgatory—a state of purification. Marriage remains sacred to Christians and necessary for the social order. It provides women relative security to engage in reproduction, so they can pass on the gift of life to their children. Men, on the other hand, find marriage a support system for their work in the world. All in all, Van de Velde supports a traditional view: men are in the workplace and women are in the home nurturing children. The essential element in marriage is finding the right partner. A man needs to find a spouse who shares his attitude toward marriage and the world as well as a similar style of parenting. Both must also want a good sexual life. It helps married couples to have other interests such as stamp collecting, but children work best for holding a couple together (1–2, 5).

Sexual intimacy, simply put, provides a basis for marriage. Marriages vary but exist within a normal range. In his descriptive chapters Van de Velde will define what exactly constitutes this range. Even within this range, some might think a particular activity "debauched," but physiological soundness corresponds to ethical acceptability. The truth of this assertion, of course, turns on the meaning of the word "sound." Van de Velde neglects to define it for the moment, but his definition will undergird the entire text. He notes that he will maintain a scientific tone throughout *Ideal Marriage* and assumes all his introductory qualifications again (6–9).

Warming to his subject, Van de Velde argues that the erotic drive aims at reproduction, though reproduction and sexual impulses have lately become separate. This reproductive urge proves strongest in mature women and manifests itself as a desire for motherhood. Men, on the other hand, experience this urge mainly as a wish to have children by a particular woman. In Van de Velde's view, the sexual/reproductive dyad is species-wide, and women bear responsibility for maintaining it, since the maternal drive is part of their nature. The partners in an ideal marriage can achieve a union of souls, and thus a type of psychic immortality. Van de Velde next addresses the contrary argument. Some argue, as he says, that the urge to copulate can be divorced from reproduction. Van de Velde disagrees, but he also constructs a vast smokescreen. In parsing these distinctions Van de Velde at first distinguishes between copulation and "complete intercourse," and by implication equates mere copulation with incomplete intercourse. On the other hand, he does note that some prefer other types of sexual activity than normal intercourse. On page 12, however, he contradicts himself and announces that he has separated reproductive urges and sexuality. Van de Velde goes on to define the sexual urge as an *"impulse to sexual activity . . . [with] its irradiations not only in the genitals, but in the whole body and the whole psychic personality.* Hence its power is almost supreme, [and] almost divine." But he also claims that maternity is necessary for femininity or wholeness of being. Since maternity defines part of a woman's being, Van de Velde can then ostensibly drop it out of his definition of the sexual impulse while retaining it at the same time. His equivocal stance on the relationship between copulative and reproductive sexuality underpins the entire work, much as it will Dr. Ruth's *oeuvre* in the 1980s and 1990s. Only by understanding this contradiction as a rhetorical strategy can we decipher *Ideal Marriage* (12–14; italics in original).

Drawing on new research at the time, Van de Velde postulates that the sexual urge depends mainly on sex glands and their secretions. Though the sexual urge originates in these glands, it is combined with heredity and conditioned by the psyche. In the evolution of women the correlation between sexual desire and ovulation has been weakened, but the relationship has not been completely sundered. When the impulse to approach another person merges with the desire for consummation, love blossoms (14, 16).

Marriage is a "permanent form of monogamous erotic relationship" and an evolutionary force. It makes people work toward the welfare of others such as spouses and children. Sexual feelings not only attract men and women but can also repel them at the same time. Van de Velde suggests that married couples deal with this tension by maintaining strong emotional bonds and enhancing attractive factors so as to minimize incompatibility. To avoid unpleasantness and achieve happiness, couples should constantly renew their courtship; they also must compromise, satisfy each other's needs, and create an erotic culture.

Van de Velde will deal only with normal sexuality: "morbid deflections, twisted and abnormal desires have no place in the physiology of marriage." He supplies no examples. Since his concept of ideal marriage includes reproduction as an element of sexual union, however subtly he makes this part of women's nature, Van de Velde declines to acknowledge nonreproductive expressions of the sexual impulse and labels such things morbid (12–19, 32).

Van de Velde tells men to give sexual pleasure to their wives, but he also knows that the root of women's pleasure is clitoral, not vaginal. Like numerous others who take this approach, he must then either normatize vaginal intercourse by arguing that maternity enhances a woman's being or teach that other needs are fulfilled in addition to the maternal one. Van de Velde deploys both approaches. Reproductive or vaginally penetrative sexuality certainly can satisfy a woman's maternal needs. He adds that a woman's being and pleasure are enhanced when she serves as a spermatic receptacle: "For a woman (in coitus) the odor of the beloved man's semen is delightful and excites her anew; but that of an unloved mate fills her with loathing." Men, on the other hand, accept the odor of their own semen, but not that of others. This, of course, calls into question birth control devices like condoms, any technique that flushes sperm from the vaginal area, or any chemical that kills or neutralizes sperm. All these techniques reduce a woman's delight and excitement (32).

As previously noted, Van de Velde portrays the clitoris as the locus of a woman's sexual pleasure. He terms it "an organ of voluptuous sensation exclusively." The clitoris, however, attains full development only with regular use. Clitoral smegma, much like semen, appeals to the opposite sex. He goes on to note an aphorism in Latin, both here and later in the text, that ovaries define a woman's being. Just before the follicle bursts a woman undergoes intense sexual desires. Van de Velde, of course, reads this as an evolutionary necessity. Nature, in his view, expects every egg to be fertilized (54, 55, 86, 88, 95, 113).

Reflecting on menopause causes Van de Velde to scale lyrical heights about a middle-aged woman's fulfillment. He praises her experience and intuition, among other things: "And she has now learnt to know and understand her husband perfectly: to encourage him in his life's struggles, to forgive his faults, to meet his wishes." After menopause a woman should be able to meet her husband's reasonable sexual needs. Van de Velde now disregards his earlier linkage between reproduction and sex and even suggests that the connection can burden women. Middle-aged women—in spite of the end of their ovarian function—still appreciate sex. Since these women need no longer fear pregnancy, they may even appreciate sex more. Even so, *"propter solum ovulum mulier est quod est"* (111–12, 113).[1]

Nature does not dominate men's lives as it does those of women. While motherhood marks women's destiny, men are mainly responsible to support and preserve their families. While sex remains fundamental for women, for men it is an accessory (115 , 119).

Vaginal tissues absorb semen, which vitalizes women. It also accelerates metabolism and has an overall tonic effect. Women also benefit from the corresponding increase of their own secretions during intercourse as well as from better psychic health in general. This, of course, necessitates penetrative intercourse and precludes some barrier methods of birth control such as condoms, but might allow for diaphragms. Diaphragms, however, benefit women by allowing seminal discharges but disallow their full experience of self in maternity. Spermicidal jellies would also deny women benefits both ways, while sponges would at least deny maternity. Women both want and need sperm.

In a position reminiscent of the late Victorians, Van de Velde holds that men reabsorb some of their own vital fluids, and this promotes their vigor and mental acuity. Internal secretions cause men to experience sexual emotions and make them want to share their élan vital. (Skeptics might argue that if all this is true, gay men should be very vitalized as well as have heightened mental acuity, while lesbians would be doubly deprived.) Van de Velde believes that unless male organs are moderately used, they can atrophy, and this leads to senility and degeneracy. Unless morbid symptoms appear, men should engage in intercourse until they are fifty or sixty (139, 141).

Having established the physiological basics, Van de Velde goes on to define sexual intercourse as the "full range of contact and connection, between human beings, for sexual consumption." He is, of course, discussing only *"normal intercourse between opposite sexes."* Though he will make occasional references to abnormal practices, his purpose remains "to keep the Hell-gate of the Realm of Sexual Perversions firmly closed." Ideal marriage, on the other hand, permits the full scope of normal activities, which in Van de Velde's view includes a reverence for chastity. Normal intercourse requires a man and a woman whose activities exclude cruelty as well as artificial modes of stimulation. Their activity must directly or indirectly seek consummation and conclude with ejaculation of semen into the vagina. He also values the simultaneous enjoyment of climax and makes men responsible for achieving this feat. Later he notes that communion has its "acme" and purpose in depositing the "seed of life." The biological purpose is pregnancy, though not every occasion causes it. Similarly, intercourse is not absolutely necessary for impregnation; thus Van de Velde conveniently allows for virgin births. His insistence on ejaculation into the vagina without any impediments rests on his earlier muddied distinction between copulative and reproductive sexuality. Having understood this equivocation, we can take Van de Velde as a conservative writer much like Dr. Ruth. Pleasure, the supreme acme in mutual culmination, is firmly fixed within the reproductive matrix (144–45 and n. 1, 146; italics in original).

Van de Velde allows some variation in sexual roles. He even lists various positions for intercourse and the amount of pleasure that each induces as well as each one's potential for causing pregnancy. In *Ideal Marriage* a man and a woman "should merge into a melodious *mutuality*" as they experience equal joys (145; italics in original).

In his discussion of erotic kisses, by which he means deep penetration of the mouth by a tongue, Van de Velde claims that substances injected into the vagina become part of a woman's saliva. A husband can increase the retention of his own vital fluid and reduce his net outflow by reabsorption; if he is repulsed by it, he can determine that his wife is adulterous. Sperm, in other words, brands a woman. Only a condom can hide adultery. Men, as he has already told us, are repulsed by the semen of others.

Though Van de Velde accepts some variation in sexual roles, his discussion of "love bites" reinforces traditional gender/power roles. Unless husbands act emotionally overwhelmed, their wives will not believe that they are truly loved. Van de Velde cites Havelock Ellis, Margaret Sanger's mentor, to the effect that "a certain pleasure in manifesting his power over a woman by inflicting pain upon her is an outcome and survival of the primitive conquest of courtship, and an almost quite normal constituent of the sexual impulse in men." Men, in other words, cannot stop, even in inflicting pain. To sum up: "What both men and women, driven by obscure primitive urges, wish to feel in the sexual act, is the essential force of *maleness*, which expresses itself in a sort of violent and absolute *possession* of the woman." "Both of them . . . exult in a certain degree of male aggression and dominance . . . which proclaims this essential force." Lurking behind this is a basic "repulsion" and "antagonism" between the sexes. This elemental disjunctive force is more real and permanent than the attraction between women and men. Underneath love, in other words, lies violence. Brownmiller will make this case in the conclusion of *Against Our Will*, a study of sexual assault (Van de Velde 1930, 154, 158–59, 161; italics in original; Brownmiller 1976).

Van de Velde frankly discusses different types of stimulation such as that directed at the nipples and glans of the clitoris. All the while he stresses reciprocity. A woman who is fully possessed by her husband will quite naturally reciprocate and try to stimulate his organs. Her husband's full erection "is a supreme psycho-erotic joy to her." But if she is too assertive in her stimulation, she just might repel her husband as well as cause ejaculation. Male arousal becomes a woman's responsibility. All women revel in male power and must do the dance of the Seven Veils (163, 165 –66).

Women, on the other hand, require local stimulation, including genital kisses. After receiving such intense pleasure, the wife may offer reciprocity. Men, as Van de Velde qualifies his gender distinctions, are essentially active, while women are mostly passive, with the exception of feminine assertiveness in genital kisses. Both should enjoy an equal share of pleasure, and women have equal rights of consent. Van de Velde appeals to self-interest to convince men to attend to their spouse's pleasure. Her active participation actually increases his own pleasure. He also makes an argument that happiness results from love, since emotional and psychological happiness depends on its bodily realization. In all of this, all of it, husbands should educate their wives and instruct them in the mysteries of eros (169, 171–72, 174, 176).

Both clitoral and vaginal orgasms create pleasure, but like two wines, they differ. Both involve the same internal mechanisms, local and cerebral discharges and relief. "Perfect and *natural* coitus" consists of a blend of both types of orgasms. Ideally, stimulation focuses on the vagina, which is "fully adequate" for orgasm. Of course, Van de Velde must equate the two, since his not quite so hidden agenda consists of defending reproductive sexuality, which requires unimpeded vaginal penetration (180; italics in original).

In another blow to birth control, Van de Velde teaches that the initial "jet of life-giving fluid against the urethral walls may give the signal for the orgasm and even intensify sexual excitement." Van de Velde argues that orgasm depends on ejaculation into the vagina, but once again he equivocates. Orgasm can occur without ejaculation and some

women may experience several before ejaculation. In normal communion, however, ejaculation heralds the woman's orgasm. A husband's
muscular contractions while ejaculating or the impact of the vital fluid
triggers his wife's orgasm. Van de Velde acknowledges that only a minority of women experience orgasm as a function of male ejaculation,
but he argues that it would be wrong to deny any importance to the
fluid's impact.

Since earlier in his book Van de Velde held that seminal fluid enhances
a woman's being and potentially satisfies her maternal instinct, it comes
as no surprise that he explicitly rules out birth control after his discussion
of the acme of the sexual impulse. Condoms and rubber caps may cause
irritation and congestion. Psychic and mental disturbances are the logical outcome. Besides, women miss the balm of the seminal fluid. Other
birth control techniques also frustrate nature and cause men to commit
a fraud upon their spouses. Even if the wife consents to these practices,
she does not fully understand the consequences. Every action that does
not bring the couple to normal orgasm causes injury and can permanently damage both body and soul. Couples who engage in these practices without perceiving any harm are really degrading and destroying
their marriage. Van de Velde pays a good deal of attention to the monthly
cycle so as to pinpoint the risk of conception. By using the rhythm
method, his readers can engage in coitus with a reduced risk of pregnancy
but still enjoy the other benefits of sharing the élan vital. If the husband
ejaculates too soon, he should use genital friction and caresses—unless he
proves potent enough to reenact the whole sequence. If genital stimulation fails to bring the wife to acme, then "autotherapeutic measures" are
better than nothing (186–87, 191–92).

Van de Velde explicitly agrees with most Roman Catholic theologians
and emphasizes the progressive nature of his book, certainly one suited
for the times. Science teaches that wives are not "*a passive implement, receptacle and incubator*, and . . . [modern thinking has] recognized and
accepted her as *an active, adult and equivalent sexual being.*" Van de
Velde, however, undermines all this with his teaching that women must
have sperm, jets of it coating the vaginal walls, and that both partners
seek the essential force of maleness expressed in violent and absolute possession. Van de Velde has mainly constructed a physiological basis for the
incubation and receptacle roles; unlike his late Victorian colleagues, he
does not draw directly from theological premises (193, 195 ; italics in
original).

Van de Velde goes on to gender the "supreme moment." This instant, in his view, can even erase the effects of age and give people maximum attractiveness and charm. Men experience power, while women feel tenderness. Husbands on their honeymoon should teach their new wives how to behave and also what to feel during intercourse. Men need to exercise self-mastery along with patience. Advanced instruction comes after the honeymoon. Having made his point, he deploys his Purgatory metaphor again (247–48, 262, 263).

Van de Velde engages his rhetorical strategy by instructing women about the critical role of pregnancy in their lives as well as their need for sperm. His overall goal is to maintain the linkage between sexuality, marriage, and reproduction. Sexual activity itself, as he notes, favorably influences feminine minds and bodies. Sexual activity, however, also has drawbacks such as pregnancy, which is a mixed blessing. Pregnancy defaces a woman's body while it also changes many of the body's processes. It also can make women morbid and cause anxiety neuroses. On the other hand, pregnancy allows women to experience *"Motherhood,"* a woman's "most overwhelming and wonderful experience." Pregnancy plays a huge part in sexuality and is a racial necessity. Women are responsible for maintaining the species, more so the white race. Intercourse becomes all that it can be only when couples free themselves from worrying about pregnancy, a fear that can even destroy a marriage. Van de Velde could allay these fears by recommending birth control, but he breaks off the argument with the ambiguous statement that "vigorous and harmonious sexual activity" cannot occur if the wishes of both husband and wife regarding pregnancy are not respected. Intercourse may be enjoyed during pregnancy, and Van de Velde recommends this since sperm still functions as a balm. He authorizes the use of condoms if seminal substances turn out to be harmful during pregnancy. Suppressing sexual desire, after all, can cause anxiety neuroses (263–67, 271, 287, 288 and n. 1, 295–96, 299–300; italics in original).

After reiterating all the benefits that accrue to women from vaginal intercourse, Van de Velde draws the line between exertion and excess. This line will vary among women as well as from time to time. Crossing this "Rubicon" remains the responsibility of men, generals, and conquerors (in terms of his metaphor). Once married, women experience desires equal to those of their husbands, which spur their husbands/conquerors on to greater heights of happiness.

Having implicitly opposed birth control from the beginning of his book, Van de Velde now confronts the subject directly. As known and practiced in his day, birth control contravenes ideal marriage, "diminishing stimulation, disturbing and dislocating normal reactions, offending taste, and effectually ruining spontaneous *abandon* to the act of communion." This conclusion, however, proved evident long before Van de Velde's three hundred pages of exposition. Birth control can also lessen a man's spermatic reabsorption. Though men reabsorb some of it themselves, deep kissing provides another route. If this tonic is not absorbed in the wife's vagina, preferably jetting against the walls, and transferred back during deep kissing, then intercourse certainly reduces the husband's quantity of the élan vital. Adopting the bank account metaphor from the late Victorians, Van de Velde like Sanger has found a way to make deposits. Only a very selfish and/or stupid wife would want to waste this life-enhancing elixir as well as deny her maternal nature and reduce her own pleasure. Van de Velde does not make an explicit argument at this point. He merely concedes that birth control requires its own monograph. On the other hand, all of *Ideal Marriage* functions as an elaborate argument against birth control, and Van de Velde even acknowledges that his position is compatible with traditional Roman Catholic teachings. Van de Velde quite disingenuously states that he has excluded birth control from his present study. This assertion will be given the lie in the introduction to his third volume, where he recants (317; italics in original).

Times have changed, but Van de Velde still tries to discourage birth control and views religious truths as coequal to those of science. In *Ideal Marriage* physiological norms equal what is divinely ordained, which equates with what is morally good and ecclesiastically lawful. The converse is also true: physiologically abnormal acts equate with divinely prohibited ones, which correspond to morally evil and ecclesiastically prohibited acts.

Sexual love is not an end in itself. Its delights and pleasures remain merely a necessary means to reproduction. Pleasure itself fails to bring nourishment to the soul. In his lyrical close, Van de Velde shows the way to spiritual love, which he considers a higher pinnacle. The acme of the sexual impulse consists of the violent and absolute possession of one's wife. Though positions can vary somewhat, the experience of power remains the traditional one. Essential maleness, as Van de Velde puts it, consists of force. Erections and ejaculations remain the fundamental experience of male power. Though a new sexuality was emerging due to a loosening of sexual norms and availability of birth control, Van de Velde supports the traditional linkage of sex, marriage, and reproduction (317–19, 321).

Van de Velde, like some of the late Victorians, subscribes to a spermatic political economy. Unlike the late Victorians, Van de Velde does not think that withdrawals from the account are limited, so he celebrates frequent sexual intimacy. In his assertion about vaginal absorption of semen, which can be reabsorbed by the husband during deep kissing, Van de Velde even finds a way for men to get back some of their vital fluid. In this sense, Van de Velde reduces the net outflow of semen caused by frequent intercourse. Sperm, however, brands women. A husband, in Van de Velde's view, would naturally be averse to the smell and taste of another man's semen in his wife's mouth. Van de Velde makes adultery without the use of a condom most dangerous for women. Even if a man's wife commits adultery while using a condom, the paramour would be repelled by the foreign semen he detects if they engage in deep kissing.

Ideal Marriage is modern in its emphasis on the joys of sex and in its presentation of great detail, as indicated by the exhaustive table of contents. The evolution of this approach reaches its pinnacle with Alex Comfort's *Joy of Sex* series. Comfort's basic alphabetical organization within general categories (French kisses before nipples) facilitates instant reference, not a frantic search through an elaborate table of contents. Yet Van de Velde's emphasis on male power, his rejection of birth control, and his insistence on maternity as part of woman's nature make his *Ideal Marriage* an amalgam of late Victorian thought along with some modern viewpoints. It represents an attempt to re-create the pre-1920s world for a lost and jaded generation—a world where theology, philosophy, and science still constituted a coherent worldview.

Like Hunchbacks and Cripples

Random House published Van de Velde's *Sexual Tensions in Marriage*, the second volume of his trilogy, in 1931. The book belongs to the defense of marriage genre that marks the late 1920s. His goal in this volume is to repair marriage, and he begins by explaining gender differences. In *Ideal Marriage* he had relied primarily on physiology, however misogynist, which he now combines with depth psychology and natural philosophy to guide his readers around the obstacles to successful marriage.

Men, according to Van de Velde, have a strong sexual impulse conjoined with a "will to power." Striving marks their lives. Men do this for their own reasons and as a result of natural necessity. Unlike women, men have well-developed mental skills, such as an ability to concentrate, and their thinking is logical, clear, and objective. Men are also aggressive. Their lives are marked by ambition and egocentricity (Van de Velde 1931b, 39–41, 44).

Women experience life differently. They have strong emotions and also seek out situations that ignite them. In an explicit reference to Genesis, Van de Velde suggests that women seek "forbidden fruit," implicitly reading original sin into feminine nature. Their love of emotion leads women to appreciate theatrical drama and even the suspense of smuggling. Their minds have a smaller range than that of men, and they tend to be fully absorbed by any issue. On the other hand, women are blessed with tact, intuition, and suggestibility. Impulsiveness marks their lives, which can lead to harm and is associated with "violent emotional storms (anger, etc.) for which there is no sufficient reason." Women also are indecisive. As in *Ideal Marriage*, he writes that the ovum itself expresses female vulnerability, plasticity, and sensitiveness. Once again, "*Propter solum ovulum mulier est quod est.*" Physiology defines the feminine mind; biology remains destiny. Van de Velde also genders mental energy. Corresponding to the monthly cycle, women alternate between equilibrium, when the mind operates below normal level, and times of action and power. When it comes to these perceived defects, women feel like "hunchback[s]" or "cripple[s]." Conflating theology, philosophy, and science much as the late Victorians did, Van de Velde constructs gender to make women inferior and less fully human than men. Once such an image of gender is implanted in consciousness, women's feelings verify Van de Velde's original construction. Much later, Wolf will chronicle the price women pay for such views of gender. Some one hundred and sixty thousand breast operations as well as seventy thousand face lifts attest not only to the plasticity of the female body, but also to feelings of inferiority (Wolf 1991, 242).[2] Collins, writing several years before Van de Velde, argued that such constructions loaded into consciousness serve to control behavior, and he offered psychiatry as a way for women to gain authenticity and freedom. According to Van de Velde, women's natural inferiority, however, is not tragic; it is counterbalanced by opportunities for happiness, and though they are inferior in the primary cerebral functions, women can develop the secondary ones such as intuition and a deeper interior life (Van de Velde 1931b, 51–53, 59–60, 63, 65 , 67–68, 72–75).

In a summary all in uppercase, Van de Velde trumpets the natural inferiority of women and teaches that their rightful role lies in subordination and submission to men. Though relationships are marked by a struggle for power, a woman really desires "SUBMISSION WITH HER WHOLE SOUL." If she wins a marital power struggle, she consequently loses the most elemental thing she wanted in the first place: a man's protection and support. Male superiority reflects both biological and natural facts. Though men must stop oppressing women, the roles prescribed by biology cannot be reversed (76–78).

In this volume Van de Velde addresses homosexuality. Though he remains within the medical model, which takes homosexuality as an illness, he does not display hostility comparable to that of Collins. If a man has experienced a same-sex liaison and then marries to combat this homosexual tendency, the situation proves difficult. Such marriages collapse. A woman who grows addicted to "abnormal stimuli" cannot then experience orgasm with a man. Such failures only strengthen both her inhibitions and her "unnatural tendencies." Latent homosexuality in women is the more frequent situation. Such women are not completely "inverted," but rather bisexual. Sometimes husbands do not notice this deviation. If they do, techniques like those discussed in *Ideal Marriage* will help develop normal sexual desires. If all this fails a physician should be called. Latent lesbians, in other words, can be cured by the right man with good erotic techniques, which is a persistent part of patriarchal folklore. Latent homosexuality proves more serious in men, especially if combined with "feeble normal instincts." Treatment often does not generate potency/power, that is, erection. Van de Velde then takes up the subject of impotence. He concludes by suggesting a topology of erectile problems, of which male homosexuality is a distinct category (98–100).

As he previously noted, feelings, thoughts, energy, and striving in men and women are bipolar. For example, men strive, women do not. This accounts for many of the tensions discovered in marriage. Gender bipolarity as engraved into personality guarantees some discord in marriage. Several pages later Van de Velde undermines his bipolar vision by suggesting that gender forms a continuum. As he puts it now, "An absolutely masculine man and a wholly feminine woman do not exist. There is only a plus or a minus in masculinity and femininity." "Man is woman too in his soul, and woman, man." This provides some common ground for harmony in marriage. Men, however, typically repress their feminine feelings and drive them from consciousness or transform them in sublimation. Despite this potential common ground, Van de Velde holds that "men and women *are* and *remain*, in spite of their bisexual constitution, strangers in their inmost souls to each other." Only those with insight and self-control can negotiate the gender boundary (106–7, 112, 116–18; italics in original).

Though Van de Velde considers sexual issues to lie at the core of most marital disputes, he goes on to consider other discordant factors and offers conventional advice on selecting a partner. He recommends selecting from the same social class and nationality as well as religion. Van de Velde, who styles himself a moralist, reiterates the gender roles that comprise marriage. He denies that he has a double standard, but states that nature does. Marriage doctors, unfortunately, do not exist, and Van de Velde calls for such a specialization. He recommends gynecologists who also have psychoanalytic training. As this genre develops, it will remain dominated by medical doctors and psychoanalysts until the advent of Dr. Ruth (129–30, 208–10, 305 , 314).

Van de Velde attacks feminists in the latter part of the book. Authoresses—he leaves them unnamed—are wrong to seek equality in marriage. Even if such equality could be achieved, it is only apparent. Gender roles and sexual behavior proclaim nature's dictate. He then defines the marital union as a power relationship. "Sexuality is always present in man and woman, and upper and lower place is inseparably allied with it. It is not matter of chance that the relationships in a mental or physical struggle, as well as in sexual connection, are expressed in these words." Nature dictates that women occupy the subordinate position in marriage and sex. Solving marriage problems, in other words, requires the subordination of women. Like some of the late Victorians, Van de Velde goes on to scorn modern women.

> The modern woman who enjoys herself outside her own home, who is spoilt and thinks of nothing but dancing, who has short hair and short skirts, painted cheeks, lips and eyebrows, who understands how to steer a motor car, but not how to guide her children, who flirts with a mass of adoring men, but does not understand how to attract her own husband, who pours out tea at bazaars, has all sorts of little hobbies and understands how to adapt herself to anything except to her household duties. We all know that this type is by no means the worst.

In seeking freedom women are being "insubordinate." The feminist movement had not yet peaked, but Van de Velde discerns that the tide has begun to turn. According to the doctor and moralist, most women do not want freedom and others only think they do. Women in reality flee from "independence" (142, 171, 175; italics in original).

Professional women often do not wish to sacrifice their careers upon marriage. Many women writers argue that women do not desire to combine motherhood with a career. As before, Van de Velde does not name these writers. Women should give up their careers upon marrying or soon after. Van de Velde rejects the option of not having children or leaving their care to others as injurious both to women and to marriage. Van de Velde then seems to relent and provides guidelines for suitable professions for married women. None of them, however, can interfere with motherly duties. He recommends work a couple can do together. Education, of course, should fit this reality. It helps for girls to learn languages, stenography, typing, file indexing, and bookkeeping. These may well help her husband or prove useful if she remains unmarried or becomes a widow. Women already in professions should give them up gradually after marriage (192–98).

Feminism itself proves an impediment to ideal marriage. As Van de Velde writes, "It produces . . . a state of mind . . . which is definitely opposed to the outlook dealt with above. I am, therefore, convinced that Feminism has a more or less unfavorable influence on the foundations of marriage, and on the mental disposition in many marriages." The pursuit of pleasure, another mark of the times, also frustrates ideal marriage (289).

Overall, Van de Velde distrusts women. In *Ideal Marriage* he even finds a physiological basis to discover a wife's adultery, provided that a condom was not employed. In *Sexual Tensions in Marriage* he mainly reinforces traditional gender roles, opposes any separation of marriage and maternity, and requires that women remain housewives. His suspicions of modern women are summed up by his suggestion regarding life insurance examinations. Given the times, many women were not virgins and may even have contracted a venereal disease that could make them sterile. Since a man must always avoid shocking his betrothed, Van de Velde recommends a medical examination ostensibly for life insurance purposes. This examination will also include a surreptitious gynecological investigation. The doctor, of course (but not the fiancée), must be told the real purpose of the examination (224, 288–89).

Nature has a double standard; Van de Velde does not. Women, feeling like cripples and hunchbacks, muck their way through life trying to find the right man to offer submission to. Marked by Eve's sin, they seek what happiness they can achieve in secondary cerebral functions and motherhood. *Sexual Tensions in Marriage* more fully articulates the rigid gender distinctions of *Ideal Marriage*, but Van de Velde creates a conundrum. Though he supports a bipolar understanding of gender and its norms, he also articulates a theory of bisexuality that undermines these very norms. "Man is woman too in his soul, and woman, man." If men and women are bisexual, why must the norms be so rigid and the silences within marriage so complete? Van de Velde suggests an answer for men. They repress their bisexuality or sublimate it. And he implies, though he does not state explicitly, that women act out their masculinity in power struggles within marriage. This view outlines another approach to rescuing marriage that Van de Velde largely ignores. If men and women learned to accept and experience the other gender in their own constitutions, then the silences in marriage could be broken. This, however, would lead far afield from Van de Velde's purpose, which is to shore up the traditional institution of marriage and to subordinate women. It would also force him to reevaluate his view of feminists. Feminists, usually unnamed, serve as the villains in this volume. Equality cannot be had. Feminists stir up a tempest for no good reason.

Sexual Tensions in Marriage, unlike *Ideal Marriage*, does take notice of homosexuals or inverts. Though Van de Velde is unsympathetic to inverts, his text lacks the passionate homophobia of Collins. Van de Velde, unlike Collins, does not mean to eliminate homosexuals. Perhaps feeling like cripples and hunchbacks themselves, they can achieve some type of limited happiness. Later, in the 1960s, Reuben's *Everything You Always Wanted to Know about Sex* will revive Collins's passionate homophobia.

Van de Velde Recants

In his book *Fertility and Sterility in Marriage*, also published in 1931 by Random House, Van de Velde announces that he has arrived at a parting of the ways with organized religion. In his previous volumes, as he states now, he selected his words carefully and limited himself to certain themes to keep his work congruent with religious teachings. He remains convinced that "*in normal sexual relations there is complete consonance be-*

tween physiological health and religious righteousness; indeed that 'the sets of equations; *physiologically normal—divinely ordained*—morally good—ecclesiastically lawful (as with their exact opposites) are positively startling." But he now considers religion an illusion in the Freudian sense. Religious illusions, however, are necessary for human happiness. Humankind cannot adequately deal with its helplessness before nature as well as its desire for justice and permanence without projecting gods as a wish fulfillment. Van de Velde regards it as wrong to disillusion people, and hence he states that in his previous volumes he avoided disputes with religious doctrines. This is no longer possible due to the Roman Catholic Church's "absolute prohibition . . . of certain measures which as a doctor I consider unavoidable; and the very similar, though less definite and explicit attitude of the majority of Protestant theologians towards those measures and methods." Van de Velde, making his complaint more specific, now disagrees with traditional religious teaching on artificial insemination and birth control (Van de Velde 1931a, 4–8; italics in original).

Van de Velde acknowledges the hold of large families on the popular imagination, but he points out that conditions have changed. Happiness in marriage results "when both physique and finances are vigorous and prosperous." Couples, as he now sees it, have a moral obligation to limit their families to protect the mother's health as well as to safeguard the family's finances. He specifically recommends the use of birth control to space births. Three or four children are plenty, and should be timed at intervals of two and a half years. He sees three alternatives when it comes to human fertility: absolute abstinence, unrestricted intercourse with its consequent large families, and the control of fertility. Of these alternatives, birth control, that is, controlling fertility, causes the least damage. Van de Velde, in a very erudite section, goes on to discuss Roman Catholic and Protestant theology on this issue (11–14 and appendix). He is very familiar with the arguments in Roman Catholic and Protestant circles. He includes copious citations and excerpts in Latin, and his anguish over the issue has a contemporary note. He goes on to attribute the core of the problem to moral zealots among Roman Catholics and Protestants. After considering the theological arguments, he concludes that *"Therefore, I advocate the use of preventive methods, with wholehearted conviction."* Birth control forestalls abortion, prevents "unwelcome" lives, and avoids the worse evil of abstinence. "Medical men" (women of course remain unsuited) have an obligation to offer information and advice. Doctors should not recommend abstinence to their patients to satisfy their own religious scruples (11–32, 34–35 ; italics in original).

Both parents and the state have an interest in birth control. Quality of offspring, of course, is a major concern. Overpopulation, as Van de Velde now sees it, can be a problem. Increasing the death rate is unacceptable, so birth control remains the only viable option. Underpopulation and imbalance between races can also cause problems. Van de Velde recommends that states adopt a family planning policy that will also serve eugenic ends. Such policies should encourage proper population growth among elite classes. Van de Velde understands modern individuals to be realistic and materialistic, prudent calculators of their self-interest, so he advocates wide availability of birth control. He assumes that lower, less privileged classes will realize that having fewer children improves their economic situation. Materialism and selfishness, thus, will propel the voluntary adoption of birth control, a prophetic pronouncement first made by Sanger. He recommends using the tax system to provide incentives for the elite and disincentives for others. Like Sanger, he never defines fit or unfit or enumerates the qualities of the elite (50–54, 57, 60, 63–68).

Though Van de Velde recants on birth control, he does not fundamentally alter his misogynist views, intertwined as they are with physiology and now psychoanalysis. Women still need maternity for fulfillment. Suppressing the maternal urge completely can cause "morbid symptoms." Men also desire children, but for different reasons. Children confirm virility and provide a "memento of moments of ecstasy." They can also provide support and comfort in old age. So in his revised view Van de Velde holds that happiness in marriage does not depend on children, but they remain "a natural and necessary accompaniment." Motherhood, in this context, remains woman's work (79, 81–84, 92).

Van de Velde also elaborates his teaching about homosexuality. Male homosexuals abhor women. They have such an "innate horror of intimate body contact . . . that . . . [they] cannot kiss a woman, not to mention copulate with her." If a homosexual attempts to cure himself through heterosexual intercourse, his erection will fail and the experience quickly becomes "grotesque." Artificial insemination could be attempted, but for reasons of eugenics doctors should refuse to perform such procedures. Van de Velde implies that a homosexual parent might transmit a proclivity for the condition. Radical therapeutic interventions usually fail. Van de Velde, however, holds some hope for "milder pathological cases." Psychotherapy might work and at least engender *"procreative potency."* In a footnote Van de Velde cites Stekel, who believes that the condition is acquired, while he also refers to Hirschfeld, who believes it to be inherited. Bisexuals, however, are another matter. Young men, experiencing the normal tensions of bisexuality, may be enticed by their companions or older homosexual men and become persuaded through mutual masturbation that they are, indeed, homosexuals. Even though such young men can be aroused by the opposite sex, autosuggestion may make them impotent. Psychotherapy "can save them from impotence and their married life from sterility." In this view, true homosexuals recruit young bisexuals but not heterosexuals (236–38; italics in original).

A Modest Revision

Just two years before the "Summer of Love" in 1967, Random House published a revised edition of *Ideal Marriage*. According to the dust jacket of the 1965 edition, Dr. Margaret Smyth, a British physician, revised the work. The title page does not acknowledge her contribution. At the end of the original personal introductory statement, Smyth quite seriously adds that Van de Velde's work had a large impact on the current revolution in sexual thinking (Van de Velde 1965, xx).

According to the revised edition, couples must solve the parentage problem because it can destroy marriages. After acknowledging the birth control pill, Smyth excludes it from the study in order not to complicate the discussion. Immediately following this exclusion, the text reaffirms the linkages between ideal marriage and the Roman Catholic position on contraception, as well as Protestant and Jewish moral teaching in general. Smyth does not call attention to Van de Velde's revised view, which remains buried in the introduction to *Fertility and Sterility in Marriage*. Intercourse, as in the original edition, remains not an end in itself, but a means to the end of intimacy and pregnancy. An appendix contains favorable references to the birth control pill and continues the first edition's focus on "safe times" for intercourse. In other words, Smyth appends a hesitant acceptance of birth control to an anti–birth control text. The revision proves inadequate: Van de Velde changed his mind. In this regard the revision of *Ideal Marriage* is somewhat comparable to the revised edition of Guernsey's *Plain Talks on Avoided Subjects* (Van de Velde 1965, 247, 253, 297–98, 301, 308, 311).

Smyth carried a heavy burden. She edited in a period defined by the availability of the birth control pill as well as one of increasing consumerism, including the use of sex as a marketing tool. *Playboy,* for example, with its stylish consumerism blended with hedonism, had been available for years. She worked with a text that originally proved hostile to birth control and whose author later changed his mind. Smyth does not revise enough to change the underlying attitude toward birth control or remove the intertwined layers of misogyny masquerading as physiology. All of this in a time when the norms of conventional morality were due to suffer a renewed assault. Two years after Smyth's revision, hippies in San Francisco's Golden Gate Park would offer a glimpse of an alternative sexuality rooted in pleasure, celebration, and even spectacle. Somewhat like the 1920s, participants in this assault would assert that pleasure served as a coequal purpose of sex. The birth control pill divorced sex and reproduction for everyone, regardless of marital status. Smyth's task was doomed from the start. She softens the more extreme teachings, such as the one about the spermatic political economy, while she largely leaves undisturbed the main tenets of the book. She uses the appendix to suggest options such as the birth control pill, but retains the linkage between femininity and motherhood. It was precisely this linkage that was due for a renewed challenge. On the other hand, she could have rewritten large portions of the text, removed the support for the existing sexual regime as well as the misogyny and focused on physiology and erotic techniques, but this would have created a new text. *The Joy of Sex* in 1972 will be this new text.

D'Emilio and Freedman, relying largely on Gordon, note that marriage manuals began to change in the 1920s and 1930s. The emphasis shifted from the control of sexuality within marriage to the pleasurable expression of the sexual impulse, which became a prerequisite for happy marriages. Authors such as Van de Velde, then, began to supply "elaborate instructions." The goal became mutual orgasm, and the literature is dominated by searches for the best method to achieve this goal. Gordon considers *Ideal Marriage* "the most detailed and rationalized treatment of sexual behavior to see the light of print." He refers, as many commentators do, to its table of contents. According to Gordon, Van de Velde turns marital sex into "virtually an academic discipline." He uses the term "hedge" to describe Van de Velde's position on birth control. On the contrary, the premises of *Ideal Marriage* are anti–birth control, as

Van de Velde himself acknowledges in *Fertility and Sterility in Marriage*. At best *Ideal Marriage* can only be taken to support the rhythm method within marriage. In a chapter about Van de Velde entitled "He Taught a Generation How to Copulate," Breecher writes that his later books, *Sexual Tensions in Marriage* and *Fertility and Sterility in Marriage*, "added little to his reputation, and need not concern us here." Breecher, like Gordon, overlooks Van de Velde's change of mind as well as his acknowledgment of the hidden premises in *Ideal Marriage*. The misogyny of Van de Velde's trilogy remains plain, layered as it is with a veneer of physiology and depth psychology (Gordon 1978, 77; D'Emilio and Freedman 1988, 267; Breecher 1969, 88).

5

One Step Forward, Two Steps Back

Sex and Pleasure in the 1950s

The decade of the 1950s, perhaps more than any other period in this century, represents a golden era in the minds of many Americans. The 1950s conjure up images of small screen TVs in wooden cabinets, of Ozzie and Harriet, of Joe DiMaggio. Families lived—or were supposed to live—in suburban houses with yards. Dad went off to work every day, Mom stayed home and kept house. The couple had two children, a boy (older) and a girl (younger), and a dog. There were two cars in the garage, one of which was a station wagon. Boys went to Cub Scouts and Little League. Girls took ballet lessons and went to Brownies. Families took two-week vacations together using the family station wagon as cars became the preferred mode of leisure transportation. The median family income was between $3,000 and $4,000 a year. The young parents of the 1950s family had been reared during the Great Depression and came of age during World War II. These two overwhelming social experiences set the stage for the attitudes and values espoused in the 1950s. During the depression people learned the necessity and value of sacrifice and making do. Children reared in the 1930s saw people working very hard, often for little or nothing. They also felt the grind of poverty and the despair that comes with having no work. The war years reinforced the value of sacrifice, this time for the war effort, but if one was still sacrificing things, at least there was work. The experiences of the 1930s and 1940s translated in the 1950s into the desire for stability and security and an end to sacrifice. Young adults in the 1950s were determined to leave behind both the poverty of their childhood and the turbulent war years of their adolescence and young adulthood. A booming postwar America was only too ready to help.

The GI Bill provided returning servicemen with money for education.

The Federal Housing Authority revamped its loan policy. Supplemented by the GI Bill and the Veterans' Administration, millions of Americans were able to buy homes for the first time. Young couples quickly got on with the business of settling down and working hard to achieve financial success. Stable and conservative patterns of living, which often revolved around earning and acquiring, were quickly established by couples living in the ever expanding suburbs (Coontz 1992, 77).

This postwar pattern and the newfound prosperity were reflected in changes in the spending patterns of Americans. In 1950 *U.S. News & World Report* noted that American families were now spending more on housing and on home furnishings and less on clothing, movies, and eating out. A nation recovering from the population shifts of wartime mobilization was ready to settle down and stay put. Young couples set their sights on a comfortable home complete with stylish, comfortable furniture and convenient appliances. Money to support this new lifestyle was provided by the husband, who worked hard at a good job.

By 1950 Dr. Spock's book on infant and child care, first published in 1945, was hugely popular. In the first twenty years of publication over sixteen million copies in 155 printings were sold. His more relaxed approach represented a break from that of previous experts on childhood. For Spock, moderation was the key. Spock advised mothers to pay close attention to their children, who would essentially set their own schedules and communicate their likes and dislikes. Not surprisingly, women left alone in the suburbs with their children sometimes forgot about moderation. Children became the focus of an intense and concentrated attention, the likes of which has not been seen before or since. This focus on motherhood served as an antidote to the freedom women had experienced in wartime, when many had worked and earned real money for the first time. In spite of the fact that maternal attention was the ideal, this attention from mother was also vilified, as articles about "momism" and the feminization of American men demonstrate. The ramifications of this attention would manifest themselves later in the turbulence of the 1960s as these children confronted the harsh realities of adult life, but in the 1950s it served to re-anchor women to maternity and home in a new way.

Parents worked to imbue their children with values they thought important for future success. Children, while indulged, were nevertheless expected to be circumspect in many areas. They were expected to follow the rules, one of which was to control emotion. Boys were supposed to be unemotional, strong in victory and stoic in defeat. Girls, always given more latitude, could be happy, even "gushy," or sad, shedding a tear or two, but generally their emotions were not supposed to be about anything truly important. Anger was a forbidden emotion that had to be kept under control. Sexual feelings were simply ignored. Perhaps war and depression had taught the parents of the 1950s that there was no point to emotional displays.

An important value and the focus of much attention was the ability to work in groups. Boys, especially, were encouraged to be on teams and to engage in various group activities to acquire leadership skill. It was not enough to be able to function in a group, one had to be a member of the "right" group, a rule that applied equally to parents and children.

The veneer that covered life in the 1950s was, however, quite thin. Nostalgia blinds us to the fact that Americans of the 1950s were not at peace with themselves or with the world. The threat of nuclear attack was very real, and the government responded with a policy of containment (see May 1988). Communists with nuclear bombs could be rendered impotent if America could continue to control its sphere of influence. Joseph McCarthy (R-WI) and his (antihomosexual homosexual) aide Roy Cohn reiterated all the dangers and the ubiquitousness of the Red Menace, a threat from within rather than from without. To combat the internal threat, political leaders stressed the need for strong families and unified communities. This served to further solidify parental obligations, which included ensuring that children conformed to the appropriate values and belonged to the right groups.

Families were given the additional task of planning for survival in a nuclear holocaust. The ideal family home was not complete without a bomb shelter, though in truth few families actually built them (May 1988). Children in schools were familiar with the duck and cover exercise, routinely throwing themselves under their desks with their arms over their heads in an officially sanctioned method of protecting themselves from nuclear explosions. In a real air raid, children were told, they would be allowed to go home after the all clear signal.

Women of the 1950s were also supposed to learn first aid skills for use after nuclear bombs fell. Civil defense programs identified specific skills for men and women. Women were given tips on cooking for large numbers of people in the communal kitchens that would surely be required. Men were supposed to learn about fire fighting and construction. The point was to reassure Americans that they could survive a nuclear attack and defeat the enemy. A key to American defense was the strong family. This political motive reinforced the tendency already present in couples of the 1950s to form stable families whose members had specific roles. Deviation from norms of any kind, especially the sexual norms, not only was frowned on, but was even dangerous.

Sexual Subversives: The Enemy Within

The fifties saw the euphoria that swept the world at the end of World War II replaced by the consciousness of millions upon millions of casualties as well as Germany's extermination of European Jewry. Attention shifted to the countless refugees and the shattered European economies with their infrastructures reduced to rubble. The vision of the Nazi menace and horrors that united the allies, however, was quickly replaced by fear of communism. The Soviet Union, formerly a glorious ally, soon became the new evil force in the world. Western powers came to view the Soviet Union with its revolutionary ideology as a threat to Western civilization itself as attention focused on subversion from within as well as conquest in Europe and then throughout the world. This vision of the enemy within soon led the United States as well as its allies to adopt severe security measures.

In 1947 President Truman established a loyalty program, and his Justice Department soon issued a list of subversive organizations. The House Un-American Activities Committee held hearings on this new menace and sought to identify the enemy within. Communists were an obvious target; homosexuals were a close second. Naming names and exposing traitors were central to the mission of the committee. During one congressional hearing an undersecretary of state, John Peurifoy, said that in 1950 homosexuals accounted for most of the ninety-one employees fired from the State Department. Republicans, anxious to find issues with which to attack the Democratic ascendancy in Washington, quickly raised the hue and cry. In June 1950 the Senate authorized an investigation of homosexuals and "other moral perverts" within the government. The committee viewed homosexuality as a pathological condition that disqualified one for federal employment. In the committee's view, homosexuality entailed emotional insecurity, and fear of exposure and blackmail made homosexuals a security risk. As a consequence, the number of federal employees fired for homosexuality increased. Newly elected

Dwight Eisenhower issued Executive Order 10450, which declared that sexual perversion precluded federal employment. Many states as well as industries with government contracts adopted the federal standards. About 20 percent of the labor force eventually underwent loyalty investigations. Soon the Federal Bureau of Investigation began conducting background checks for the Civil Service Commission and networked with local vice squads to identify sexual subversives. The bureau maintained lists and sought information on homosexual groups and gathering places.

Naming names, for example, became a central ritual with the Florida legislature's Johns Committee as it sought to purge homosexuals from 1956 until 1964. The committee began with an attack on the National Association for the Advancement of Colored People (NAACP) as a communist front organization, but the NAACP struck back with a blizzard of lawsuits. The committee then sent its agents all over the state to sniff out sexual abnormality. "Its suspicions were endless, its curiosity insatiable." The committee tapped phones, took testimony from children, and even investigated a teenaged girls' slumber party. Local police and public officials, eager to prove their own sexual orthodoxy, cooperated with the committee. Employers often sat in on the questioning sessions of employees. Sometimes students and professors were actually taken from classrooms and brought to motel rooms to be questioned about their political beliefs and sexual practices. The committee "employed police state tactics, browbeating victims with threats and coercion." Committee operatives also entrapped students at Florida State University by inviting them to parties and then photographing them in compromising situations. They were then pressured to name names ("Papers Show" 1993; "Gay-Bashing" 1993).

By 1964, seventy-one teachers had lost their teaching certificates and fourteen university faculty had been fired. The purge also included thirty-seven federal employees. At the end, the committee had investigations pending against another 14 state employees, 19 university faculty, and 105 public school teachers. Witnesses faced the threat of twenty-five years in prison for perjury. Governor Farris Bryant applauded the committee's work. "This office is doing everything it can to control or wipe out homosexuality. You know how difficult it is and I hope that what the legislative committee is trying to do will result in better enforcement." Naming names became a central ritual in this new embattled Americanism; sexual orthodoxy became part of the national creed ("Many Joined"

1993; "Light of Day" 1993; "Papers Show" 1993; "Gay-Bashing" 1993).

Twenty-one states required registration of persons convicted of homosexual-related crimes. Loyalty oaths included references to moral turpitude, and states commonly denied licenses to sexual subversives. Local police enforced sodomy statutes and other restrictive legislation with relish as they raided gay bars and trysting places. "Every evening spent in a gay setting, every contact with another homosexual or lesbian, every sexual intimacy carried a reminder of the criminal penalties that could be exacted at any moment." In Washington, D.C., for example, police arrested a thousand sexual subversives a year in the early 1950s. This practice continued for at least two decades. In 1969 a police raid on a gay bar in New York City inadvertently launched gay liberation. The demonization of lesbians and gay men helped make them vulnerable to theft, robbery, and blackmail and provided an opening for organized crime to gain control of gay bars and other establishments. Ironically, the growing visibility of lesbians and gay men in urban enclaves helped make them convenient targets, and Kinsey's studies showed that America swarmed with sexual subversives. All of this impacted lesbian and gay male identity and changed them from Collins's misfits to the enemy within. Federal and state repression (Florida was merely one example) denied lesbians and gay men participation in any legitimate social order, and every raid on a gay bar proved that they lacked power and honor (in general see D'Emilio 1983b, 40–52; Shilts 1993, 7–11, 106–11).

Gender Roles

The communist threat to American life was ever present, as demonstrated by other events in the 1950s. For many Americans, the Korean War further illustrated the threat to peace posed by the communists. At the same time it made clear the necessity of preparedness. The possibility that the "police action" in Korea would result in a confrontation with Beijing or Moscow was very real and fostered a siege mentality. Then in 1957 the Russians launched Sputnik, the first successful earth satellite, touching off an uproar about the inferior quality of American science education that lasted through the next decade.

In spite of the social and political pressures, the 1950s are often remembered as a halcyon time in America, a time of ice cream socials and sock hops, and brownies in the kitchen after school with Mom. These same 1950s give us visions of spirit-crushing segregation, communism run rampant, controlling mothers emasculating the men of America, and polio, a disease so feared that it shut down public swimming pools everywhere.

Traditional gender norms were in full force after the brief but heady war years, when women held all sorts of jobs and sexual mores were more relaxed. By the 1950s most women were out of the factories and settled back into their pink-collar jobs of secretary, teacher, and nurse. Pants for women, far more accepted and common during the 1930s and 1940s, fell almost completely out of style. The 1950s teenage girl at home wore jeans and bobbie sox with loafers and sometimes one of her father's dress shirts. Anywhere else she wore a dress or a tight straight skirt. According to TV, all moms wore shirtwaist dresses, heels, and pearls, whether they were vacuuming the house, making a cake, or serving dinner. In spite of the intensity of gender distinctions off screen, dads on TV were often portrayed as sort of ineffectual bumblers who often succeeded, but usually by accident. Frequently family members colluded to maintain the impression that Dad had been right all along. Mothers, on the other hand, were often portrayed as schemers who used indirect manipulation to get what they wanted. The roles portrayed in TV sitcoms served as a model for the balance of power in the typical middle-class home, and reinforced the need for enforcing the rigidly drawn gender lines. The relationship between men and women, as portrayed on TV and in film, was a kind of war, with constant skirmishing. On TV the contest always ended with the reinforcement of traditional gender roles. When the wife won, she won by artifice and the use of feminine wiles. What she won was her man. When the husband won, most often it was by asserting his power or influence. In the movies the skirmishes often ended in a final surrender symbolized by the lights going down or a door discreetly closing, symbolizing female capitulation to that great solver of all problems, sex.

Regardless of who won in any given week, the combatants' roles were clear. Women fought for the upper hand, achieving it—when they did—through manipulation and deceit. This was tolerated by the men, even the bumbling ones, because it was culturally defined as "cute" and because what the women wanted was not important. Who could take seriously the continuous efforts of Lucy Ricardo to be in Desi's nightclub show? How important was it that Donna Reed get a world-class pianist to play at her fund raiser? In countless sitcoms stretching over the decade of the 1950s, women were depicted as illogical beings who raised tempests in domestic teapots.

The TV sitcoms had something else in common: each loving couple slept chastely in twin beds. While there might be erotic tension depicted on the screen, it was never explicitly sexual. What then can we say about the behavior of real people in their bedrooms? Alfred Kinsey thought he knew. His now famous works, *Sexual Behavior in the Human Male*, published in 1948, and *Sexual Behavior in the Human Female*, published in 1953, ushered in a new era. Although it would not fully manifest itself until the 1960s, Kinsey's works paved the way for free discussion of sexuality. Kinsey offered a new way to judge sexual behavior, and in spite of the fact that the volumes were filled with charts and dull scientific jargon, both sold well. Although more copies of the first volume on men were sold, more controversy surrounded the volume that dealt with women's sexuality. It was as if the whole idea of female sexuality, especially data covering topics like masturbation and extramarital affairs, was too outrageous and horrible for some people to contemplate. In the Cold War era female sexuality outside conventional marriage was viewed by some as an assault on the family itself and therefore an attack on America. While the 1950s wife was supposed to be her husband's sexual playmate, the idea was for her sexuality to exist only within the context of marriage. Thus the Kinsey reports were received with a predictable mixture of enthusiasm and revulsion.

It was not an era of much frank discussion about sexual matters. Even novels tended to shy away from descriptions of sexual activity. The curious or the uninformed had few places to go for information. Kinsey certainly offered no help in the "how-to" area, reporting instead on the "how much and what" side of things. It is not surprising, then, that marriage manuals of the traditional type continued to be popular, even as society glimpsed a whole new array of sexual activities on the horizon.

A Practical Guide

One of the most widely sold books was *A Marriage Manual: A Practical Guidebook to Sex and Marriage* by Hannah Stone and Abraham Stone, a husband-and-wife physician team. They first published this guide in 1935 but completely revised it in 1952. It sold extremely well and had achieved a prominent place by the 1950s. According to the preface to the

1952 edition, the book had already gone through twenty-nine printings and was translated into numerous foreign languages.

Written in a question-and-answer format, the marriage manual was a forerunner of Reuben's *Everything You Always Wanted to Know about Sex.* Unlike Reuben's book, which was meant to entertain as well as to inform, this book makes it clear that sex is pretty serious business. The authors seek to provide readers with the facts about sex and reproduction. It does this without much in the way of embellishment. The text is not completely staid and conservative—as befits a book written by physicians affiliated with the Margaret Sanger Research Bureau and Marriage Consultation Center.

According to the Stones, the first thing one should consider when thinking about sex is whether or not one is actually fit for marriage. This does not, however, only mean fit for reproduction, although that is surely important. Marriage is for more than that. It is also for love, companionship, and sexual intimacy. The reader is assured early on that information on birth control will be forthcoming. Vestiges of earlier ideas remain, however. The Stones give with one hand and take away with the other. Immediately after the offer of birth control information comes the matter-of-fact statement, "Eventually, of course, you will, like every normal couple, want to have children and you will then plan your family accordingly" (Stone and Stone 1952, 4). Birth control, then, is for planning and spacing children, not avoiding them altogether. The link between sex and reproduction, hanging tenuously for a perilous second, is firmly reestablished and with it a boundary of normalcy. Thus the Stones popularized Van de Velde's recanted view.

Nevertheless, the Stones do emphasize the importance on being sexually fit, especially for men. In a reversal of Van de Velde's "insurance examination" for women, a man's potency must be established either directly or indirectly before marriage. Women are not required to pass any such tests regarding their sexual abilities, but both men and women should pay attention to eugenics. While acknowledging that Cupid may sometimes determine one's choice of a mate, they recommend that readers avoid marrying someone who has a serious defect that can be inherited. The Stones do apply eugenics fairly liberally, noting that it is not terribly clear yet what specific defects should be avoided, and they advise caution against the mistaken notion that socioeconomic class is equivalent to biological fitness. After all, in different circumstances, there is no telling to what social heights an individual might climb.

The discussion of eugenics and environmental influences echoes Sanger's earlier writings. Both Sanger and the Stones believed that the grossly abnormal, which includes those of very low intelligence and psychotics, should be prevented from reproducing. Neither Sanger nor the Stones care to be more specific than this about what it means to be fit or unfit for reproduction. The eugenics theme reappears in the chapter on family planning. The Stones reassure readers that the contraceptive information is offered only as an aid to spacing and regulating the size of the family. The not so hidden message is that those with defects should avoid children altogether.

Like the 1950s, in which this edition of *A Marriage Manual* found its readership, the text presents a mixture of old and new. The section on fertility and infertility contains a fairly lengthy discussion of artificial insemination. While the facts and information on the exact procedure are scant, the tone is quite contemporary, not unlike what might be found in any brief discussion of the subject in the 1990s. But the section on reproduction harks back to the Victorian idea of the healthful and curative nature of seminal fluid. Echoing Van de Velde, the Stones declare that it is possible for at least some seminal fluid to be absorbed through the vaginal walls. The salutary effect this has on the female constitution is not proved as yet, although there are proponents of the theory. The absorption of seminal fluid is healthful, as shown by the well-known tendency of women to improve in health and gain weight after they get married. The Victorian idea of the conservation of seminal fluid and the preservation of male vitality through limiting intercourse disappears. They replace "save it for posterity" with "use it or lose it." The Stones note that the earlier a boy shows interest in sexual matters, the more frequent his sexual activity in later years. They recast the early expression of male sexuality as a positive sign, with potential side benefits for the woman who will be his partner later on.

No such prescription exists for women. In *Sexual Behavior in the Human Female*, however, Kinsey openly suggested that the most responsive women are those who have engaged in various forms of premarital sexual behavior. In a discussion of the problem of lack of sexual response in women, the Stones inform the reader that "one has to realize that the sexual impulse of the woman may normally remain dormant for a long period." They do not suggest that early sexual expression, even masturbation—a behavior only recently off the taboo list—might help awaken sexual responses and prepare women for marriage. Instead, we are told that it is up to the husband to awaken his wife's passion. The Stones agree on this point with Stopes, Sanger, and Van de Velde. Passion can be difficult to awaken, and a substantial number of women will not reach orgasm, or at least not frequently. *A Marriage Manual* assures us that there is no need to fear because conception is not linked to female orgasm. One wonders what the benefits of a more sexually experienced male are for a woman who is herself not sexually responsive (206).

As befits a book popular in the 1950s, *A Marriage Manual* is not particularly graphic. Compared to Van de Velde's *Ideal Marriage*, it is not explicit and is filled with reassurances that it is perfectly respectable for married people to want general information. The Stones acknowledge that some topics are controversial. They inform the reader that they intend to discuss the medical not the social aspects of issues, especially any controversial ones. This, of course, is not entirely possible, as we have seen in the discussion of birth control and the links to eugenics, which were controversial then and remain controversial now. Nevertheless, they acknowledge that people have different opinions about some of the topics covered in the book, and everyone is entitled to their own opinions. They believe that it is up to the couple to decide about these issues based on their own beliefs and preferences. To reinforce this idea, the Stones cite information and advice given to people in other cultures, thus demonstrating that these things are essentially matters of taste.

Readers of *A Marriage Manual* are left with some commonsense suggestions, information about reproductive organs, suggestions about techniques, and ideas about eugenics. They also receive permission to do more or less what pleases them, when they want to, and as often as they want within the confines of the marriage bed. In some ways this book provides less information than Van de Velde's. The recommendation to use some form of birth control to at least space births, however, is unequivocal.

Fearless Love

Eustace Chesser wrote another popular manual. Like both the Stones and Van de Velde before him, Chesser was a physician. His manual, *Love without Fear: How to Achieve Sex Happiness in Marriage*, was originally published in England in 1940 as two separate volumes. In 1942 he was hauled into court on an obscenity charge but was acquitted. The trial probably helped to popularize the manual. A single volume comprising the two earlier works was published in the United States in 1947, accompanied by little adverse reaction. The hardcover edition was in its fourth printing by 1952 and had sold three quarter of a million copies. A paperback edition did even better.

Different in emphasis from the Stones' work and in many ways far less conservative, Chesser's book focused on what might be called the psychology of love and marriage. While the term "free love" is often associated with the 1960s, there have been calls for free love by social reformers at various times throughout history. Chesser notes that the current talk of free love and even freer divorce totally ignores the idea of free marriage. Free marriage is not to be confused with open marriage popularized in the 1970s. Chesser means a marriage that is free from the chains of what he terms infantile romanticism. Women must not believe the Prince Charming myth, nor should men believe the Fairy Princess idea. Marriage is for two emotionally mature people who want to share their lives. Concentration on the mythical ideals can only lead to disappointment, since no one can live up to the idealized image except, perhaps, during the early days of the relationship while infatuation reigns. That is why he advocates getting to know each other well before marrying and suggests that couples must have the will to love. Both partners must accept responsibility for keeping love alive and helping it grow.

A striking difference between the Stones' work and Chesser's is the incorporation of some feminist ideas, although the notion of equality does not yet extend to the bedroom. While "today's" woman does not want to feel subordinate and wants equal pay for equal work (this fifteen years before the Equal Pay Act), the wish for equality espoused by feminists can be taken too far. Chesser rejects what he terms "sex equality." Men and women are definitely not the same, and promiscuity is wholly opposed to woman's true feminine nature. Some intersexual types of women, however, do seem able to behave much as men do. Fifty years earlier, Guernsey called any woman who felt any sexual desire a nymphomaniac. By 1950 only promiscuous women are deviant (Chesser 1947, 44).

Demonstrating the prevalence of Freudian theory so common in medical writing in the 1950s, Chesser terms the desire for sex equality, especially the abolition of the double standard, an infantile wish on the part of feminist leaders. Women, however, do not really have leaders because "in the main they do not follow their sex." His presumably mature solution to the problem of the double standard is for women to say to men that they must "play fair" and be chaste themselves, just as they want women to be. After all, men who behave this way are really not happy. They will yield to the chastity argument because they know in their consciences that it is true. This is the only way to get "sex equality." Not surprisingly, there is no empirical evidence to support the efficacy of this suggestion (47–48).

Chesser's appeal to men to be faithful is followed by the assertion that sex for men is just one act. Sex encompasses multiple stages for women, ending in lactation and maternity. The use of birth control will unalterably change a woman because she will have interrupted the chain of events prematurely. She will have experienced only wooing and courtship and the sex act. Contraception divorces intercourse from conception, pregnancy, childbirth, lactation, and maternity. The elimination of concerns about conception leads to a greatly increased desire for sexual intercourse. Promiscuous women and feminist women who want sex equality run the risk of having these very strong desires aroused, since by definition promiscuous sex will fail to satisfy their intrinsic need for home and family. Hence, promiscuous sex can never be truly satisfying for women (Pym, as quoted in Chesser 1947, 50–51).

In contrast to the Stones, who make it clear that women may be difficult to arouse, Chesser seems to worry that unleashed in the wrong circumstances outside marriage, female sexuality may be difficult to control. Even a single rape may result in "an insatiable hunger for a repetition of the experience" (Mace, quoted in Chesser 1947, 51).

Chesser is not against birth control under some circumstances. He devotes an entire chapter to the positive effects of modern birth control techniques on married women, children, and their families, although not a single actual technique is identified. With regard to sex before marriage, Chesser advocates that an engaged couple take an extended vacation together to see whether they are sexually compatible. Presumably, the couple will use some form of birth control during this vacation in case they turn out to be poorly matched. His concern is not premarital sex but casual sex or, more accurately, sex between people who do not intend to marry. Chesser is far more worried about women and the negative consequences of such sexual behavior on them. While promiscuity is undesirable for men, there is no talk about the importance or even the existence of the steps of wooing and courtship, the sex act, insemination, and paternity. These, save the sex act itself, are not mentioned and appear to be unrelated to intercourse for men, for whom the act of sex itself "might be a mere incident" (51, 92–93).

He identifies other differences between men and women once promiscuity is out of the way. Having already noted that some equality is probably acceptable as long as it is confined to work-related issues, Chesser frequently reminds readers that men are men and women are women. One difference between the sexes is that physical appearance for men is not as important as it is for women. A man's temperament is more important than his looks. Chesser warns against the "nervous lover." Such a lover fails to seek conquest. If he does marry, the nervous lover is constantly worried about everything, especially intercourse. Usually his timidity comes from feelings of inferiority, which are often tied to physical appearance. Chesser makes it clear that nervous lovers need not worry, since in men physical appearance counts for little in love. Chesser designs these paragraphs and assurances to "go far towards restoring your (his) confidence." Maybe so, but Chesser still warns women off the nervous lover or a fat man on the grounds that one is too timid and the other too slow to make a good husband (86).

Women, however, do not need this warning. They have an unusual kind of intuition that warns them away from poor mates. In spite of a number of more forward-looking concepts, Chesser endorses the idea that women are not especially rational creatures. Intuition, rather than some logical assessment of a potential mate's capabilities, warns them away from weaker mates. Physical appearance in a potential husband is not important. Physical fitness, health, strength, and freedom from defects are critical. Women discern these things indirectly through "that strange intuition of women"; they may also make the discovery unconsciously (85).

The female counterpart of the nervous lover is the woman who is pretty and bright but does not believe that love is for her. She is in far worse shape than the nervous lover. He only runs the risk of being a dreadful husband. The woman may develop perverted habits, possibly even with other women. No such risk threatens the nervous lover, who is merely destined for mediocrity. There is something uncontrolled about these women—as if the female who faces the prospect of no male lover must find some sexual outlet, no matter what.

Ugly women get no comfort from Chesser. In contrast to what Chesser tells men who are not physically attractive, he assures readers that even the ugliest woman can find a man who will be willing to have intercourse with her. He may even enjoy it. If the ugly woman simply keeps this in mind, she will have the necessary confidence to find a mate. Unfortunately, less than two pages later Chesser states that "most men seek physical perfection in those they marry," which is hardly a confidence builder for women who consider themselves ugly (89).

Also abhorrent to men are women who are masculine in mind or physique. Here Chesser reflects some of the ambivalence inherent in his position. Earlier he stated that it is fine for women to have their own careers and professional lives if they want them. At the same time, men abhor women with masculine minds. Since the professions were defined as masculine in the 1950s, it is not possible for a woman to follow one without having a masculine mind. Chesser appears to be trying to suggest a way to balance the pressure for role change with that for specific, definable gender roles. Women should have careers and do what they wish, but they should be careful not to give up their femininity. Like many of his contemporaries in the 1940s and 1950s, Chesser does not seem to realize that his definition of femininity by and large excludes professional or career behavior.

Chesser goes on to note that the only type of man who is willing to be sexually involved with a masculine woman—later referred to as a he-woman—is the so-called masochistic type. He suffers from an abnormality the complement of which is found in the woman with whom he falls in love. Although one might be tempted to think that this is a happy pair, we are assured that their union is based on dual abnormalities. Here is another version of the philosophy reflected in the sitcoms of the 1950s. The ideal pair—indeed the only normal pair—comprises a manly man and a conventionally feminine woman.

In all his discussions, women are perceived as the ones who have the most to lose. The 1950s were not the decade of change that the sixties became, but it was one in which the pressure for change began to rise. In *The Feminine Mystique* Betty Friedan described the dissatisfactions and frustrations of 1950s wives. Attacked as neglectful mothers if they did not play the role of full-time Mom and attacked as smothering mothers if they did, women were becoming more conscious of the contradictions embedded in their lives. Perhaps the television situation comedies of the time, with their rigid roles for men and women, were popular because they affirmed the existence of a stable world, a world yearned for after the depression and war, but actually experienced by few.

Since women's roles were the most fluid, it is not unexpected that writers of marriage manuals would spend time discussing them. Chesser voices opinions that are ahead of his time when he encourages women to have a career and suggests that couples take a long holiday together before they married. Nevertheless, other parts of his advice are more traditional. For example, in the chapter on love play Chesser reverts to the nonrational nature of women again. He notes that a woman knows by instinct just how much coquetry can aid in encouraging her partner. He feels that it is necessary to point this out since some "modern women" despise coquetry (127).

On the other hand, Chesser is careful to point out that love play, what more modern writers would identify as foreplay, is very important to sexual satisfaction. Love play is critical if the female partner is to be fully aroused and then satisfied, which does not happen in the majority of cases, according to Chesser. His advice is in the tradition of Van de Velde. A man should not rush an inexperienced partner. A woman should not be too forward since a man expects to take the lead in intercourse and may be turned off by attempts to stimulate him that are too direct.

At the same time, Chesser takes care to advise readers to keep sexual behavior normal. He quotes Van de Velde's definition of normal sexuality in full to illustrate what he means. Thus he agrees with Van de Velde that normal sexual behavior involves a mature male and a mature female, is free of artificial aids to stimulation, and ends in more or less simultaneous orgasm with semen ejaculated into the vagina. He cautions the reader that a very thin line exists between the normal and the perverse. Perversity by Chesser's definition is more or less restricted to sadistic or hurtful behaviors. In this context, Chesser again reveals the prevailing notion regarding the irrational, uncontrolled nature of women: "any woman could make a pervert of any normal man within six months." There is no suggestion—and it seems not to occur to him—that a man might be able to pervert a woman. The underlying theme is that woman's sexual nature is, or can be, ungovernable once awakened. While successful sexual experiences depend upon the awakening of a woman's sexuality, it seems by implication a dangerous task, to be undertaken carefully. In some senses we have come full circle from the days when Victorian writers claimed that women lacked sexual feelings (143).

In spite of all the good advice, it is still possible to have sexual failures. Men may suffer impotence due to nervousness. This can be easily cured with the proper psychological reassurance. A man can prevent premature ejaculation—so common among highly creative men that it has been called the "literary man's impotence"—by distracting his mind. Chesser suggests that men recite the multiplication tables in order to prolong erection. The reciter is cautioned against doing it out loud (201).

Frigidity in women can also be a problem, although most women are not truly frigid. Here Chesser is using the word "frigidity" in the broadest sense. He means an inability to feel at least some pleasure in the sex act, since he quotes data that about 50 percent of women fail to be orgasmic. While he views men's sexual problems as curable, those of women are viewed as more diverse and potentially lasting. He divides frigid women into three categories. The first category consists of women who are simply uninterested in the sex act and view it only as a way to procreate. These women make good mothers and bad lovers. This is not necessarily harmful as long as the husband gets the appropriate amount of sexual stimulation. The second type of frigid woman is repulsed by the sex act. She may enjoy the preliminaries but finds consummation distasteful. Still, she does not want her marriage ruined by her dislike of sex, which may be what sends her in search of help. The third type of frigid woman may be a victim of her husband's ineptitude. This type of frigidity can be cured only with the husband's cooperation. Otherwise, he runs the risk of having his wife turn to other men, lesbianism, or masturbation (206).

For the woman who is truly happy without an orgasm, there is the time-honored method of simulation, which is "in the power of any intelligent woman." Chesser has already said on several occasions that for lovemaking to be truly satisfactory, both parties must play their part. Pretended orgasms are part of the role, at least for women who do not care about them. Decades later Dr. Ruth will revive this idea. This pretense is hard to reconcile with the honest and uninhibited responses Chesser recommends in other contexts. On the other hand, he implies that women who do care about orgasm should hold out for the real thing (205).

An entire chapter deals with the prolongation of intercourse. Primarily a discussion of a technique called karezza, Chesser seems to include it because it is one of the few areas in which he disagrees with Van de Velde. Karezza was advocated by John Humphrey Noyes and served as a form of birth control. He and his followers formed a community that controlled population through this practice, which is also known as coitus reservatus (D'Emilio and Freedman 1988, 165). Karezza involved prolonged intercourse of several hours, eventually resulting in one or more orgasms for the woman and a gradual subsidence of sensation, without orgasm, for the male (Dickinson, as quoted in Chesser 1947,189). Chesser believes that Van de Velde's opposition to the practice reflects the negative effects of stimulation without orgasm. In Chesser's version of karezza, however, orgasm is avoided only when the couple is using the practice as a contraceptive technique. In any case, Chesser assures his readers that the dire warnings are very much an exaggeration and that the technique, although it requires practice and self-control, particularly for the man, remains perfectly acceptable.

Although *Love without Fear* was written in the late thirties and published in the forties, its American audience was made up of 1950s couples. By the 1950s masturbation was not viewed as the insanity producer of earlier years. Nevertheless, Chesser keeps his chapter on "youthful follies" in the American edition, just in case. He is reassuring about the practice. Mostly everyone does it, no one goes insane, and it is definitely not a perversion. In fact, if one feels intense desire and avoids the practice, one runs the risk of impotence.

Most of the information in the chapter on so-called youthful follies is about women and masturbation. There is no denial that men practice youthful follies, but Chesser pays virtually no attention to them. Even so, masturbation should not become a habit, especially in adults who have the opportunity for intercourse. That it should not become habitual is especially true for women. Again, Chesser's more progressive ideas have trouble breaking completely away from older views of female sexuality. The woman who masturbates, so the story goes, runs the risk of becoming excited only through stimulation of the clitoris, "the vagina being dead to stimulation." Many years later Dr. Ruth makes congruent remarks about vibrators. While Freud viewed female excitation through clitoral stimulation as a sign of arrested or fixated development, Chesser does not. For him it is an inconvenience that can easily be overcome by proper sexual technique on the part of the woman's lover. Chesser is somewhat unclear about the effects of clitoral versus vaginal stimulation. He describes the clitoris as "the equivalent of the male penis pleasantly sensitive, and the seat of voluptuous sensations" (305). The vagina "is somewhat funnel-shaped [and] is capable of contracting to accommodate itself to the size of the penetrating male organ or relaxing sufficiently to permit the passage of a fully developed child." Chesser never mentions the sensitivity of the vagina. His description makes clear which organ is most sensitive. This chapter closes with a set of questions and answers for parents about what to tell their children regarding "youthful follies." It contains advice far superior to the fare of years before, which warned about insanity, wasting diseases, and nervous disorders, although Chesser still advises wise to avoid spicy foods after puberty (229, 305–6).

People can have sex problems. The main problems of nonperverted people stem from the same causes as neurosis, namely, spoiling, fear, and anxiety. Chesser advises that afflicted individuals must believe that they can be helped and then seek such help. This is sensible advice in an era when experts were eagerly sought and psychotherapy was enjoying a boom in popularity. This advice is reserved, however, for those who are nonfunctional, not perverted.

Since he warned earlier of the ease with which a woman can turn a perfectly normal man into a pervert, it seems appropriate that there be some information about what Chesser terms the byways of sex. In agreement with Van de Velde, he writes that variety is important in sexual behavior. There is often a turning toward the perverse if there is no variety within normal limits. Chesser affirms that sex should culminate in mutual orgasm (if possible) through vaginal penetration. Chesser views other activities that lead to orgasm but that do not involve penetration as potentially, if not actually, perverse.

Perhaps because it is so easy to become perverse oneself, Chesser counsels sympathy for the pervert. Punishment is not helpful, but treatment may be. People cannot help their perversions and should be aided in overcoming their sickness. Sadomasochism comes in for special consideration as the most common of the then current perversions. It is especially interesting to Chesser since it represents the normal aggression and submission (passivity) in intercourse carried to extremes. Thus it is easy to see how this perversion can occur. Focusing only on the aggression and submission can eventually lead to the need to hurt someone or to be hurt to achieve orgasm. Alex Comfort's *Joy of Sex* series will later focus on sex as playful violence, which Chesser portrays as extreme.

Chesser also deals with homosexuals, or "she-men" and "he-women," in his chapter on sexual byways. His approach is carefully moderate. He agrees with Freud that homosexuals are often created by the circumstances and events of their lives. He asserts, however, that this happens when there exists a predisposition. In a return to the rape theme mentioned earlier regarding women, Chesser notes that many men become homosexual as a result of sexual assault at school. Women too can be raped by other women, which can result in a tendency to want to repeat the experience. This in spite of the fact that both men and women tend to intensely dislike it. In the case of lesbianism, a single girl can sometimes introduce the practice to an entire school. In general, lesbians appear more dangerous than homosexual men. At least they merit more discussion from Chesser, perhaps because women are more sexually naïve and open to seduction. Chesser is concerned about the strength of the unleashed sexuality of women in general. Lesbians often direct their sexual urges toward normal girls, having a strong dislike for other lesbians. Some lesbians have seduced many, many girls, and Chesser cites the case of a Polish woman physician who boasted that "she had seduced more girls and women than anyone else in Poland." Homosexual men do not appear to try, or to be able, to seduce normal men. At least it is not among the topics that Chesser chooses to mention (255–56).

The discussion of rape, in both a lesbian and heterosexual context, is somewhat curious. Chesser seems to believe that an intensely disliked sexual experience can forever change the course of an individual's sex life. It can cause a woman to become a lesbian, or it can cause her to develop a taste for violent—in his view perverted—sex. He does not explain why wedding night experiences are different. Unpleasant experiences on the honeymoon may result in reluctance to engage in sexual activities again rather than a taste for the perverse or an urge to repeat the bad experience. We are left with a vision of women who are so sensitive that great care must be taken not to distress them unduly during first intercourse lest all sexual desire be killed. On the other hand, women who have been raped are in danger of developing preferences for perverted acts, promiscuity, and violent sex (164).

Chesser, nevertheless, tries to take a more modern view of sexuality, particularly what he terms the "by ways." He warns the reader against making judgments about people based on their appearances since not all homosexual men are effeminate, nor are all homosexual women mannish. Almost parenthetically he adds that modern girls may look somewhat mannish, but they are not necessarily homosexual. While making it clear that homosexuality is not criminal, medical professionals agree that it is pathological and deep-seated. After all, homosexual men dream about men, and homosexual women dream about women (243, 253).

All of this creates a complex picture of feminine nature. No longer without sexual responses, women are instead endowed with a sexuality that is not under their own control. They are easily seduced by women or men. Such experiences can either lead to permanent distaste for sex or make women virtually insatiable, even if the experience is a violent one such as rape. Women who do not need to have an orgasm to feel fulfilled should simulate one so that their husbands are satisfied.

In many ways, Chesser's book and the Stones' manual reflect the struggles of society to cope with the changing role of women in the area of sexuality. The struggles arising from changing roles account for some of the contradictions, especially in Chesser's work. While the Stones were basically content to have their manual reissued with few revisions, Chesser published several other works on similar topics. These are not simply a reworking of *Love without Fear*. In these later works he continues to modernize his thinking and embrace the sexual practices of the time. He gives advice on topics he perceives to be relevant to people grappling with new sexual mores. For example, his book *Unmarried Love* (1966) discusses premarital sex approvingly and includes sections for both men and women. Through this and other books Chesser begins to work out the contradictions of his earlier writing. Couples who read *Love without Fear* get a traditional view of love and marriage without the benefit of many of Chesser's later, more progressive ideas.

Women of the 1950s were urged to be sexual playmates to their husbands. The job description of the housewife included being a willing and enthusiastic sexual partner. This represented a quantum leap from earlier attitudes and beliefs that suggested that good women did not experience sexual desire, or if they did it was only after years of faithful marriage to a loving and kind husband who had carefully taught them to be responsive. Both the Stones and Chesser try to find the thin line between assuming all women were terribly inexperienced and naïve and acknowledging that some women might have sexual experiences. Chesser is by far the more open about this, suggesting that experience on the part of women is not necessarily a bad thing. Still, it is not very likely.

In the era of the Cold War it was terribly important that sexuality be contained in the family, and that the family unit remain strong. Only then could people resist the many bad influences that could lead to the moral decay of the nation. The late Victorian image of national decay resulting from sexual transgressions once again haunted American consciousness. Yet at the same time, Kinsey's work suggested that not all sexual behavior occurred in the context of the family. A nation that took pride and assurance in its family structure epitomized by the virile man and the feminine woman was about to erupt into an unbridled, no-holds-barred sexuality. The marriage manual genre was about to be transformed into a much more explicit sexual one.

6

Sexual Upheaval in the 1960s
Counterculture, Counter-Sex

Following the deprivation of the Great Depression and the triumphant struggle of World War II, the American middle class began its exodus to the suburbs and sought happiness in material well-being combined with good, secure jobs. Despite the sense of well-being reflected in the mirror of television sitcoms, dissident voices soon challenged the complacency of bourgeois America.

The Beats, for example, understood themselves as poets protesting the mindless conformity of the period (Halberstam 1993, x–xi, 509–12). Allen Ginsberg first howled in 1955. Only San Francisco's North Beach Beats recognized his agonal struggle at first. In his 1955 poem "Howl," Ginsberg raged at the forces that destroyed the best minds of his generation. Moloch, a fire god, "bashed open their skulls and ate up their brains and imagination." America had become Moloch's altar, "an incomprehensible prison." Finding himself trapped in the mind of Moloch, Ginsberg celebrated what America called madness (see Miles 1986). William Burroughs (1966) and Jack Kerouac (1958) also knew Moloch, and other writers, such as Ken Kesey, came to recognize America's structure of powerful unfeeling. In *One Flew over the Cuckoo's Nest* (1962), Kesey visualized America as a psychiatric ward ruled tyrannically by Nurse Rached, a dispenser of mental health. Beats such as Ginsberg, Burroughs, and Kerouac rejected the 1950s emphasis on acquisition, conformity, and obedience to authority. Jim Morrison, lead singer of the Doors, who once called himself an "erotic politician," expressed his horror of Moloch in his music and his life.

Ginsberg's song of himself lunges toward an empowering discovery that arises from socialist conceptions of consciousness and is more fully articulated in feminist theory. The personal is political. The authorities, of course, busted Ginsberg's poem as obscene. Comstock's legacy lived long after him. The erotic possibilities that Ginsberg howled toward the heavens threatened the established sexual regime.

Prelude to Change

In the late 1950s student populations swelled. Between 1956 and 1967 the number of graduate and undergraduate degrees awarded by American colleges and universities had doubled. Freedom Summer in 1964 brought some one thousand of them to the South under the auspices of the Student Nonviolent Coordinating Committee (SNCC). Two of them, along with a local African American man, were assassinated in Mississippi. Now northern mass media began to report the violence of American apartheid. This portrait of institutionalized hate clashed with the "evangelical idealism" sparked by President John Kennedy. Though conditioned to defer to authority, some white students began to see structural flaws in America, deep fissures that their African American friends knew well. The activists' experience of institutionalized racism shattered illusions: lawfully constituted authority was lawless; violence masqueraded as right. The civil rights movement sparked a conscious sense of opposition that built on foundations laid by the Beats as well as the Old Left (see *Sense of the Sixties* 1991; Branch 1988, 1998; Gitlin 1987, 83).

A cadre of newly radicalized students returned to their northern campuses and took on local issues. They organized civil rights actions and began to attack universities' authoritarian ideology of *in loco parentis*. The Free Speech Movement (FSM) took hold at the University of California at Berkeley in 1964. When university administrators refused permission for several veterans of Freedom Summer to recruit demonstrators and collect donations on campus, Jack Weinberg sat down at an unauthorized table on Sproul Plaza on October 1, 1964, and was promptly arrested. The police put him in the back of their squad car, but other students blocked the way for thirty-two hours. When the battle for Berkeley ended in January 1965, about eight hundred students had been arrested. In a pattern often repeated, administration miscalculations mobilized students, who then became radicalized by police violence. The FSM sparked fundamental reforms in curricula and university governance. Similar movements arose on other campuses and led to more reforms as well as student empowerment. Like African Americans, white middle-class students knew by their own experience that the system was repressive. It institutionalized Moloch's unfeeling. As the Vietnam War mounted in intensity, many student activists shifted to antiwar efforts. Evangelical idealism fed the nascent movement. The war seemed as unjust as the reign of southern sheriffs or university administrators over their counties or campuses (see *Sense of the Sixties* 1991; Gitlin 1987, 163–64; Isserman 1987, 202–5; Sale 1973, 162–63).

Tear gas, nightsticks, and police dogs recruited for the antiwar movement much as they did for the civil rights struggle. During one street action to shut down the military's Induction Center in Oakland, California, two thousand police charged into the demonstrators. From time to time the police commanded the demonstrators to disburse: "In the name of the people of the State of California" began the legalistic formula. The mob roared back, "we are the people" (Gitlin 1987, 251). Indeed, a new people had formed who rejected the legitimacy of cultural, sexual, and governmental authorities, a revolutionary new people bent on fundamental change. Though reminiscent of the 1920s, this rebellion proved more broadly based as the media publicized every major event on the evening news. Much like the Wobblies, rebels attacked the alliance of government and industry. America's "ethic of authority" was at stake (DeBenedetti 1990, 402–3).

In howls of protest, many of America's youth came to realize the madness of middle-class normality. As Kesey wrote, the system defined and dispensed mental health; lobotomies awaited real resisters. Some turned inward, others to action in quests for personal and political liberation. The antiwar movement as a whole fed on disillusionment and sought intellectual nourishment in the New Left. The attack on "traditional cultural authorities," whether in the antiwar movement or the counterculture, created new possibilities for alternative lifestyles. Amerika was Kesey's madhouse, or as Ginsberg put it, an "incomprehensible prison" (see DeBenedetti 1990 for the antiwar movement; Isserman 1987 for the Old Left; Sale 1973 and Miller 1987 for Students for a Democratic Society).

The Left, both old and new, launched devastating critiques of bourgeois reality. Theories of oppression, alienation, and false consciousness molded their working tools; capitalism was the usual suspect. In an intellectual ferment similar to the 1920s, large numbers of students recognized false consciousness in themselves and searched for alternatives. They sought the vision of Students for a Democratic Society's (SDS) Port Huron statement: a world of "abundance, reason, love and international cooperation." Failure meant the horrors of Vietnam's daily body count or even nuclear Armageddon. The New Left attacked middle-class consciousness and its alliance with church and state. This rebellion, along with the availability of birth control pills, approved by the Food and Drug Administration in 1960, doomed repressive sexual mores. As Bob Dylan sang, the times were a-changing (Miller 1987, 329–74).

In 1967 the Summer of Love erupted in San Francisco's Haight-Ashbury neighborhood. The human potential aspects of the movement took the fore, ever to the chagrin of the Berkeley political types. Hippies, offspring of the Beats, frolicked in Golden Gate Park and sought love and happiness. In their view happiness resulted from changing consciousness; conventional perceptions had to be altered. LSD did it all.

The media focused national attention on the Summer of Love, and soon every American city had a local equivalent of Haight-Ashbury. Love became a "public phenomenon." What was formerly private now became public, and sexual imagery flooded popular consciousness. The goal was to fully experience life, to test and enjoy its limits (Oliver Stone cited in *Sense of the Sixties* 1991). Anything went; what happened, happened. Haight-Ashbury provided an environment of unrestrained freedom, an enactment of the polymorphous perverse. Two years later, in 1969, Woodstock finally marked the end of the counterculture (see Didion 1968, 127; Cohen and Bowen [1967?]; Gitlin 1987, 213; Hinckle 1991; see Wolfe 1968 for Kesey's "Merry Pranksters").

Hair length came to symbolize one's political values. Blue jeans and denim work shirts defined the radical uniform. *Reefer Madness* did not speak to this generation. Marijuana and other drugs quickly became sacramental and spread among college students and the middle class. Rebellion soon fed on itself. *Hair* became a Broadway musical in 1968. It condemned the Vietnam War, celebrated drugs and sex, and prophesied a utopian age of Aquarius, which was soon to dawn. Scandalous when it opened, the play had a scene with full frontal nudity (which was risqué even for New York at the time) as well as a song celebrating sodomy.

Broadway's *Hair*, however, mainly popularized and merchandised the counterculture. The *Living Theater*, on the other hand, confronted repressed consciousness in the hope of finding "Paradise Now." The Living Theater drew no distinction between actors and audience. The actors mingled with the audience and baited them to respond. As opposed to the dead theater, the Living one combined Dionysian mysteries, nude encounters, antiwar politics, and emotional assault. Theater confronted life much as a thesis confronts antithesis. Audience reaction to statements of powerful prohibition supplied the synthesis in "permanent revolution" (Epstein 1991, 368).

"I am not allowed to travel without a passport."

"I cannot travel freely, I cannot move about at will!"

"I am separated from my fellow man, my boundaries are set arbitrarily by others!"

"*The Gates of Paradise are closed to me!*"

An audience in Los Angeles in 1969, angered by their recognition of unfeeling repression, shouted for "Paradise Now." The actors briefly withdrew, then returned.

"I don't know how to stop the wars!"

"You can't live if you don't have money!"

"I'm not allowed to smoke marijuana!"

"I am not allowed to take my clothes off!"

"The body itself of which we are made is taboo!"

"We are ashamed of what is most beautiful, we are afraid of what is most beautiful!!"

"We may not act naturally toward one another!"

"*The culture represses love!*"

"*I am not allowed to take my clothes off!*"

The actors stripped. They enacted the cultural prohibition by covering the legally stipulated minimum. "*I'm not allowed to take my clothes off! I am outside the Gates of Paradise!*" The Los Angeles police stopped the performance at this point. They enforced the prohibition and thus became part of the drama. Jim Morrison sat in the front row all week during the Los Angeles performance. (Hopkins and Sugerman 1980, 222–23 transcribed this experience, and as befits the Living Theater, they do not distinguish between actors and audience in their quotations. The italics are theirs. Also see Epstein 1991, 365–85 for a New York experience.)

As the Living Theater demonstrated, public nudity was certainly charged with politics. "Longhairs" often went much further and advocated "free love." The phrase referred to sex divorced from marital responsibility. This responsibility, in turn, was viewed as a social cost. Having sex, in the older view, entailed the risk/cost of pregnancy/marriage. This revival of free love had a broader base than in the past and represented a new sexual ethic first glimpsed in the 1920s: pleasure and authenticity divorced from fear of pregnancy/marriage. The pill made it possible (see also D'Emilio and Freedman 1988, 301–25).

The Zeitgeist Shifts Course

The sexual revolution continued. Like some computer programs, it had been running in the background all the while. Like all social movements, antiwar fervor brought previously private issues into public light. Authenticity, for example, called for free expression of one's sexual nature. In fact, sexual pleasure became an end in itself as a peak experience, Van de Velde's revised edition to the contrary. Advances in medical science had already divorced sex from reproduction as well as most fears of sexually transmitted diseases.

Hugh Hefner edited the first issue of *Playboy* on his kitchen table in 1953. Even though a new Hollywood star, Marilyn Monroe, adorned the foldout center page (a picture from before her rise in Hollywood), Hefner remained unsure about his chance for success. He put neither his name nor a date on the first issue so if initial sales proved sluggish, he could keep the first issue on newsstands an extra month. With seventy thousand copies in print, Hefner hoped to sell thirty thousand at fifty cents each. He ended up selling fifty-three thousand copies. The second issue displayed Hefner's name as editor and publisher, and within a year the magazine sold one hundred thousand copies monthly. Within two years, *Playboy*'s circulation soared to four hundred thousand. Every month the magazine presented new airbrushed visions arousing to the "male gaze" (see Williams 1989 for the phallocentric male gaze and its ordering power). Hefner became the first American to get rich by "openly mass marketing masturbatory love through the illusion of an available alluring woman." The magazine connected to its subscribers from "erection center" in Chicago (Talese 1980, 22–23). Government approval of the first birth control pill in 1960 as well as the liberalization of obscenity rulings fired male synapses. Hefner went on to create Playboy Clubs in major cities and popularized his "Playboy Philosophy."

A law review article by Hefner summarizes his arguments and focuses attention on the sexual regime. Hefner argues that moral questions involving private consensual sex between adults are not the business of the government. Resolution of such issues resides with individuals. Around the time of the article in the mid-1960s, forty-eight states and the District of Columbia prohibited nonmarital and extramarital sexual intercourse between consenting adults. The states used adultery, fornication, and lewd cohabitation statutes to enforce the sexual regime. Thirty-one states specifically prohibited cohabitation and penalties tended to exceed those for fornication. Sodomy statutes, according to Hefner, most clearly displayed the interplay between sexual regulations and religious proscriptions. At the time forty-nine states and the District of Columbia prohibited sodomy, "the abominable and detestable crime against nature," and these statutes did not make any distinction between heterosexual or homosexual criminals. Only the state of New York differentiated between married and unmarried perpetrators. Hefner, not surprisingly, vigorously defends heterosexual criminals. The logic of his argument as well as the temper of the times then moves him to defend homosexual ones. He called for tolerance for those whose inclinations differ. Since contemporary erotic practices quite often departed from the norms of the old sexual regime, the country overflowed with sexual outlaws and *Playboy* provided new fantasies on a monthly basis (Hefner 1968, 199–221).

Hefner, his empire ever growing, promoted consensual, guilt-free sex. If it felt good, it was good. *Playboy* presented sex "as not only legitimate but as a sophisticated lifestyle." Hefner struck "a powerful new chord in post-war American life: the changing attitudes about sex and a steadily more candid view of sexuality. Hefner was fighting that part of the Puritan ethic that condemned pleasure." *Playboy* also helped define a new concept of the good life. Its pages abounded with advertisements for the latest hi-fi sets and proffered advice about how to order fine wines in expensive restaurants. Its pages conjoined sex and consumption. "Ordinary Americans could afford to live better than they ever had before, and they now wanted the things that had previously been the possessions of only the very wealthy; and they wanted the personal freedoms the rich had traditionally enjoyed too. In the onslaught, old restraints were loosened." Hefner "preached pleasure. He touched the right chord at precisely the right moment." *Cosmopolitan*, with Helen Gurley Brown as its editor, came to mimic *Playboy*'s brassy sexuality (Halberstam 1993, 570–76 for the citations; Talese 1980).

Two years after the approval of the first birth control pill, Helen Gurley Brown penned a *succès de scandale* entitled *Sex and the Single Girl*. Several hundred years earlier, Mary Astell (Hill 1986) pleaded and argued for a retreat for women that would function as a refuge from patriarchy. Women, after all, had no alternative to marriage. Helen Gurley

Brown, on the other hand, thought it was finally time to have some fun. Brown acknowledges that both single and married life are "hell" for women. She also notes economic inequalities that would soon receive a great deal of attention from the (not quite yet established) National Organization for Women. Brown advocates that women tease men ("she doesn't have to deliver"), but she also breaks with traditional norms. Good girls do! "In Los Angeles, where I live, there is something else a girl can say and frequently does when a man 'insists.' And that is 'yes.'" As Brown sees it, virginity can become a trap that reduces a woman's chance for happiness and/or marriage. Affairs can begin in two hours or two years and can last from one night to forever. It no longer matters that a man thinks a girl is a virgin as the tradition had it. As Brown says, "is *he*?" Likewise, in bed it's "silly" to pretend to be inexperienced. During an affair, "if you are not going to marry him, it's insane not to keep date channels open." Brown considers multiple affairs a possibility. Girls should avoid "disturbed" boys, but "one thing a single woman *can* have is a good sex life." She does not have much advice to offer lesbians, but her view is relatively progressive for its time. She assumes that their problems are numerous, but "it's *your* business and I think it's a shame you have to be so surreptitious about your choice of a way of life" (Brown 1962, 234, 225, 231–32, 234; italics in original).

Helen Gurley Brown's work certainly advocates a world in which women can seek pleasure more on their own terms. Yet, as Andrea Dworkin noted twelve years later, the pill mainly reinforced patriarchal bondage. "It made us more accessible, more open to exploitation. It did not change our basic condition because it did nothing to challenge the sexist structure of society, not to mention conventional sexual relationships and couplings" (Dworkin 1974, 82). Given the reality of gender-based economic discrimination, Brown's questioning of the linkage between sex and marriage also boded ill for what little economic security many women did have. Brown chipped away at an essential enticement for men to get married. But, as a *Cosmo* girl might say, it's "hell" either way.

"Sex and Caste: A Kind of Memo"

Radical feminism developed from the antiwar movement. One catalyst was a 1,500-word essay called "Sex and Caste: A Kind of Memo from Casey Hayden and Mary King to a Number of Other Women in the

Peace and Freedom Movements." Hayden and King argue that women also constituted an oppressed class. Women in SDS, for example, became enraged when told that their position in the movement was "prone." "In 1968, the 'druggy' White Panther Party manifesto declared: 'Fuck your woman so hard till she can't stand up.' Liberation News Service excised the offending line, but the word and the text got around." Male leaders typically relegated women to supporting roles such as typing, supplying food, and providing sexual services.

> The atmosphere was reeking of barricades, the burning possibility (and temptation) of death, the desperate passion to "break on through to the other side" [as Morrison sang]. . . . If the earth was going to glorious hell, sexual conquest was the garden (or last ditch?) of earthly delights. Orgasm was the permanent revolution, the grand finale that led to the next grand finale; or was it that The Revolution was orgasm writ large? With their knack for riding the Zeitgeist, the Rolling Stones seized the transition—from 1966's 'Let's spend the night together' to 1969's 'oh, dears, it's just a shot away. . . . Love, sisters, it's just a kiss away." (Gitlin 1987, 372 for the citations)

Women activists began meeting in consciousness-raising groups and circulated papers such as "The Politics of Housework" and "The Myth of the Vaginal Orgasm" that challenged their subservient role (Gitlin 1987, 367–71; Sale 1973, 566–77). In 1968, reflecting a sea change in consciousness, SDS's national conference resolved that the '"oppression of women through male supremacy' was both qualitatively and quantitatively greater than the oppression of working people in general." Women, in other words, were the real proletariat (Sale 1973, 526).

Radical feminism, a vibrant force from 1968 to 1973, stressed participatory democracy (an early SDS concept), consciousness raising, and the development of counterinstitutions. It also provided devastating critiques of patriarchal power structures as well as patrifocal conceptions of sexuality and marriage. Radical feminists understood sexuality not merely as a reflection of choice or custom, but as a locus of personal and institutional power. In their experience, a woman's identity actually depended on internalized self-hatred. They struggled for personal and political transformation and an end to gender distinctions that supported patriarchy. They sought their authentic selves, the selves trapped within conventions of self-loathing. Women should not feel like cripples and hunchbacks as Van de Velde would have it, and Sanger's vision of free womanhood finally reached toward the limit of its logic (see Echols 1989, vii–29; Gelb and Klein 1987, 4; Sale 1973, 526–624; Shilts 1987, 13).

Orgasm as Permanent Revolution Becomes Sex as Recreation

The sexual eruption continued in mainstream culture. Drug use, in the interim, had become "recreational." As the Vietnam War diminished in intensity, constraints imposed by the necessity of mobilizing against it fell away. Political contexts were slowly forgotten. Hedonism, the norm that so frightened Van de Velde, supplanted movement activism. The "ethic of authority," whether patriarchal, cultural, sexual, or political, had been discredited. If something felt good, it was good! Consumerism (even of forbidden/illegal things) fulfilled the contented consciousness. The commercialization of "uninhibited sexuality" soon provided Disneylands of erotic delights.

Commercial considerations drove the singles scene in large cities.

> Throughout the country, singles bars began to populate the urban landscape, providing a setting for men and women to meet and form liaisons. Publishers threw together guide books for the unattached, computer dating services sprang into existence, and builders constructed youth-oriented apartment complexes so that the modern singles could party without complaints of concerned parents or older Americans. Although for some this new singles culture served to facilitate the quest for a spouse, its contours made it more of a sexual, than a marriage market.
>
> (D'Emilio and Freedman 1988, 304)

A raw, more predatory eros permeated American life. Mary Quant, the designer of the miniskirt, put it simply: "Am I the only woman who has ever wanted to go to bed with a man in the afternoon?" "Any law-abiding female, it used to be thought, waits until dark. Well, there are lots of girls who don't want to wait. Mini-clothes are symbolic of them" (quoted in D'Emilio and Freedman 1988, 306). American culture traditionally assigned women the role of urging sexual restraint. Now, as Quant makes clear, many no longer did. Eros permeated the culture. The divorce between sex and marriage/reproduction continued, while the zeitgeist marched on toward the limits of liberation.

Sexual consumption increased dramatically. Plato's Retreat offered the bathhouse choice—clothing-optional adult recreation centers—to couples in New York City. Bookstores appeared with dark windows and neon signs simply declaring XXX. Erotic massage "became a national preoccupation—it was the fast-food business of sex." Chicago had a massage parlor near the Loop that was decorated to resemble a church. The reception area was furnished with prayer benches and enclosed within a Gothic confessional. What would have formerly been considered sacrilege now became just another variation on arousal, merely one more powerful taboo to be broken. Los Angeles had its Circus Maximus with thirty scantily clad masseuses. Its advertising stated that "men haven't had it so good since the days of Pompeii." A short drive into the Santa Monica mountains led to Sandstone Retreat, a fifteen-acre enclave that provided erotic delights within a group marriage. Plans called for eventually charging admission. Margaret Sanger's Wantley, a refuge for freethinking intellectuals and artists, thus became democratized. Television talk shows took up formerly taboo subjects such as orgasm. A pornographic film, *Deep Throat*, gained national attention. *Playboy* evoked competition. America now had *Penthouse* and eventually *Hustler*. Scatological images in *Hustler* even lost their power to shock. Consensual adultery, formerly a grave sin, became known as swinging, and many couples indulged in it. Los Angeles even had a bar called the Swing, which networked the action. Sex came to be viewed as good in itself, a matter of consensual pleasure. Hefner's vision had proved prophetic. Entrepreneurs eagerly supplied the hungry marketplace. In this context David Reuben published his *Everything You Always Wanted to Know about Sex* at the end of the decade. His question-and-answer format and frank language catered to a mass audience. The days when anxious publishers added inserts adjuring readers about the contents had finally passed (Talese 1980, 222–23, 224–39; Altman 1984, 115).

A Sex Manual for the Times

In *Everything You Always Wanted to Know about Sex but Were Afraid to Ask*, David Reuben, M.D., explains things people feared to ask in 1969.[1] As the title page makes clear, he understands himself not as an author, but merely an explainer of things. He will, in fact, provide explanations rooted in psychiatry. According to Reuben, ignorance about sexual matters prevails in America—a standard observation in this genre—the least qualified, such as Anthony Comstock ("a psychotic legislator") and the Reverend Bowlder ("a sick man") try to control the sexual relations of other people. Reuben, on the other hand, seeks to provide information that will give people the greatest possible sexual satisfaction. By locating sexual repression and control in the past, Reuben implies that his own work presents a new view marked by personal freedom. According to Reuben, God's design includes copulation. "An active and rewarding sexual life . . . is indispensable if one is to achieve his full potential" (Reuben 1969, 4). Hanchett's, Kellogg's, Guernsey's, and Van de Velde's (*Ideal Marriage*) religious reasoning falls away as Reuben like Collins uses psychiatry to ostensibly redefine the sexual regime. As Collins predicted, the construction of female sexuality had changed somewhat by the latter 1960s, but psychiatry and medical science had yet to eradicate inverts/homosexuals. Reuben devotes a good deal of attention to orgasm, and he builds upon Van de Velde's work and American folklore since [Pseudo] Aristotle.

> Suddenly the master switch is flipped and it happens! Indescribable sensations race from the vulva, vagina and clitoris throughout the nervous system. The primitive areas of the brain seize control. The back arches, the pelvis lunges forward, the muscles surrounding the vulva expand and contract and send waves of feeling racing over the entire body. The pelvic veins empty rapidly, droplets of sweat burst out on the skin, and a sense of relaxation flows through the entire body.

Male orgasm, according to Reuben, tends to be all-or-nothing, while women experience not only this type of climax but also "skimming"— like a flat pebble skipping across the surface of a lake. In Reuben's view, which builds on some of Van de Velde's physiology, sexual feelings flow from the clitoris, labia minora, and the outer part of the vagina. The clitoris, however, remains the focus of all sexual pleasure. After rejecting Freud's concept of an immature sex object choice focused on the clitoris and not the vagina, Reuben moves on to explain heterosexual intercourse (Reuben 1969, vii–42; Altman 1984, 117).

Reuben postulates three purposes for intercourse: reproduction, love, and fun. True feeling, according to Reuben, exists only in the brain within bundles of neurons, and he recommends the use of all available pathways to this center. These pathways are additive and reciprocally reinforcing. Oral-genital stimulation, for example, is acceptable as a prelude to penetrative intercourse. Since Reuben accepts sexual intercourse for purposes of recreation, why does he valorize vaginal intercourse above all other possibilities? Reuben explains that vaginal intercourse keeps the birthrate above zero and that real sexual satisfaction depends on penetration, which provides a transcendent experience. "The ideal act of sexual intercourse combines reproduction, deep mutual love, and profound physical pleasure. Most people will experience this combination less than a dozen times in their life span" (44–63).

Male sexuality consists of a "confidence game." "An erection is so perishable that a sudden noise, a critical word, even a rejecting look can demolish it." In what can be called the Medusa effect, Reuben explains that fear of the vagina explains impotence (82–96).

Frigidity is contrary to instinct. "Human destiny is constant relentless copulation, in spite of all the barriers and the obstacles." The instinct to breed cannot be thwarted. Here Reuben provides another reason for his valorization of penetrative vaginal intercourse. If orgasm was the only goal of sex, then masturbation would become an ideal form of it. "[Masturbation] . . . is cheaper, cleaner, and saves a lot of time." It does, however, lack emotional involvement. Thus, instinct demands vaginal penetration for breeding, while this is best done in a secure—no frightening noises—emotional relationship (107–27).

Reuben entitles chapter 8 "Male Homosexuality." No chapter is specifically devoted to lesbian sexuality or female homosexuality. He does, however, discuss lesbians in his chapter on prostitution. Though homosexuality in Reuben's view includes a wide range of behaviors, most male homosexuals sometime or other act out the female role. He does not distinguish between gender inversion and same-sex object choice. Reuben rejects the explanation that homosexuality is genetic (as it partially is in Collins's work and possibly in Van de Velde's). Reuben relies mainly on a hormonal imbalance theory, but his explanation never transcends surmises. Regardless of their genesis, homosexuals need to find the right psychiatrist (for a horrific example of such "treatment," though only one of many, see Duberman 1991).

Homosexuals typically engage in mutual masturbation for five to ten minutes. Reuben discusses examples of sex in public bathrooms.[2] Urgency drives homosexuals. "The primary interest is the penis, not the person," and "homosexuals thrive on danger." Assault, blackmail, and robbery are common; even murders occur. He compares practitioners of sadism and masochism to Hitler's Gestapo and S.S. Sometimes sadists get carried away and the outcome is death. This, sadly enough, is just part of the lifestyle. Though male homosexuals have tried every physiological possibility, they mostly try to make the anus a vagina. Reuben implicitly argues that this is not natural. Anuses unlike vaginas are not elastic, and consequently, anal penetration causes pain. The resulting sensations rarely generate enough pleasure to spark climax for the man penetrated. Though promiscuity defines homosexuality, gratification never actually occurs, since no vagina is involved. "Penis or vagina, that's it right there. No other options are available." Thus homosexuals seek encounter after encounter in public toilets in a doomed search for a "penis that pleases." Reuben defines homosexual couples as rare, and speculates that homosexuals never stop looking for sexual partners. After fourteen pages of explanation, Reuben finally mentions female homosexuals. He merely asks how they get along with the male variety.

Since sex cannot satisfy male homosexuals, they masturbate a lot, but most of their activity, as Reuben fantasizes it, focuses on the anus. Reuben also thinks that male homosexuals stand enraptured at the produce counters of supermarkets. Insertible fruits and vegetables include carrots and cucumbers. Insertions of whiskey glasses, pop bottles, flashlights, and even light bulbs result in trips to hospital emergency rooms. He goes on to reject sexual reassignment surgery as "bizarre," and like Van de Velde he states that "nature resents meddling" (129–51).

Masturbation preoccupies Reuben next. Any stimulation except penile-vaginal penetration is masturbatory. It mainly preoccupies the young and old, while adolescents tend to outgrow it. According to Reuben, masturbation is acceptable for convicts, old people, and the blind. Being consistent, Reuben grants that candles and cucumbers can be inserted vaginally, but once again denies the possibility of pleasure from anal intercourse. He reiterates that homosexual sex, presumably his male variant, consists entirely of masturbation (152–71).

Reuben reserves his next chapter for "Sexual Perversion," which he takes as a misnomer for "sexual variant." This includes "anyone who isn't interested in the penis-vagina version of sex." Sexual variants need to grow up! In this category Reuben includes peepers, female impersonators, and fetishists. Implicitly he also includes homosexuals.

Reuben finally pays attention to lesbians in his prostitution chapter. Female homosexuals are as frustrated as the male variety. "Just as one penis plus one penis equals nothing, one vagina plus another vagina still equals zero." (Alex Comfort will further develop this genital algebra in his *Joy of Sex* series.) Female homosexuals usually engage in mutual masturbation. "(This is of course the curse of the homosexual, male or female. No matter how imaginative they are, their sexual practices must always be some sort of imitation of heterosexual intercourse)." Though female homosexuals can maintain relationships for slightly longer periods than male ones, both male and female homosexuals are searching "for love where there can be no love and looking for sexual satisfaction where there can be no lasting satisfaction" (200–268).

Everything You Always Wanted to Know about Sex does note the effectiveness of birth control pills, but, somewhat surprisingly for a text published in 1969, focuses on their side effects.[3] He calls for "retrospective" techniques of birth control such as abortion or a "morning after" pill. Even granting this, Reuben notes that women fulfill their biological destiny in copulating, whether or not pregnancy results. Reuben's hesitation regarding the pill is comparable to its limited endorsement in the appendix of Van de Velde's revised edition some four years earlier (244–68). Alex Comfort in his *Joy of Sex* series will be one of the first widely read authors to celebrate the pill.

Homosexuals and African American men mainly account for those with venereal diseases. According to Reuben, research will increase when more prominent people get these diseases. Reuben then combines racism and homophobia in a simplistic formulation. "Homosexuals [males presumably] are capable of prodigious promiscuity. Simply by the laws of probability, sooner or later a wide-ranging white homosexual will come in contact with a similarly inclined black homosexual. The infection then passes to both their partners and their partner's partners and their partner's partner's partner and so on." The only reason to include race as well as promiscuity is to imply that African Americans somehow serve as a repository for venereal diseases (270–87). (For an infamous example of racism conjoined with science in the Tuskegee experiment, see Jones 1981.)

The text concludes with advice about one's golden years, and once again Reuben seems to consider gender a function of hormones. As he puts it, "once the ovaries stop, the very essence of being a woman stops." Van de Velde expressed a similar sentiment in Latin. Similarly, testosterone makes a man what he is. In a male, testosterone replacement can bring back self-confidence, determination, and optimism, not to mention sexual prowess. Like the late Victorians, Reuben links sexual potency with success in business. Women, lacking the same testosterone levels as men, will presumably be disadvantaged in business. Unlike Van de Velde, however, Reuben does not assert that women have less mental acuity.

Reuben's very first question in this volume indicates his agenda: "how big is the normal penis?"

Doctor Reuben's Explanation

Reuben discusses the genital areas as vast depositories of nerve endings. He even believes that a woman without a clitoris can have an orgasm. All these synapses terminate in the brain, where people really experience sexual feelings. So why must men penetrate vaginas when the same effect in the brain can be achieved other ways? Reuben implicitly argues that men experience their own power in sexual penetration and ejaculation, and this corresponds to their power in the realm of commerce. Though in Reuben's view it does not matter which neurons fire from the genitally rich areas, male power demands vaginal penetration to fully satisfy itself. The instinct to breed/copulate also requires penetration of an elastic orifice.

The denigration and demonization of other alternatives reflects the weakness of his explanation as well as the fragile nature of this power. Reuben does not argue or develop a teleological view of nature to support his views, but he does assume such a position at times. He merely states that nature rejects meddling. Mainly he develops an explanation that relies on psychiatry and roots itself in the instinct to breed/copulate. As many others have noted, medical science, especially psychiatry, had by now come to supplant religion as a basis for normatizing sexual behavior. Curiously enough, however, Reuben's general conclusions mainly differ from the late Victorians in that women can now have orgasms as powerful as those of men. He does not diverge all that much from Van de Velde or Collins, except for matters of style, tone, and presentation. He also shares Collins's homophobia. Reuben presents a sexual trinity: reproduction, love, and pleasure, with pleasure implicitly subordinate to reproduction. The late Victorians, on the other hand, mainly acknowledge reproduction. All of them link penetrative vaginal sexuality and success in commerce. Reuben substitutes Collins's tolerance of natural homosexuals with a call for therapy, but Reuben's hormonal approach also implicitly imagines a world without homosexuals. Hormonal therapy may just provide a cure. In the work of Collins and Reuben, psychiatry links recognition of homosexuality with its elimination. Some things, however, do change. Reuben, unlike Collins, does not feel any need to attack religion explicitly. That battle might have seemed won in 1969. For the late Victorians, God and nature command maternity, while Reuben in a more modern mode relies on instinct (for a contrary view see Weinberg and Hammersmith 1983, 317).

Stand by Your Man

In 1971 Reuben published *Any Woman Can! Love and Sexual Fulfillment for the Single, Widowed, Divorced . . . and Married.* In this work he follows the same question-and-answer format as in *Everything You Always Wanted to Know about Sex*, but this work lists him as the author, not an explainer. Utilizing Reuben's own methodology, we pose the following questions.

What is it that any woman can do?
Get married by skillfully applying the techniques outlined in the book.

How does this book clarify or add to his earlier explanation in Everything You Always Wanted to Know about Sex?
Reuben, much like Van de Velde, presents reproduction as a powerful instinctual drive in women. "From the instant of conception onward, the primary thrust of every woman's being is to be fertilized, to conceive, and to reproduce. No force on earth can stand in her way." He links this drive to the menstrual cycle and the flow of estrogen. According to one example, "Beth is coming into heat. . . . Each month just before her egg is ready to be released, Beth has the compelling necessity to make herself available for fertilization." Often this drive is redirected, but it makes its demands every month. It also invites every woman to "experience the sheer euphoria and animal exuberance that dwells within her" and provides the "key to eternal femininity." Nature obviously intended the penis and the vagina to be brought together. "During the excitement and abandon of sexual intercourse a woman has the full force of thousands of years as the bearer of children working against her. Every ounce of her being is directed toward fulfilling her sexual role with absolute disregard of everything else around her." Orgasms, rooted in clitoral stimulation, satisfy a woman's need for "animal exuberance," while penetration allows for instinctual gratification through fertilization (Reuben 1971, 9, 31–32, 73–74, 76–85).
According to Reuben, single and divorced women find themselves in

a sexual state of nature, "a modern jungle." They feel frustrated every month when they come into heat, and the possibility of rape is much greater for single women than for married ones. "If she uses every one of her abilities to the utmost, not only will she survive but she has a chance for real happiness." Her "critical" and "urgent" need consists of finding a husband (146).

According to Reuben, sexual feelings in men are much more compelling and urgent than those in women. "When a man has an erection, there is no putting it off until tomorrow night—it's a question of right now or suffer." "By blending the desperate urgency of the male sexual drive with the incentive principle . . . [keeping him constantly in a low state of arousal] and using the combination to provide what no other woman can offer: genuine sex: the only type which really satisfies and offers lasting value," a woman can rope her man. Female power thus consists of erotic teasing. "When he is desperate to discharge his sexual excitement, a woman—and what she can offer—becomes the center of a man's entire world." Premarital sex, according to Reuben, removes the most important incentive to marry. "Sex outside of marriage is like throwing a steak to a tiger—easy to give, but hard to take away" (247, 248–50, 253, 256).

As in the earlier explanation, erections remain fragile things. "It all hinges on his ability to obtain and maintain an erection," but a man's "phallic magic wand" is beyond the control of his conscious mind. For a woman to experience pleasure herself and gratify her maternal instincts, she must give her husband the strongest possible erections by providing a wide range of stimulations combined with emotional security (316, 321).

What about Mom?
Both female and male children bond primarily with their mothers, and this relationship sets the pattern for all others. Men act out this primal relationship in their attitude toward food—symbolic mother—and especially milk. "For every man the world of the subconscious is ruled by the symbol of milk," "a vital nourishing food synonymous with love." Women who skillfully manipulate food and mother stimuli have a "psychological hydrogen bomb" at their disposal to lasso a man into marriage. A man who cannot tolerate milk often displays "a complete denial and renunciation of the mother-child feeding relationship, and it may leave a girl nothing to build on." Men who totally reject milk are questionable marriage prospects (100, 211–13, 239, 242, 243).

What is Reuben's basic view of gender politics?
He presents two ways of dealing with the problem of sexual marooning, that is, not having a man. A woman can attempt to change society, but "from a practical point of view it would be much easier to make Niagara Falls flow uphill." On the other hand, a woman can rescue herself through marriage and return to civilization from the sexual state of nature. Women need to marry to fulfill instinctual needs and discover happiness as well as to avoid sexual assault. Though women may work part-time as long as it does not interfere with family responsibilities, Reuben, like Van de Velde, assigns men the burden of supporting the family. While women marry for instinctive and emotional fulfillment as well as safety, men do it to get erections as well as to gain power over Mom. Erections, it seems, really express feelings about Mom and are symbolically acted out in a man's relationship to food, especially milk (24, 166, 205).

What about erections?
On the whole, women must come to grips with society's alliance against them and manage what they can in a man's world. A woman's emotional and instinctual fulfillment depends on being a mother and maintaining a household. To accomplish this, she must give her man good erections and deal with his anxiety about them. A woman must never criticize her husband's sexual performance even if she does not experience orgasm, for once she sparks sexual insecurity there is no getting over it. Try to get him to do better next time! If all else fails, try fellatio. This method partially bypasses the brain and works directly on the penis (17, 28).

Pay careful attention to his Mom when you first meet her. Your whole marriage will be modeled on how he interacts with her.

"How does a girl identify a homosexual?"
Some "dedicated" ones do not even try to hide. Others have to be found out. Perhaps, as Van de Velde thought, some try to cure themselves by marriage. Watch out for men who do not make sexual advances and who avoid the "usual wrestling bouts" of new relationships. Reuben considers homosexuality a problem, but declines to make any moral judgments here, unlike his earlier book. Women must be alert for homosexuals who can handle the limited sexual demands of dating. They really cannot be helped. There is, however, a chance of change through psychotherapy for those not "resigned" to their condition (162–64).

What about bisexuals and transgendered people?
Reuben does not discuss bisexuals, and this book, reflecting the times, makes no references to transgendered people.

So what does all this mean?
Though Reuben, like Van de Velde, grants that women should receive pleasure from sex and that orgasms are clitoral, he presents the traditional teaching based now on psychiatry rather than religion. Given the sexual eruption of the 1960s, the work is reactionary and seeks to keep women dependent on men for their economic, emotional, sexual, and physical well-being and security. Women like Beth come into "heat" and need to breed. This need accounts for why Reuben discounts birth control techniques and always lists their many hazards as well as limited effectiveness. Dr. Ruth, writing in the next two decades, will employ a similar approach. Though Reuben grants that pleasure has a great deal to do with sex, he declines to affirm the movement of America's sexual zeitgeist.

The text tells women how to ensnare a man and then use him to provide for their own happiness. Women do this by manipulating a man's erotic drive. Overall, Reuben presents a consumer model that rests on supply and demand. He advises women, despite the rapidly changing sexual ethos, that it remains in their best interest to keep demand high, which increases the price of their product. Both male and female happiness depends on how skillfully women can play this game.

What about women who remain sexually marooned?
In the sexual state of nature, they run a higher risk of sexual assault and dry up emotionally. Their lives, to cite Hobbes, are undoubtedly solitary, poor, nasty, brutish, and short.

Why does Reuben write this way?
His tone seems conversational; it is almost as if one is talking to a psychiatrist. Reuben's constant references to his patients and extensive quotations from them not only provide a common touch, but also help his readers identify with the issues under discussion. His question-and-answer format is meant to be skimmed and read in parts, and it aims to teach women how to get and stay married. Along these lines, Reuben places the responsibility for male arousal on women. Men cannot experience their potency/power without an "educated" wife. The text also

implicitly attacks the 1960s sexual revolution and seeks to ground traditional morality in nature and psychiatry. Religion has apparently disappeared from the old trinity, as foreseen by Collins in 1926.

The question-and-answer format also gives Reuben the opportunity to change the topic when it suits him. Logic does not drive this text. Reuben's format also allows inconsistencies to remain more easily hidden. For example, he never clarifies the relationship between copulation and reproduction. Reuben refuses to grant that the birth control pill effectively sundered sex as a pleasurable activity from sex as a reproductive activity—at least for women with access to the medical system. He employs various rhetorical strategies to value penetrative heterosexual intercourse over all other methods of ejaculation/orgasm.

By using this technique, Reuben undoubtedly sought to attract a large audience, and he did inspire Woody Allen to make a film of the same title (Allen 1972). He probably influenced the behavior of many women and drove some homosexuals into therapy. As compared to Collins's *Look at Love and Life* in 1926, Reuben's explanation does not offer freedom from gender norms to women or toleration for some homosexuals. On the other hand, part of Collins's vision had come to pass. Many homosexuals in 1969 undoubtedly understood themselves as inverts and had internalized at least some of the values of "victims" and "misfits." But also in 1969 at the Stonewall Inn in New York City, some of these "misfits" rebelled against victimhood and empowered themselves as gays by means of a riot. From the new gay perspective, the psychiatric association functioned as a colonial oppressor, certainly not a learned society that dealt with scientific facts (Bayer 1987).

7

Joy through Peak Experiences in the 1970s

In *The Doors*, Oliver Stone (1991) presents Jim Morrison as personifying the zeitgeist of the 1960s. Jim defied limits. With the energized rush of an enraged adolescent, he attacked cultural precepts as if they were parental commands to return home at eleven. Jim consumed magisterial amounts of LSD, and he sang dark songs about breaking through to the other side and "The End," his beautiful friend. His dark vision matched his black leather pants and suffused his relationships. As presented in Stone's movie, psychological pain remains his one constant, and he continually entices death. Stone also presents Jim in terms of sexual excess. As Stone remarked in an interview, "No matter what time you live in I think you're always ready for Dionysus to come down from the mountains and lead you into the wild, swirling orgy" (Dieckmann 1991, 33). As Jim sang his musical poems, he often made his state of arousal obvious. His leather pants hid little and arousal was part of the act. He consumed sex the way a crack addict smokes rocks. Jim, however, embraced eros in its broadest sense. He taught "utter abandon, total will. He wasn't just talking about sex; he meant desire in the broadest, most troubling sense—as in, *beyond good and evil*" (Goldstein 1991, 35; italics in original). Sex as a socially constructed activity contains cultural commands writ small. Sexual politics presents the ultimate/intimate arena for struggles between repression and liberation. Though Jim understood his sexual challenge to parental authority, his demands for erotic freedom heralded a more radical cultural and political rebellion. He foreshadowed an erotic challenge to all authority rooted in administered structures of desire. "He defied the system with his dick" (Goldstein 1991, 35–37). Though Stone leaves the ending of his movie ambiguous so as not to challenge the Morrison legend, Jim probably died of a heroin overdose in Paris on July 3, 1971. His grave at Père-Lachaise remains Paris's fourth biggest tourist attraction (Jones 1990, 23, 146).

Sometime in this period, the zeitgeist altered course. No one event marks this shift, though in retrospect many events heralded it. The sexual regime with its rigid gender roles and restriction of sexual pleasure to marriage seemed to crumble. Sexual excess as lived by Jim Morrison came to define the times. The collapse of the old norms did not happen all at once; it was more like a slow disintegration. More and more people seemed to disregard the old commands. What was once scandalous behavior slowly became acceptable or at least tolerable. Sexual activities once enjoyed primarily by aristocrats became more commonplace. In this sense, sexual gratification became democratized. The media, of course, trumpeted these changes and in doing so amplified the very thing that caught their interest. One key event in this evolution began at a dinner party organized by Margaret Sanger.

In early 1951 Sanger brought together a gynecologist, Abraham Stone, coauthor of *A Marriage Manual: A Practical Guidebook to Sex and Marriage*, and a researcher, Dr. Gregory Pincus of the Worcester Foundation for Experimental Biology. Later John Rock, another medical doctor and a prominent Roman Catholic, became part of the research effort. Sanger already knew Katharine McCormick, a very wealthy widow, who had previously aided the movement by smuggling diaphragms into the country. With money from McCormick, eventually some two million dollars, Sanger launched the effort to create a birth control pill. The birth control pill was approved by the government in 1960. By the end of 1961 about four hundred thousand American women were taking it; by 1963 the figure had risen to over two million. Vast numbers of women could now enjoy intercourse relieved of the fear of pregnancy. In a characteristic overstatement Norman Mailer remarked that "we're in a time that's utterly divorced from the past. There's utterly no tradition anymore. It's a time when our nervous systems are being remade" (Asbell 1995, 8–9, 12, 58, 168, 184 for the Mailer citation, 206–7).

Sexual Joy

Alex Comfort's first edition of *The Joy of Sex* in 1972 illustrates Americans' evolving mores. Based on an extensive analogy to cookbooks and a variety of mixed metaphors, the book plans to describe in frank detail solutions for impotence and premature ejaculation. Comfort will also explicate techniques of oral sex and teach readers how to play sexually aggressive games that include bondage and discipline. Along the way, he will show his readers how to deal with fetishes. And, as he promises, he will do all of this in a fun and entertaining way. Comfort, a medical doctor, aims to provide solid information to those who already know the basics. In his view those who cannot accept sex as a play activity are simply "hungup." Though Comfort focuses explicitly on sex with love, *The Joy of Sex* actually endorses a more promiscuous agenda. Good-quality sex, according to Comfort, results from love, and love provides for feedback, empathy, and mutual knowledge. Comfort goes on to add that his book is about "valid" sexual acts, but he never supplies a crisp definition of the term (Comfort 1972, preface, 8, 9, 10).

Comfort, publishing a mere three years after Reuben, does not dwell on any potentially harmful side effects of birth control pills. Rather, for the first time in this genre, Comfort says quite enthusiastically that the pill makes "carefree sex possible." Before the pill only infertile couples could enjoy the varieties of sexual play that Comfort endorses. Once women experience the security offered by the pill as well as the fun that uninhibited sex provides, they will certainly not want to return to the old days with their restrictive norms and unwanted pregnancies as punishment for transgressions (54).

Reflecting evolving mores, Comfort quite explicitly broadens acceptable behavior between lovers. There are a multitude of ways to experience sexual pleasure. "Sex must be physically the safest of all human activities." In general, he advises hip initiates to avoid using labels. Sadism, masochism, narcissism, and bisexuality mark all people. Comfort writes that only two things matter. Are you comfortable with what you are doing and are you bothering other people? Even though Comfort makes mention of herpes, he regards it mainly as a "nuisance"—prevalence was much lower in 1972. Toward the end of the book, he suggests that venereal diseases "have been covertly fostered for several generations by straight Society as God's punishment for sin." They are, however, a real hazard when you have intercourse or even heavy petting with people you are not familiar with. Venereal diseases could be eradicated relatively quickly if they were treated as ordinary maladies and moralists stopped trying to use them to control behavior. Comfort goes on to make practical suggestions: wash thoroughly, use a condom, and try prophylactic penicillin.

Though "carefree," sex definitely matters. According to Comfort, it expresses the entirety of the self and can be therapeutic. "Bed is the place to play all of the games you have ever wanted to play, at the play-level." In Comfort's view, orgasm provides the peak religious experience of life, and sexual love remains the "supreme human experience." The main event is "loving, unselfconscious intercourse—long, frequent, varied." He favors the "good old face-to-face matrimonial, the finishing off position, with mutual orgasm." Besides not doing silly, antisocial, or dangerous things, good sex has only two rules: enjoy what you do and fulfill your partner's needs. In his attempt to assuage the view that common sex needs are odd or weird, Comfort helps define the new mainstream. After he establishes the ground rules, Comfort goes on to write a sex manual for the sexually sophisticated. His book represents a departure from the traditional form of this genre as represented by Hanchett, Kellogg, Guernsey, Collins, Chesser, Stopes, and even Reuben. In his assertion that pleasure serves as the fundament of sex, Comfort breaks with his predecessors. Though Comfort imitates Van de Velde's exhaustive table of contents, he alphabetizes his own table of contents by general categories following his menu metaphor. His main sections include starters, main courses, sauces and pickles, gadgets and gimmicks and, last, problems. He discusses bisexuality and fidelity in the problems section.[1] He then proceeds with an instrumental approach, using frank and colloquial language combined with explicit illustrations (8, 10–15, 51, 73, 85, 252).

Comfort also raises formerly taboo topics like bondage and explains devices and activities that were formerly limited to pornography and prostitutes. For example, Comfort recommends a bed with posts for bondage. He scorns the standard twin beds of the 1950s as depicted in television sitcoms. He recommends setting up a sex/play room so couples can avoid having to explain rings in the wall—useful for bondage—to curious relatives. He also discusses "penile rings," though he remains unenthused. They do help, however, to stiffen an erection after ejaculation. Swinging weights can be interesting; he recommends trying them on the nipples, labia, or clitoris. Ice cream and custard work well on the skin, "grapes in the pussy." Bondage gives sexual aggression a harmless outlet. "A slow orgasm when unable to move is a mind-blowing experience for anyone not too frightened of their own aggressive self to try it." Chains and handcuffs are all right, but Comfort has practical concerns. Harnesses provide an easy restraint system for those who are not adept at knots or merely appreciate the look. Wash carefully before "feuille de rose." Be gentle in anal sex. Comfort likes leather and approves of mirrors. In cars and vans, count orgasms per gallon (50–67, 113, 118, 121, 158, 165, 173, 188–90, 197, 200, 242).

In his preface Comfort extols the joys of sex with love, but his definitions as well as his hip swagger undercut this restraining qualification. He applies the term "love" to include any relationship of mutual tenderness, respect, and consideration, ranging from total dependence to a nice night together. Comfort sees no reason why pairs of friends cannot make love. It is a matter of personal preference. Comfort thinks this works best with either very good friends or total strangers. Orgies typically do not allow for "instinctive feedback" because strangers are involved, or they tend to collapse into a closed circle. Though Comfort does not view these options as providing high-quality sex, "there is no reason why sex should not be social if you wish." Promiscuity is a matter of personal taste. He notes that regular swingers seem to get bored after a while and return to closed relationships. Overall, fidelity depends on a couple's needs, situation, and anxieties. In a position that will be adopted throughout the *Joy* series as well as *The Joy of Gay Sex* and *The Joy of Lesbian Sex*, Comfort says that individuals have to define their own standards of fidelity. Partners need to discuss this issue and at least understand where the other one is coming from. On one level *The Joy of Sex* embodies the openness and experimentation of the 1960s as symbolized by San Francisco's Summer of Love. Comfort's view of pornography illustrates his frankness and his rejection of repression. He defines pornography to include any suppressed literature. "Most normal people enjoy looking at sex books and reading sex fantasies which is why abnormal people have to spend so much time and money suppressing them" (69, 180–84, 233).

Though Comfort considers the vulva as magical as a penis, he finds it slightly scary to children, primitives, and males generally. "It looks like a castrating wound and bleeds regularly, it swallows the penis and regurgitates it limp, it can probably bite and so on. Luckily, few of these biologically programmed anxieties survive closer acquaintance, but they are the origins of most male hangups including homosexuality" (98). Comfort never explains what he means by a "biologically programmed anxiety," or his thesis that homosexuality arises ultimately from fear of the vulva. Writing from a patriarchal perspective, Comfort valorizes the penis. "The penis has more symbolic importance than any other human organ, as a dominance signal and, by reason of having a will of its own, generally a 'personality.'" Lovers, according to Comfort, know this and come to treat the penis as something like a third party during sex. Comfort also makes the penis the locus of male self-esteem and identity and associates dominance with the penis. This provides the key to understanding his focus on playful violence. On the implicit level, male arousal reflects dominance and playful violence. Cruelty is out, but a little violence is fine. "Since we all have some aggressions, good sex can be wildly violent. . . . A little frightening helps some people sometimes." Tenderness, in his view, does not prohibit violent sexual games, but it does "exclude clumsiness, heavy handedness, lack of feedback, spitefulness and non-rapport generally." Comfort rejects the view that women wish to be raped and suggests that both parties can play the aggressor role. He views violence as an instinctive thing that finds expression and satisfaction in his new religion of hip sex. Jim Morrison would agree. In actuality Comfort articulates the strictures of patriarchal sexuality as a game and invites women to play along. Even though Comfort envisions women dominating their male partners some of the time, all women in his view lack a man's locus of dominant identity. Love becomes much more like rape, but as Brownmiller (1976) tells us, it had been all along (Comfort 1972, 80–81, 98, 103, 129).

Despite his savvy swagger, Comfort reaffirms patriarchal norms and mainly extends the range for permissible gratification. Though he endorses a more active role for women and even switching roles, he does not consider women equal and active partners (for a contrary view see Weinberg and Hammersmith 1983, 314, 317). Since he aims to legitimize more violent sexual expression, Comfort must, of course, deal carefully with concepts such as "normal." Employing the term "normal" suggests that sex ought to take place in a particular way. Since people exhibit wide variation in terms of their sexual needs as well as their capacities, the term "normal" proves meaningless except as an attempt to sanction certain behavior. Having assaulted conventional conceptions of normality, Comfort goes on to discuss lesbian and gay sex. He finds it odd and suggests that it restricts one's range of enjoyment. After several curious analogies, he summarizes. "We don't have a single 'normal' pattern of sex behavior, but a bunch of responses." After rejecting rape and the seduction of children, he postulates four criteria for "normal" sexual behavior: there is mutual enjoyment, nobody gets hurt, it causes no anxiety, and it does not reduce scope. Earlier in his discussion, when Comfort noted that lesbian and gay sex restricted one's range of enjoyment, he compared it to a man who could only experience orgasm by getting into a bath of cooked spaghetti, though he pointed out that the gentleman enjoyed it like this. But later, after he introduces the concept of scope, he analogizes lesbian and gay limitations to people who will have intercourse only in the dark, in one position, and with little pleasure. Yet following his own logic, exclusively lesbian and gay male partners who enjoyed it that way would really be no more limited than similarly situated heterosexual ones. On the implicit level, however, Comfort suggests that good sex, this peak experience, requires not only two bodies, but also three personalities. The penis, as noted above, not only symbolizes male dominance, but also has a will and personality of its own. Lesbian sex involves two bodies, but is missing the additional personality. Gay male sex involves two bodies and four personalities, which is one too many. Comfort might also note the lack of a "valid" orifice for the "good old face-to-face matrimonial." Gay men, in other words, have too many personalities involved, lesbians too few. Comfort valorizes trinities, but he never explains why. To avoid these difficulties Comfort should have entitled his work *The Joy of Heterosexual Sex*. Comfort's discussion of perversions reverses the traditional understanding, but does little to clarify his concept of homosexuality, except that he declines to apply the term to lesbians and gay men. Since everyone is bisexual, play activities in a two-couple setting run little risk of getting participants "stuck like that." Overall, it's a matter of taste. Do what's comfortable, but avoid getting in a rut.

A mere three years after gays rebelled during New York City's Stonewall riot in 1969 and a year before the American Psychiatric Association decided that homosexuality was not a mental disease after all, Comfort's ambiguities as well as his curious analogies demonstrate that the old strident condemnations of lesbians and gay men no longer resonate quite as strongly as they did for Reuben and Collins. The times had changed. In fact, Comfort had written a graphic sex manual whose illustrations alone would have formerly gotten it banned like Ginsberg's "Howl" (78, 80, 184, 247).

Even More Joy

Why did Comfort write another book?
More Joy, as indicated by its subtitle, *A Lovemaking Companion to the Joy of Sex*, aims to serve as an independent companion to *The Joy of Sex*. While *The Joy of Sex* is the "first explicitly sexual book for the coffee

table," *More Joy* develops areas neglected in the first volume, such as a focus on relationships (Comfort 1974, preface, n.p.).

What does More Joy add to our knowledge of relationships?
More Joy, unfortunately, does not resolve any of *Joy*'s ambiguities. Good sex, as in the earlier volume, requires a relationship, which can consist of a lifetime thing or a "casual romp between friends." It means "knowing what resources turn some people on and roughly why. If you have a lot of partners you need to start with this knowledge and can check it in practice." Talk first, then play.

Does Comfort ever qualitatively distinguish between sex with a life part-ner and a "casual romp"?
Not really. As he puts it, "the idea that no pattern of relationship or be-havior, conventional or otherwise, suits everybody is the most important one we have to get across." Even in a casual encounter, good sex by itself generates a relationship. Fidelity in this context means maintaining con-fidence and unity while avoiding things that provoke anxiety. With a partner's consent, fidelity does not require monogamy, and institutions like monogamous marriage are dying anyway (11, 47, 98).

Is the penis still a dominance signal?
Yes, like antlers. "It's almost impossible for men not to regard an erec-tion as a performance, an achievement, and a general badge of mas-culinity." During deep penetration, however, the penis becomes "joint property" and resolves all anxieties about who is entering whom. Com-fort also links penile endowment with self-esteem (72, 77, 79, 130).

If reproduction is only an optional goal, why value deep vaginal pene-tration above other forms of erotic pleasure?
Comfort assigns this to a hypothesized biological nature of gender. Though gender mainly reflects roles, hormone levels push a person in either a mas-culine or feminine direction. Masculinity, understood as high dominance, comes to mean taking the initiative and being penis/penetration centered, while femininity resides in "penis seizing" (56–57, 67, 72, 84).

How can hostility be love?
Hostility, as distinguished from assertion and dominance, equals love in that adult relationships require some defense against being "taken over."

Why does Comfort value relationships?
Since good sex by itself can create a relationship, his emphasis on them is meaningless. The term includes a monogamous heterosexual couple happily partnered for fifteen years, as well as two strangers coupled in the darkness at Sandstone. Ultimately the issue is moot, as indicated by Comfort's embrace of the wisdom of Fritz Perls: "I am I and you are you, and neither of us is here to live up to the other one's expectations. But if we meet it's beautiful" (53, 57).

Does Comfort's understanding of lesbians and gay men change?
No, but he presents a fuller view that is more consistent. "All of us are biologically and socially male, female or both at once." He explicitly undermines the heterosexual/homosexual binary and suggests thinking in terms of a continuum. "You don't have to line up with either battalion—the flags are phony anyway." According to Comfort, people think this odd only if they consider reproduction the only function of sex. Comfort, however, urges caution instead of exuberant celebration of homoerotic desire. As he notes, cultural norms will not change overnight, and he advises against upsetting a good pattern for an unrealized potential. On the whole, he remains ambivalent on the issue (13, 60, 62, 63; Seidman 1989, 309).

Given all the cultural change, why isn't everyone bisexual in practice?
Because masculinity, both biologically and socially, demands deep vaginal penetration. Tension ejaculations that make a man "feel like one huge penis" require penetration. As opposed to muscle relaxation orgasms—the general feminine experience—tension ones build on hostility and assertion (Comfort 1974, 36–38).

So how does Comfort distinguish at all between homoerotic and heteroerotic relationships?
He still valorizes heteroerotic relations even though his position is not supported by his text. To make such a case, Comfort would have to demonstrate qualitative differences between vaginal and anal intercourse and explicate more fully the necessity of deep vaginal penetration. In Comfort's mind, it is probably a matter of culture and personal response to risk taking as well as learned and inborn gender imperatives. In a few years, Silverstein and White in *The Joy of Gay Sex* will build on many of Comfort's distinctions. They will note that the anus contains neurons

and that deep penetration stimulates the prostate. Reuben, of course, denies all of this and believes that anal intercourse causes pain and does not lead to mutual ejaculation. Silverstein and White will stridently disagree.

Does milk matter?
In this nonpsychoanalytic construction, no.

New Joy

Alex Comfort published *The New Joy of Sex* in 1991. He opens on a triumphal note. The previous editions sold eight million copies. As in the original edition, he divides the text into sections and entitles them ingredients, appetizers, sauces, venues, and, last, health and other issues. In this edition, however, he does not alphabetically arrange items within the categories. The first item under "ingredients" is now "love," followed by "fidelity," which fell under "problems" in the first edition. Safe sex comes next. Comfort includes bisexuality and transvestism at the end in the renamed problems section, which is now designated "health and other issues."

In the new edition Comfort finds that problems with sexual technique have changed little, but there have been changes in the sexual revolution itself. There is now even a backlash against it. Unfortunately, in an oft repeated lament in this genre, Americans remain unwilling to talk about sex. Unlike the first edition, which relied on drawings to illustrate Comfort's points, *New Joy* adds photographs to the drawings. This volume, like *Joy* and *More Joy*, presupposes an ethnological theory that makes all sex a play activity. Frank talk and sexual variations should not embarrass adults so long as their play activities are neither cruel nor hostile. Couples should vary control, because sex no longer means something that men do to women, who are supposed to lie back and enjoy it. Sometimes sex occurs as "loving fusion," at other times lovers are mutual "sex objects." Balanced sexual relationships embody maturity and have proper portions of personal and impersonal arousal. According to Comfort, sex understood as a form of play also allows men to stop domineering and performing, while also permitting women to be in control (Comfort 1991, 6–7).

Sticking with his earlier cookbook metaphor, Comfort aims to provide a menu, not merely rules. His goal remains to demolish the idea that ordinary sexual needs are abnormal or odd. Once again, he postulates that sex has no norms except enjoyment. The menu, like those in fine restaurants, has many pages. Specialty items are also available. Before AIDS, sex had few risks. He longs for the day when this will be so once again (8–9).

Good-quality sex, as in the previous editions, requires love. "Either you love each other before you come to want it, or, if you happen to get it, you love each other because of it, or both." Good sex also requires feedback and, hence, Comfort once again laments America's sexual silence. Only empathy and slowly developed mutual knowledge can produce the frisson of good sex while retaining the core identity of the participants. Comfort can teach skills and techniques, providing, however, the participants come already supplied with tenderness. Just as in his earlier editions, Comfort notes that he is writing about "valid" sexual behaviors (9).

Sexual play bonds partners together. He calls this "love," and compares it to birds building nests. Labels, as he says again, do not help matters. Everyone is sadistic, narcissistic, masochistic, and bisexual. It only matters when any of these needs bothers you or your playmate. Comfort teaches that sex play deals with anxieties and aggression and that bed remains the place to act out these fantasies. But in a startling generalization even for Comfort, he adds that the alternative to acting out these behaviors is My Lai or Belsen. One is the site of a mass murder committed by American soldiers in Vietnam, the other a Nazi death camp. In other words, if Heinrich Himmler, head of Hitler's *Schutzstaffel* (S.S.), only had flexible, masochistic playmates, the Holocaust may well have been attenuated (10).

Love, as in the earlier editions, still serves as the entree "Unselfconscious intercourse—long, frequent, varied, ending with both parties satisfied" defines the event. As in his first book, the *pièce de résistance* remains the "good old face-to-face matrimonial." Sex still has only two norms (besides avoiding things that are antisocial or dangerous): avoid things that you really do not enjoy, and meet your partner's needs if you can. Relationships, in other words, assume compromise at least in terms of meeting someone else's needs.

Writing now in the 1990s, Comfort must deal with AIDS. If two people are virus negative, then the entire menu can be consumed with gusto. If either partner carries the virus, then only mutual masturbation is safe. He goes on to add that safe sex means avoiding carriers of the virus. Since this proves difficult, condoms remain necessary to prevent body fluids from mixing. Since the advent of AIDS requires a time-out in the sexual revolution, Comfort proposes that his readers use it to focus on the affectionate side of their relationships. Comfort even adds a new section designated "Safe Sex." People know that until AIDS becomes curable, self-preservation demands limitations on play activities. Even "mouth music" (oral sex) can be dangerous. Comfort reiterates his advice about condoms; as he bluntly puts it, "no argument no exceptions: no glove, no pussy" (13, 15, 37).

Labeling sexual behaviors sick does not help matters. Love is found in "any relationship in which there is mutual tenderness, respect and consideration—from total interdependence . . . to an agreeable night together." All of it is love and part of human experience. Love involves psychological risks and remains an open-ended experience. Traditional morality exists to keep the number of "casualties" down, but it does not work all the time. Comfort feels no need to classify different types of relationships. He finds no love between two manipulative people playing control games, but he does find it between a prostitute and a client when there is genuine tenderness and respect (34–35).

Fidelity, as Comfort sees it, characterizes few men and only slightly more women. It depends on the needs, situations, and anxieties of the partners. Any situation that excludes a partner proves harmful. On the other hand, partners cannot completely fuse with each other, and here he repeats the wisdom of Fritz Perls. He ends by suggesting that couples discuss this issue.

Violent games, as in the earlier editions, are still acceptable, and Comfort reiterates his limiting factors. In a section titled "Women (by Her for Him)," he presents the penis as a "shared possession," not a weapon. Size of the organ is of no consequence, but its personality is. Social pressure, not nature, makes women masochistic. He reiterates that good sex can be "wildly violent," but role changing remains the norm. Women should be treated as both people and equals, but do probably differ due to their more complex sexual apparatus. In a parallel chapter designated as "Men (by Him for Her)," Comfort says that men respond more briskly and automatically to sexual stimuli. Almost anything can trigger an erection. In this construction, women appear to men as body parts and nonpeople. Male sexuality depends on performance and focuses on the glans of the penis. Comfort reiterates his view of the vulva. Once again, he suggests that fear of the vulva represents biological programming and underpins "hangups" like homosexuality (38, 41, 43, 44, 49).

Comfort still presents the penis as a "dominance signal" and as having more symbolic importance than any other organ. It still has a will of its own and in good sex becomes a joint possession. The penis also has an aesthetic function and serves as the locus of male self-esteem and identity. Size does not matter since the unstretched vagina is merely four inches, nor does it correlate with race or big muscles. Just as men are captivated by breasts, women feel similarly about the penis. "It's a fascinating toy quite apart from experiencing its main use" (58–61).

Continuing with his cookbook metaphor, Comfort suggests experimenting with "custard or ice cream on the skin, [and once again] grapes in the pussy." Stiff or wiry feathers work best, especially if taken from a heron or egret. In a pinch, a feather duster will do. Occasional fighting, often physical in his view, is normal. Some couples even get aroused by it. Folklore, according to Comfort, makes the same point. Aggression is a "normal" part of sexuality. Erotic violence, however, differs from real spite or anger. The quarrel that ventilates or serves as an appeal for help differs from normal erotic violence. Comfort denies that he is defining borderline sadists, but goes on to note that some women unconsciously want violence. "To need some degree of violence in sex . . . is statistically pretty normal." The secret consists of using sex play to express normal sexual aggression, while keeping in check what he calls ordinary anger and frustration. On the other hand, women should avoid harmful violence. If this happens, they should leave and call the police. Love, as he puts it, cannot cure sadists. Some women experience erotic helplessness when tied up, others when pinned down like wrestlers. In vaginal penetration men experience sexual intercourse as violence. This range of aggression is normal and enacts the antagonisms felt by any couple living together. Good, if not violent, sex can discharge these antagonisms. Normal aggression, even when one partner is tied up or held down, however, does not exclude tenderness. "Sexual violence can be tender and tenderness violent" (90, 96–99).

At last Comfort serves up the entrée. As in his earlier volumes, orgasm provides the most religious experience in life. Nothing can match it. Sometimes, however, stop means go, while at other times it actually means cease and desist. Comfort calls this an individual language, and only sensitive "field observers" learn its real meaning (106, 114, 140).

Maximum muscle tension orgasms, though more difficult to manage, supply the most feeling. Total relaxation orgasms, on the other hand, are "overwhelming." For many women tension orgasms can actually interfere with their achievement of total relaxation ones. Comfort merely wants his readers to widen their repertoire, try an exotic dish at a restaurant. Some people experience a type of climax that totally fuses them with their partner. To achieve this, high men should do nothing after penetration (145, 148).

Fantasies remain part of the experience, a sauce for the main course. As long as they do not become "nasty," "spiteful," or "unhappy," all is permitted. Keep the game wild and exciting, for adults, unlike children, have a need for this type of play. Having accepted sex as both pleasure and play, Americans must now learn to understand its ceremonial aspects. In sexual play people can act out fantasies that still trouble society. Sex thus becomes psychodrama. Leather and bondage dramas fit well within this theatrical view (145, 148, 152, 153, 161, 165, 169, 172).

Bondage boosts orgasm and remains the second most popular fantasy after group sex. Bondage images appeal to those who need the illusion of rape to deal with their sexual guilt. Bondage games also gratify important needs. As Comfort understands it, many women enjoy helplessness and exaggerated male control, but for men bondage delivers "the mind blowing sensation of 'becoming one enormous penis,' plus withdrawal of all performance anxiety—she gets the opportunity to be in total control." Bondage can become, as Comfort notes, sadomasochism, but the most effective guarantee against this is switching roles. Really skillful bondage works like an erotic bomb. It only scares people who insist on too much tenderness. Once again, verbal cues can be misleading, and initiates must learn to distinguish between them. Since traditional books do not offer much in the way of bondage techniques, Comfort goes on to offer details about ropes and knots. He prefers cotton clothesline to more exotic and expensive hardware. Gags are fine, but must not block breathing. Comfort lists minimal rules: (1) never tie anything around the neck; (2) never use something pliable for a gag that can get caught in the throat; (3) never leave a bound person alone, especially if the person is face down on a soft surface, and do not play for more than a half hour; and (4) play heavy bondage games only with people you already know both socially and sexually and avoid group scenes. As distinguished from sadomasochism, which remains in the province of psychopathology, bondage can help heal childhood issues. Comfort once again suggests that the proper mix in bondage consists of tender and tough. Ask your partner how they like it, then deduct 20 percent as fantasy. For people who have difficulty with knots, try harnesses. The look of a harness on a person can also prove aesthetically pleasing. Chains look good on naked skin, but are uncomfortable and are only symbolically effective. Beating your partner may or may not work. Try birch twigs. Men, however, must avoid playing into the cultural fantasy that women enjoy getting beaten. Do not play this game with strangers and never mix real anger with sexual beatings. After all, it's only a game, not reality (175, 178, 180, 185–94).

Two's company and three's a crowd, but foursomes can be fun. For safety considerations, AIDS requires that two couples now merely observe each other's play. Foursomes can have psychological dangers, but Comfort endorses play activities that lead to sexual openness and lessen possessiveness. In these days of the AIDS pandemic, sexual cults, especially those in California practicing "open sexuality," prove too dangerous. Besides emotional considerations, it remains just too difficult to check out the sexual history of another couple. For venues, Comfort remains fond of using cars and still employs the orgasms per mile norm for quality considerations (195, 210).

Unlike earlier times when sexually transmitted diseases were mainly a nuisance, now they once again severely limit sexual games. AIDS threatens the banquet itself, not merely the appetizers. Women are easier to infect than men. Comfort foresees the day when the common mode of AIDS transmission in Western countries will be vaginal intercourse, as it is now in Africa and Asia. No one is safe! Readers must assume that any new partner can endanger their lives. Western countries reacted at first with indifference ("AIDS only affected gays and drug addicts, so who cares?") and moral righteousness ("AIDS was God's judgment on the sexual revolution") and are now in a panic that will only worsen as the epidemic intensifies. Moralistic approaches seek to "shut down sex altogether and confine it to marriage." Dr. Ruth, for one, employs this approach. Comfort does propose a solution to the quandary. Except for lifetime partners, avoid all activities that can transmit AIDS. If you are not sure about your partner, always use a condom. If your partner refuses to use a condom, then he or she is irresponsible and uncaring. Nonoxynol 9, a contraceptive foam, kills the virus at an 0.08 percent solution and offers some protection.

Mature adults need to avoid intimacy with members of known risk groups such as drug users, former drug users, bisexuals, and prostitutes (especially in Asia and Africa) as well as anyone who has had many sexual partners. Be sure to avoid activities like anal and menstrual inter-course. Always use a condom with a foam or suppository containing Nonoxynol 9. When you are not certain about a partner's sexual history, treat them as if they are infected. Both partners must acknowledge their common need to keep this deadly virus outside their play circle. Forget about anonymous sex! If you are positive, then you must have sex only with other positives (214–17).

Comfort emphasizes biology, because too much of the discourse has reflected psychoanalytic viewpoints like those of Reuben and Collins. Comfort calls for a focus on real human behavior as opposed to psycho-analytic theories. He reiterates that there is no single way to enjoy sex. The time has finally arrived to chuck the old-time religion that hides be-hind the traditional, repressive approaches (220–21).

In a tautology that he does not mean ironically, Comfort announces that "the propaganda about 'vaginal orgasm' is propaganda." Some women have them, others do not. In fact, some women are multiorgas-mic. Some women even experience orgasm more like men. Other women prefer breast or genital stimulation to clitoral sensations. Suit yourself.

Children can result from sexual intercourse, but are not a necessary re-sult of it. Be careful, however, when playing. Most children interpret the cacophony of intercourse as a violent assault. In the context of a segue on nudist camps, Comfort points out that a father's penis signals domi-nance to a young male, while the vulva once again proves ambivalent (223–26).

Comfort remains consistent on his understanding of normality. "Nor-mal" does not refer to any specific acts or activities. The only norm in-volved remains that sex be "a wholly satisfying link between two affec-tionate people." Both participants should experience reduced anxiety, feel rewarded, and be ready for more. People exhibit wide variation in what they need as well as their ability to achieve satisfaction. Historical reasons often account for the linkages between human sexuality and anx-iety. American culture is just starting to realize that its former moral panic reflected only fear. Past censorship limited knowledge about sexual techniques and designated quite a few techniques abnormal. "It's abnor-mal in Papua [New Guinea] to bury dead relatives and abnormal in Cal-ifornia to eat them. Yet lovers all over the world would certainly like 'to eat one another.'"

Once again Comfort distinguishes sexual behaviors that are different or restrictive, and he repeats the spaghetti and bathtub analogy from his first edition to deal with lesbians/gay men/bisexuals. Comfort also views American society as homophobic. America fears same-sex expression. Comfort suggests two criteria to delimit normal/abnormal and natural/unnatural acts: (1) does the activity hurt or ruin a person's chance of being fully actualized; and (2) can society tolerate this activity? Comfort explicitly excludes the seduction and rape of children. As he sums up, "we don't have a single, 'normal' pattern of sex behavior, but a bunch of responses." Comfort actually redefines the term to mean that both parties enjoyed the game and neither got hurt, while the play did not result from anxiety or reduce future options for different games (228–29).

In another curious analogy, Comfort states that "you can no more 'have too much' sex than you can over-empty a toilet cistern." Comfort pegs the common frequency at two or three times a week. Coital orgasm probably produces fewer ejaculations for men, while employing a variety of stimulations can often increase a man's ability to have more than one. Nature teaches that, quantitatively considered, there is no excess when it comes to sex. Nature, however, ensures some balance. Women, after all, will eventually get sore, and men cannot go on forever. Lots of good sex only makes for more good sex, and it works as an excellent sleeping pill. Nothing is better than a "violent and shared orgasm" (229–30).

Being homosexual means being turned off by the opposite sex, while bisexuals are turned on by both sexes. Homosexuality in Comfort's view is now analogous to left-handedness. He suggests that a variety of factors probably account for same-sex responses. As Comfort sees it, male to male homoeroticism has been harshly repressed. "Some 'lesbians,' are simply women who have given up on men after a lifetime spent kissing frogs who failed to turn into princes." Comfort implies that the right man may well remedy this situation, which is a common observation in the genre (241–43).

Sexual excitement can shift the pleasure-pain boundary so that crossing the barrier can actually feel pleasurable. Some people, though, desire pathological physical or mental pain. Be sure to avoid disturbed individuals and once again deduct 20 percent from any stories you are told. Comfort goes on to postulate a "normal" fantasy range, but fails to delimit specific activities. Following this inconclusive discussion, he next deals with fetishes, transvestism, and perversion. Sexual fetishes become a problem when they turn into something that is all-enveloping. "It may sound brutal, but don't, repeat don't, take on a partner with a major sex problem such as homosexuality [*sic*] or compulsive ritualism in order to 'cure him by love.' You won't." Transvestites are not homosexuals. They are usually men who want to become women, at least in appearance. Some, however, do seek sex reassignment surgery. Before the 1970s, authors listed perversions to condemn activities that they personally did not like. Such lists merely represent attempts to manipulate and interfere with other people's lives (246–47).

Birth control, of course, makes "carefree sex possible." Comfort holds that the pill remains the best and safest method of birth control. Condoms, however, remain the best prevention for AIDS. Comfort excludes only long-term monogamous lovers from this warning. When it comes to contraception or AIDS, never take risks. Comfort endorses vasectomies, and terms the rhythm method of birth control "Vatican roulette." Instead of writing directly about abortion Comfort deploys the term "termination." He blames the large number of abortions on alarmists who have frightened women off the pill. Comfort links opposition to abortion with attempts to limit research and access to birth control itself (248–49, 252–53).

The Party's Over

Published in 1991, *The New Joy of Sex* mainly restates the arguments and repeats the ambiguities of the earlier volumes, while it adds several new ones. Comfort's earlier work depended on "carefree" sex, which assumed the antibiotic revolution of the post–World War II era. Carefree sex meant, among other things, sex without medically harmful consequences and assumed the availability of effective birth control. In this new work, Comfort must deal with what some commentators term the sexual counterrevolution, and he tries to blunt the use of AIDS to justify a "backlash politics" (Seidman 1989, 293, 294).

Once again Comfort ostensibly democratizes male dominance by supporting some sex role flexibility. Women, formerly not allowed to be aggressive, now can dominate at least some of the time. The cost of this flexibility is the acceptance of overall male dominance focused in the penis. To put this another way, Comfort rejects concepts from depth psychology such as penis envy only to reinstall them in another guise. Phallocracy and women's submission to it constitute part of the nature of things. The world may very well be a better place if men act out their power fantasies in sex, but certainly more aggressive sex would not have attenuated the Holocaust. Despite Comfort's claim to the contrary, he now adopts the concepts of repression, the id, and penis envy.

AIDS is a large concern in this new volume. If both parties are negative for the virus that causes AIDS, then the whole menu remains available. If one is positive, then the only safe activity consists of mutual masturbation or having sex only with other positives. He also recommends building up the affectionate side of sexual relationships, while he still extends the meaning of love to cover just about any type of bonding. As in the earlier editions, he still maintains that "I am I and you are you, and neither of us is on earth to live up to the other's expectations." Thus he denies that love offers any type of substantial human exchange. Given Comfort's understanding of love, humankind's most intimate moments become truly lonely, a serious game fought over mastery and submission, with the penis, the dominance signal, a joint possession at best.

A man's sense of dominance and identity resides in his penis. Violence, even of the physical kind, can be found in all relationships, but it also has an erotic effect. Indeed, some women desire violence, but Comfort counsels women to leave battering relationships. He tries to close the matter by distinguishing between real violence and the playful kind, but never clearly defines the difference. Comfort actually writes violence into the nature of intimacy in his acknowledgment that good sex involves dominance. Nothing is better than a "violent and shared orgasm." Comfort emphasizes the violence theme by thrusting bondage into the core of intimacy as a type of therapy. America, he finds, is now more accepting of bondage. He suggests switching roles and avoiding real sadomasochism. The top/male must distinguish between cries of real pain and ones that mean keep on going. Never, Comfort advises, let real anger into the game. Despite this caution, Comfort's underlying theme remains the same. "What *The Joy of Sex* confirms is that ultimately what 'biology' urges men to do is to be violent toward women. . . . Violence conforms exactly to the dictates of man's essential sexuality" (Brunt 1982, 165). Or as Jim Morrison sang, Come on baby light my fire, it's time to set the night on fire. A little erotic violence sparks the kindling.

Why did Comfort publish a new edition so many years later? Things changed, and not for the better. AIDS, for one thing, negates his presentation of sex as a harmless and therapeutic play activity. Recreational sex can now prove deadly. Specifically Comfort points out that all activities are safe between a man and a woman negative to the AIDS virus. He neglects to mention that the HIV antibody test really means something only at the time the blood was drawn and that seroconversion—the presence of antibodies in the blood—can take six weeks to six months. For HIV positives he recommends the use of condoms, but the safest activity remains mutual masturbation.

Comfort's argument does break with the past, but it also refashions patriarchy on new ground. He remains willing to sacrifice some dominance, while he continues to support a phallocratic social structure. In fact, his work assumes penis envy, and his discussion of the vulva invites thoughts of a castration complex. Catharine MacKinnon would probably consider his work pornographic, because it mainly confirms a phallocratic regime of dominance/submission that largely equates with the male/female binary. Comfort's assertion of male prerogative, overall dominance, and a need for violence promotes a system that disempowers, if not abuses, women (MacKinnon 1993). According to Comfort, some women have rape fantasies, and men must distinguish between when a woman really means no and when no actually means yes. This logic underpins date rape and suggests that some sexual assaults result from a misreading or misunderstanding (see Seidman 1989 for a different view, which focuses more on Comfort's ostensibly humanistic approach).

Comfort also writes in the era of Presidents Reagan and Bush, when conservative activists took control of the Republican Party apparatus and sought to impose their own vision of moral goodness or virtue by law. Comfort also writes in the era of AIDS, when some argued that the wages of sin is death, and the federal government initially responded with report after report but little action. In this context, Comfort tries to revive the carefree 1970s. Soon, however, Dr. Ruth will supplant the *Joy* series with a more restrictive view of sexuality, one more in keeping with conservative times (Melody 1994a).

Comfort considers the sexual act a supreme human experience justified by its pleasurable content alone. It's a play activity for adults. Sex may provide more than pleasure, but it need not do so. In this assertion of the primacy of pleasure Comfort breaks with the tradition. Since the pill had liberated women from worries about pregnancy, they too can now join in the fun without fear of serious consequences. In this sense, Comfort's view of female sexuality proves expansive. They, too, can now play like men and even switch roles sometimes. On the other hand, Comfort emphasizes the role of dominance and violence in sex, and though he allows role playing, most of the dominance and violence is done by men to women. So the cost of more pleasure for women becomes playful pain. In this sense, the *Joy* series represents only a partial break with the tradition, since it tends to make women masochists and treats them as instruments of male domination. Comfort suggests that more violent sexual expression would even make the world a safer place. If confined to a playroom, male violence and aggression may not seek expression in the world. Rhetorically, Comfort seeks to convince women that violence is a fundamental part of the game and that by playing along they can help make the world a safer place. In his belief that sex can change the world, Comfort affirms a persistent theme in the genre.

8

Does Pleasure Demand the Conjunction of Particular Body Parts?

Gay and Lesbian Sex

On Friday, June 27, 1969, a flock of drag queens, many of them persons of color, launched a new stage of the sexual rebellion. As the legend goes, police from Manhattan's Sixth Precinct set off to raid the Stonewall Inn, a gay bar on Christopher Street in New York City's Greenwich Village. It was an election year in the city, and such raids were common. Mayors liked to preside over cleanups during elections, and homosexuals provided convenient targets. At the Stonewall a crowd gathered as police released the patrons one by one. Several of them, along with the bartender and bouncer, were hauled away in a police van. As the police herded the last patron toward a police car, s/he put up a struggle that launched lesbian/gay liberation. No one knows which transvestite threw the first punch.

Greenwich Village witnessed America's first gay riot. Police from the tactical force arrived on the scene and "dispersed with swinging clubs an impromptu chorus line of gay men in the middle of a full kick." As the riot continued on Saturday night, graffiti calling for "Gay Power" marked the Village. Allen Ginsberg arrived on Sunday. As he remarked to a reporter, "You know, the guys there were so beautiful. . . . They've lost that wounded look that fags all had 10 years ago." Ginsberg's "Howl," his celebration of "angleheaded hipsters" who rejected sexual authoritarianism, had called forth the reality of affirmation in a rebellion of drag queens (D'Emilio 1983b, 232 for the citations; Duberman 1993).

On August 12 a New Left newspaper printed the Gay Liberation Front's (GLF) declaration. The manifesto critiques sexism and calls on gays to eliminate oppressive patterns imposed by heterosexists such as limiting oneself to strictly delimited gender roles. "Sexual objectification," in the manifesto's view, "has to do with seeing other human beings in terms of the superficial alone—face, body, clothes." Gay liberation, on the other hand, "stands for the total abolition of sex-determined roles in society—and in bed." Sodomy statutes make all sexually active gays outlaws, and those in jail are political prisoners. New groups like GLF promoted consciousness-raising to help move toward the goal of liberation. Sexual freedom, according to the manifesto, is premised on pleasure through equality. Since gay relations are not bound up with male supremacy, gays "have a better chance than heterosexuals to build relationships based on equality because there is less enforcement of roles. We have already broken with gender programming, so we can more easily move toward equality" (Young 1971, 52–59).

GLF groups quickly employed New Left confrontational tactics and, among other things, disrupted an annual meeting of the American Psychiatric Association. "At a session there on homosexuality a young bearded gay man danced around the auditorium in a red dress, while other homosexuals and lesbians scattered in the audience shouted 'Genocide!' and 'Torture!' during the reading of a paper on aversion therapy" (D'Emilio 1983b, 235). Medical researchers "tinkered with lobotomies, castration and electroshock to 'rehabilitate' gay people" (Adam 1987, 60). Unlike earlier homophile organizations such as Mattachine and Daughters of Bilitis, which sought acceptance and assimilation, GLF emphasized "coming out" as a revolutionary act and sought confrontations.

The collapse of the "ethic of authority" in the 1960s destroyed the ability of the custodians of mental health to brandish illness as a weapon. In 1973, more than four decades after Collins's book, the American Psychiatric Association removed homosexuality from its list of mental diseases (see Bayer 1987 for the history of the struggle as well as Duberman 1991 and Monette 1992 for the tyranny and pain experienced by lesbians and gay men in analysis).

In his preface to *The New Joy of Gay Sex*, Edmund White reflects on his coauthorship of the first edition in 1977. In that year, White, an aspiring author, joined together with Charles Silverstein, a clinical psychologist, to write *The Joy of Gay Sex*. In retrospect White calls it a "managed book," a work put together by the publisher. The publisher wanted to imitate the elan of the *Joy of Sex* series, while obviously selling to a market niche. White calls his coauthorship "the most liberating act of my life." For the first time he identified as a "proud homosexual."

When the copyright later reverted to the original authors, they decided to launch a new edition (Silverstein and Picano 1992, xi–xii).

Children of Stonewall

In *The Joy of Gay Sex: An Intimate Guide for Gay Men to the Pleasures of a Gay Lifestyle*, published eight years after the Stonewall rebellion, Charles Silverstein and Edmund White write with a verve informed by gay liberation. At that time, the designation "gay" included both women and men. Often, however, they revert to the term "homosexual," which derives from the discredited medical model. On the whole, Silverstein and White are startled by the contrast between their own times and ancient societies like Periclean Athens. In parsing the differences, they attempt to explicate the modern breakthrough in gay life. Silverstein and White limit their remarks to exclusively homosexual men, while they also acknowledge the presence of many married gay men as well as bisexuals. Homosexuality, in their view, has been democratized in the modern era and has moved beyond bohemian and aristocratic circles. Silverstein and White go on to reject the old sissy model. Only a minority of gay men identify and dress as women. The new style is more androgynous (Silverstein and White 1977, 9–11).

Silverstein and White note the artificiality of all social constructions and make a reference to Michel Foucault, though they do not develop an elaborate constructionist argument. Many factors have contributed to the emergence of the new, androgynous gay man, including urbanization, the breakdown of religion, and the emergence of the middle class. American culture in the twentieth century has also come to mandate self-fulfillment, if not hedonism, as a norm. Some gays, according to the authors, take hedonism to its extreme and celebrate promiscuity in bathhouses, which maximize erotic efficiency. Though many men, whether heterosexual or homosexual, experience sexual pleasure within the context of a single relationship or marriage, many gay men, on the other hand, retain their freedom to seek pleasure and are known for their sexual prowess as well as the extent of their desire. The authors go on to celebrate promiscuity or at the very least enumerate the myriad pleasures of gay sex, whether an affair lasts one night or an hour. In the spirit of Alex Comfort they note that "the less pathological rewards of lust remain to be properly celebrated." Their use of "pathological" implicitly qualifies their embrace of hedonism, but they later undermine this qualification in their discussion of "compulsive cruising."

Flexible role playing figures prominently in their constellation of available pleasures, as it does in Comfort's *Joy* series. One moment, for example, you can be Superman, the next Superboy, or Batman for an instant and then Robin. Silverstein and White praise this flexibility, consider it healthy, and note that it certainly maximizes pleasure. Many gay men, however, remain hung up on their own promiscuity. Silverstein and White ask why having one lover is preferable to having many "tricks." Comfort certainly never distinguishes between the two. Hedonism, however, does spark "rage and jealousy" from bigots. They hate single people in general and merely focus and vent their rage on gay men, whom they view as subverting marriage itself (11–14).

Instead of imitating straight marriages, gay men are now creating alternative relationships. *The Joy of Gay Sex*, as the authors tell us, will explore a few of these options. Given all the changes in traditional marriage, gay men just may be trailblazers. *The Joy of Gay Sex* will tell us how to get the maximum pleasure from sex, which translates into a better sense of well-being, and it will also instruct us in avoiding mistakes. Silverstein and White aim to write a book that will serve as a friend as well as a sex manual. They use the term "joy" for three reasons: to confront hangups, to emphasize the joy that can be found in sex, and to echo the book's sister work, *The Joy of Sex*. In this context, "homosexuality is, after all, simply one more set of variations along a vast continuum of individual difference" (15–16). Comfort, however, would demur, fuss about getting stuck, and likely confuse the issue with an assortment of metaphors.

In spirit, tone, and organization, *The Joy of Gay Sex* does parallel its sister volume. The main course, however, does not consist of vaginal intercourse, so some appetizers now become the entrée. The anus, for example, receives due notice as a sensitive sex organ "with particularly responsive nerve endings" located strategically close to the prostate. Later in the volume, Silverstein and White elaborate. Gay men, it seems, particularly respond to "buns." They are "versatile, ambiguous and beautiful—cushiony when relaxed, firm when flexed, and at once soft and hard, smooth and strong, plush and steel." They recommend an exercise for building up the gluteus maximus and endorse three sets of twelve repetitions, which can turn "cassaba melons into cantaloupes." *The Joy of Gay Sex* is most interesting when it digresses from the heterosexual norms articulated by Comfort. Both volumes share the same élan, the frenzy of the hitherto forbidden, the formerly unspeakable. Both volumes transgress (17–18, 34).

The Joy of Gay Sex is arranged alphabetically rather than by category. Our discussion of the book will parallel this rather haphazard format. Androgyny gets listed first. Silverstein and White view it as part of gay liberation and an outgrowth of feminism. They also question the hetero-sexual/homosexual binary. This particular binary, as the authors remind us, produces anxiety, but they do not elaborate.

In the section on bathhouses, Silverstein and White note their erotic efficiency. Even in the highly eroticized world of bathhouses, standards of modesty do exist, and many informal social norms govern behavior. Despite their harsh honesty—speedy acceptance or rejection—bath-houses serve the "interests of pure sensuality" (17, 18).

Bathhouses once served the hygienic needs of large urban populations stranded in tenements. In the 1890s in New York City only about one in forty families had a bathroom in their house or tenement. Ritual baths served the religious needs of Jewish New Yorkers. Turkish, Roman, or electric baths catered to the privileged, and public baths served everyone else. Some of the Turkish and Roman baths also attracted gay males. They either were "gay tolerant" (in the historian George Chauncey's term) or even catered to gay men. In his important volume *Gay New York*, Chauncey reconstructs gay life based in part on the records of societies for the suppression of vice. As Chauncey puts it, "voyeurism and exhibitionism were an important part of the sexual excitement" in "cooling rooms" in bathhouses. During a surreptitious inspection one vice society official observed numerous sexual encounters, including a "fifty-three-year-old Irish pantryman [having] sex with nine different men." By the 1940s residential bathing facilities obviated the need for public bath-houses, and most went out of business. Bathhouses that served gay men, however, remained open. Chauncey reports "persistent rumors" that the Police Athletic League owned one of these establishments (Chauncey 1994, 207–18).

When it comes to bisexuality, Silverstein and White reject Freud's view. Bisexuals do exist, but the term is used with far too much impreci-sion. Homosexual men posing as bisexuals draw their indignation. Their bisexuality is merely an attempt to preserve heterosexual privilege. For other men bisexuality is transitional. If maintained too long, however, it becomes deceptive. Bisexuality does, however, allow for a greater range

of roles. Endless possibilities await a true bisexual as opposed to a counterfeit gay man. Yet bisexuals are one of the most persecuted groups and
receive criticism from both gays and straights.

In the work of Silverstein and White, the gender binary that invokes
the subcategories of active/passive, dominant/submissive, powerful/weak
is subsumed in the new top/bottom classification. "Bottoms" are acted
upon; they are passive, submissive, and weak. As Silverstein and White
put it, "for the man getting fucked, the very passivity of the position can
either be a turn-on or a bore, depending on . . . [his] mood and general
sexual make-up." "But the real appeal of the position is its posture of
submission and passivity. . . . For the majority of gay men, the feeling of
being covered and surrounded can be comforting and secure" (33).

Silverstein and White devote almost ten pages to coming out. It marks
a process that is psychological as well as one enacted in sex. For many
men, realization dawns after several sexual experiences; for some, however, self-acceptance proves ephemeral. After their first experiences many
men will reveal their sexual orientation to close friends, parents, and relatives. Yet this does not end the coming out process. The final step involves identifying with the gay community. In the next decade Dr. Ruth
will adjure readers about taking this last step. As Silverstein and White
see it, America's cult of masculinity prevents many gay men from loving
another man. The culture recognizes only two roles: straight man and
straight woman. This leads many gay men to think that they must be
women and/or effeminate. Challenges to the male/female binary that ag-
itate heterosexuals also trouble gay men. The problem resides in the
rigidness of the binary, and this accounts for the authors' emphasis on
flexibility. Due to feelings of transgression, guilt marks the lives of many
gay men. Various psychological defenses are common, such as declaring
oneself a bisexual. "Don Juanism" and alcoholism are other strategies of
denial. The reluctance to kiss another man is often "a last holdout
against a full commitment to homosexuality." Holding out allows some
men to distinguish between "getting their rocks off" and being homosexual. Silverstein and White's final advice on this subject is to go at your
own pace (47–51, 109).

The authors devote almost five pages to "cruising"—seeking casual
sex with a stranger. In some ways, "cruising" defines urban gay male life.
It has its own rituals and even a dress code. Various clichés serve as a
greeting and others allow a man to quickly exit an encounter if necessary.
Some gay men "cruise" all the time, and this can quickly become a

"nightmare." Others seem bored or lonely. They may fear missing Mr. Right if they do not go out on the prowl every night. For some men "cruising" can be a function of depression. Gay sex makes them feel guilty, which provokes anxiety, which they deal with by "cruising," which only causes the cycle to repeat. "Often the compulsive cruiser *needs* love but *wants* sex." When "cruising," avoid "danger freaks." These men seek to get arrested or even hurt as part of their arousal process (54–59; italics in original).

Depression does not figure in the *Joy of Sex* series, but Silverstein and White devote several pages to it. They link depression to too much passivity. Depressed gay men are willing to serve as passive partners, but not active participants. Their passivity and failure to initiate sex are a turnoff. Their cruising style only increases their sexual frustrations and ensures failure. Some gay men get depressed after casual encounters, known as "tricks." Fear of intimacy can cause men to ditch a "trick" as quickly as possible. Some gay men internalize America's cultural loathing of their existence and become anti-homosexual homosexuals. Roy Cohn is a case in point, though the authors prudently do not use him as an example (since Cohn was alive at the time). Bad feelings about oneself preclude sexual enjoyment. Problems with coming out are often expressed in terms of dislike for other gay men or an inability to form relationships. Some gay men hate themselves and then redirect their anger against a particular segment of the gay community. Since gay men emphasize sexual action, performance anxiety marks many. Overall, however, "gays are no more bitchy, conspiratorial, unstable, excessively emotional, disloyal, infantile, dependent on authority figures, frightened of competition, incapable of mature relationships, cold or waspish than straights." All of these are categories imposed on gay men by heterosexual psychiatrists (59–62, 65–66).

Like Alex Comfort, Silverstein and White distinguish between fidelity and monogamy. Fidelity excludes sex with other persons, while monogamy can allow for erotic escapades. Like straight couples, gay men argue most about fidelity issues, which translate into issues of ownership and possession. Friendship, on the other hand, provides a refuge from domination and possessiveness. Jealousy can also cause conflict and is often rooted in envy or possessiveness. Sometimes jealousy masks fear of abandonment. Overall Silverstein and White, much like Comfort, advise lovers to establish explicit rules that suit their needs (73, 86, 106–7).

Unlike Comfort, Silverstein and White devote almost four pages to guilt. Extreme guilt, according to the authors, is parasitic and can even lead men to loathe themselves. It often appears as chronic depression. Less extreme forms of guilt, either conscious or unconscious, can cause everything from excessive cleanliness to an inability to form relationships. Such men cannot love either themselves or others, and some even entertain a fantasy that some day they will become heterosexual. They are doomed to endlessly repeat approach-avoidance patterns of behavior. Silverstein and White suggest coming out and joining gay organizations as a tonic. If this does not provide relief, they recommend therapy (93–95).

Loneliness can mark gay lives. Silverstein and White distinguish between the cosmic variety—more properly angst—and the alone-ness that results from rejecting other people and refusing to commit. Such men seek love in self-defeating ways—from "hustlers" (male prostitutes), straight men, or strangers at the baths. Some of these men marry and live a counterfeit life. Quick, anonymous sex can defeat loneliness but also presents a trap. Having created a life defined by quick sex, some men then protest that this represents all that gay men want. To the contrary, as the authors point out, many gay men live rather ordinary, domestic lives with their lovers. Either change your behavior or see a therapist (113–14).

Lovers combat loneliness. Silverstein and White offer the image of partners locked in a passionate embrace in which they share their souls as well as their bodies. Unfortunately, many gay men believe the psychiatric ideology that says they cannot love. Some gay men desire conventional-style marriages, while others prefer open relationships. Possible variations of open relationships abound. Much like Comfort, Silverstein and White encourage their readers to talk openly about their feelings and work out accommodations. Gay relationships break apart for the same reasons as heterosexual ones. Fear of intimacy remains one prime cause. This fear can set off powerful feelings of vulnerability and loss of control. The remedy, once again, is therapy (114–18).

Gay men marry women for a variety of reasons. For some it marks an attempt, however illusory, to be cured. Some marry as part of an effort to hide their real sexual orientation. Others are trying to please their parents or even a therapist. Some gay men marry and even enjoy sleeping with their wives, but continue to "cruise" other gay men and remain uninterested in other women. Based on mutual communication, these couples should seek an accommodation that is mutually satisfying (123–25).

Orgies are easy to organize, but hard to get started. You can greet your guests at the door naked and pass joints or "poppers." If everyone is like-minded and "reasonably versatile," things will somehow work out. The authors view pornography as positive, if not therapeutic. The term "promiscuity" is not value-neutral and usually masks a condemnation. "Why having one lover rather than many tricks is considered 'mature' has never been adequately explained. If a gay man is quite unattached, then there's no harm in his having as much sexual experience as he wants" (144, 149, 150). White's more recent autobiographical *roman à clef*, *The Farewell Symphony*, adds some more depth to the treatment of promiscuity in *The Joy of Gay Sex*. In the novel the unnamed main character, a man very much like White, is asked to coauthor a gay sex manual. In reflecting on this, the character notes that he might expect transcendence but not affection from sex, and he assumes that as much sex as possible with as many men as possible is a good thing. The unnamed main character disparages relationships (White 1997, 316–17).[1]

Silverstein and White discuss role playing in the context of gender roles. The cultural norms, as the authors see it, barely function for straight couples, let alone gay ones. Gay men engage in situational role playing with "little or no carry-over from the boudoir to the rest of life." "Many gay men dispense with roles altogether and do not connect fucking, say, with dominance or sucking with passivity. To them the sensual delight is the important thing and they do not attach significance to who is doing what to whom" (Silverstein and White 1977, 158). Sado-masochism entered the gay world in the 1970s and was captured by Robert Mapplethorpe in his *X Portfolio*. It celebrated virility and violence and involved rigid role playing, parsed into "top" or master/ "bottom" or slave. Sadomasochism, according to Silverstein and White, extends well beyond gay male circles, and actually less than half the men in leather bars are really into it. The new permissiveness, however, has allowed this group to display its colors more openly. Sadomasochism does "touch deep chords in many people." Adherents can explore fantasies of power and domination as well as cruelty and subjection. Its main characteristic consists of ritual and ceremony. "Our culture is one based on a hierarchy of power, but in everyday life the power is clothed, not naked, hypocritical, not honest." S/M dramatizes these relationships. Silverstein and White readily acknowledge that they have not exhausted the subject. They also warn that some sick men engage in the practice (160–61).

The stereotypes of gay men are contradictory: powerful seducer of teenagers on the one hand, local fairy or pansy on the other. These social constructions serve to indoctrinate children and provide a basis to discriminate against those who transgress. The legal code also discriminates against gay men. Only self-loathing gays fall in love with straight men, who "worry more about their reputations than a Spanish virgin" (Silverstein and White 1977, 20–26). "Tearooms," public toilets, are not safe places to have sexual encounters, and "backrooms" in bars breed disease. But then again, "they may just be what you're looking for if you're stoned and in a mood to pig out" (26, 175–78).

Some gay men merely want sex, but most also want tenderness. The authors paraphrase Comfort: "when tenderness is involved, sex is not an isolated event, five minutes in the dark, but the intuitive continuation of a long, lively dialogue." This depends on communicating with your partner, knowing his needs, and meeting them. Tenderness is gained by experience and is nurtured in relationships, not casual encounters in "backrooms" (178–79).

Ignoring Comfort's qualifications, Silverstein and White endorse threesomes as a nice spice to add to a feast. Though threesomes do not always work out, versatility helps. The authors view "topping it off"— "sitting on a cock"—as a control issue. It makes some men feel powerless and, accordingly, they experience a loss of potency. The problem, as the authors see it, consists of "mental scripts" in which domination and control serve as central themes. Gay transvestites transcend this issue. Transvestites are misunderstood and mistreated by gays as well as straights. According to the authors, "transvestism bears little relationship to sexual behavior in bed or to gender confusion." In fact, "drag queens can be very tough." Transvestites, for example, fought the New York City police at the Stonewall Inn and launched the modern gay movement. Transsexuals, on the other hand, seek to change their gender identity and become women (179–86).

Silverstein and White tell their readers about the American Psychiatric Association's recent change of homosexuality's classification. As of 1973, the diagnostic manual no longer listed homosexuality as a mental disorder. Gay organizations can hopefully steer men toward mental health workers who are open-minded. The authors view therapy as a counterweight to cultural homophobia as well as its internalized variety. At the end of the volume and the alphabet, Silverstein and White discuss venereal diseases. Medical schools provide little training about venereal diseases that impact gay men. Some homophobic heterosexual doctors refuse to treat gay patients or discourage them in more subtle ways from coming back (186–99).

Silverstein and White, reflecting the exuberance of the decade, propose to celebrate lust, or at least its "least pathological" aspects. They translate the norms of swinging as articulated in *The Joy of Sex* and *More Joy* to gay life. "Homosexuality is, after all, simply one more set of variations along a vast continuum of individual difference." Comfort, of course, never quite endorses this observation. Besides being organized like dictionaries, all three books share common assumptions about sex as a pleasurable recreational activity and differ only in their focus on the appropriate orifice for deep penetration. Comfort holds that vaginal penetration is preferable over other types of intercourse, and he tries to root this in psychology as well as gender. Silverstein and White demur, and their argument focuses on anal as opposed to vaginal synapses as generators of pleasure.

The value of relationships becomes a central issue in all three books. Like Comfort, Silverstein and White decline to qualitatively distinguish between a one-night stand or "tricking" and a long-term relationship. Though Comfort and Silverstein and White enumerate the greater communication as well as potentially greater pleasures that can be had from a relationship, they all offer qualifications throughout their works so as not to normatize this experience. On this central point, their key break with what they see as a repressive cultural tradition, all the authors skillfully equivocate. Comfort's original distinction between fidelity and monogamy informs all these volumes. Although some items on the menu are moved from appetizer to main course, all of the *Joy* series is compatible, including equivocations. The volumes discuss the same orifices in the same general terms. They differ mainly in their emphasis on different possibilities. Such was the state of the sexual joy in the 1970s as it was propelled by a calculus of pleasure.

Silverstein and White emphasize flexible role playing in terms of the gender binary. Like Comfort, they link penetration with power, control, and domination. Some men enjoy experiencing this, others definitely do not. Silverstein and White do not propose an alternative way of understanding penetration, they merely emphasize flexibility. Gender rigidity—the protests of the authors and the promises of the Gay Liberation Front to the contrary—informs the entire *Joy* series. All of them agree that intercourse is a power transaction whether one's partner is a woman or a man. Silverstein and White differ mainly in the degree to which they emphasize flexibility. More is better.

The Joy of Gay Sex does differ from the rest of the *Joy* series in the amount of attention devoted to combating homophobia, especially its internalized component. Silverstein and White see this as the main factor that frustrates gay men in forming relationships. Though internalized homophobia is inculcated by the culture, men can change it by reading their book; if this fails, they should try therapy. The authors seek to make their readers feel good about themselves and their way of life, while at the same time validating some unpleasant feelings like loneliness. They suggest a cause, the homophobic culture, as well as solutions like coming out combined with therapy. In this sense, *The Joy of Gay Sex* has a greater therapeutic task than the rest of the *Joy* series. Comfort must merely make an argument that pleasure is good and point out how available it is, while Silverstein and White must deal with men battered by homophobia and discrimination. Fifteen years later, Silverstein and Picano in their *New Joy of Gay Sex* must deal with men battered by death and disease.

New Joy

French customs officials shredded copies of the first edition of *The Joy of Gay Sex*. Their British counterparts burned it. In *The New Joy of Gay Sex*, published in 1992, Silverstein and Felice Picano—a novelist and playwright—take note of the burning and shredding, but state that the original edition had just the right tone and note how useful it was in building gay pride. They also state that the original edition contained more essays about gay life in general than specifically sexual ones and might have been better entitled *The Joy of Gay Life*. Upon their rereading of the text, they regard it as "excessively high-spirited, even rah-rah." Despite this, the text remains a necessary political act for its time. In this new edition, Silverstein and Picano will be more pragmatic and include negative aspects of gay life such as racism and rape (Silverstein and Picano 1992, xiv–xv).

Both editions use an alphabetical organization without any categories, which makes for less coherent texts even when compared to Comfort. The new edition drops androgyny, consciousness raising, emotional problems, enemies from within, mental illness, and self-esteem. The new edition opens with AIDS (actually discussed under HIV), and adds celibacy, condoms, effeminacy, gyms, mixed HIV positive and negative couples, phone sex, piercing, sex with animals, and suicide. Some of these additions, such as the discussion of gyms, reflect changes in the gay lifestyle, while most of the others reflect the AIDS crisis. In the first edition Silverstein and White regard the new look as androgynous, which reflected gay liberation ideology about gender, while Silverstein and Picano in the second edition regard effeminacy as a problem.

Silverstein and Picano adopt a position of sexual permissiveness, but they do not endorse everything. They oppose censorship, which includes silence about the "kinkier aspects of erotic life." They also oppose non-consensual sex. Last, they do not sanction dangerous activities. They will explain the danger involved in some activities and hope readers will make informed decisions. Given these limitations, they "refuse to chastise people for their sexual fantasies and behavior. There's been far too much of that already. At the same time, we are not endorsing any specific sexual behavior." The illustrations and drawings scattered throughout the text support the legitimacy of interracial sex, an endorsement of sorts (xvi).

The anus, not androgyny, comes first in this edition. Silverstein and Picano say that gay men who do not like to be penetrated probably suffer from low self-esteem and have internalized the assumption "that only women get fucked." Not only is this belief historically wrong, it is also an insult to the male body. The section on bisexuality mainly repeats the discussion in the earlier edition, though the condemnation of counterfeit gay men has been softened (1, 5–8). In the section entitled "Bottoms Up," the authors associate feelings of comfort and security with the passive role during anal intercourse. They add that this need might be primal. They do not repeat the first edition's critique of American macho culture that makes it hard for men to accept the passive role. Celibacy, contrary to the thrust of the entire *Joy* series, is "neither physically or mentally bad." Endowment, or lack thereof, in their view has become "a tiresome obsession." Coming out receives due attention, but the discussion lacks the urgency and political imperative of the first edition. When engaging in computer sex, do not expect quick responses. Silverstein and Picano recommend condoms for oral sex and say they are necessary for anal sex (20, 25, 30, 36–38).

Lovers share their souls, and they also form a bond against the scorn and homophobia of American culture. Instead of the first edition's suggestion that internalized homophobia makes it difficult for some men to enter relationships, Silverstein and Picano blame the difficulty on a clash between two personality types: one centered in autonomy and the other in attachment. Mismatches between these types cause many relationship crises. Fidelity remains the biggest problem in gay relationships. Personality clashes can also rend relationships. Fear of intimacy remains the primary psychological problem. Many men do not deal well with feelings of vulnerability and loss of control. Open communication, as in the first edition, remains necessary, and dishonesty the culprit. Both men have a responsibility not to bring the Human Immunodeficiency Virus (HIV) into their relationship (44–45).

"Cruising" receives due notice, and the authors note the changes wrought by AIDS. "Safe sex" (not "safer," as it is usually put) needs to be discussed prior to any festivities. Elaborating on the earlier edition, Silverstein and Picano also discuss "compulsive cruising." They define it as constant "tricking," and it has more to do with longing than lust. As in the earlier edition, they suggest that loneliness is a component and that "compulsive cruisers" want sex but need love. Since times have changed, Silverstein and Picano take up the subject of "dangerous sex," which they define as potentially infectious. They also warn against practices that involve inserting breakable objects—perhaps in reaction to Reuben's book. Depression can be caused by homophobia, and if it occurs after sex it may point to a fear of intimacy. Once again reflecting the times, Silverstein and Picano discuss domestic violence, and point out that homophobia undoubtedly plays a role. The authors suggest that before ingesting drugs, the reader decide which of the following three categories he falls into: user, abuser, or addict. They note the relationship between being high on alcohol or drugs and unsafe sex. Silverstein and Picano reject the theory maintained by some gay men that abusive fathers caused their homosexuality. As far as the authors are concerned, this assertion reflects both internalized homophobia and fear of intimacy. "Face-to-face" intercourse allows for the deepest penetration, but it also makes some men feel feminine. Other men, however, find this exciting. When it comes to fetishes Silverstein and Picano suggest that gay men have fetishized their own bodies as they strive for muscle definition and the perfect tan. Gyms have become gay temples; salvation is found in repetitions. The discussion of fidelity and monogamy reprises the discussion of the first edition, which reflects Comfort's work. Friendship, according to Silverstein and Picano, is central in gay life. In an implicit comparison to lovers, the authors note that friendship "endures" and "ripens." "Fuck buddies," somewhere between partners and friends, are men one can have sex with without "emotional turmoil" or "entangling alliances" (48, 52–54, 57–62, 65, 74, 76).

Guilt, as in the previous volume, still permeates gay life. It manifests itself in "compulsive cruising," fascination with straight men, or a talent for doomed love affairs. "Guilt breeds a fear of intimacy and the self-contempt and longing for punishment that underlie so many of these behaviors." Silverstein and Picano devote six pages to "HIV disease." They accept the gender theory of homophobia, which holds that homophobia results from inflexible gender roles that bifurcate power and status and assign low positions to women and "bottoms." The authors feel that this explains not only homophobia as a cultural phenomenon, but also its internalized aspect. A self-hating homosexual feels inadequate as a man and then projects his self-loathing onto other gays. Such men can manage anonymous sex, but fail at building relationships. Reflecting necessities brought about by the AIDS epidemic, Silverstein and Picano also discuss insurance and how to COBRA a policy and then go on to adaptations such as "J.O. buddies," "J.O. clubs," "living wills," and "letting go." As in the first volume, a reluctance to kiss is "the last holdout against a full commitment to homosexuality" (85, 95, 101–2, 106, 108, 110).

The section on loneliness largely reprises the first edition, but warns readers about HIV infection and its link to self-esteem. A lack of self-respect translates into ignoring safe sex norms. Parenthetically they add that "there are also gay men who have nothing but anonymous sex, enjoy it, and don't complain about it." Silverstein and Picano see no real problems with masturbation, contrary to Dr. Ruth, who warns about becoming trapped in this activity. Masturbation allows men to define their tastes and build confidence. It also promotes acceptance of both pleasure and one's own body. Men can do this too much, but the remedy lies in listening to one's body and watching for chafing or an aching feeling (114, 120, 122).

HIV complicates relationships, especially when one partner is positive and the other negative. Shock, if not terror, greets the announcement of positive status. Besides a future of illness and disability, a partner might fear that he has infected his lover. Fear of abandonment, of course, plays an important role. The seronegative partner, on the other hand, may compensate by infantalizing his seropositive partner (124–25).

As in the first edition, the authors see no consensus about the origins of homosexuality. They specifically attack the "recruitment theory" and call it a "smokescreen, designed to hide the fact that most child molestation is heterosexual and occurs within the family." Medical explanations, like the hormone imbalance one popular in the genre, invite skepticism. Silverstein and Picano argue that most medical explanations have a hidden agenda: to cure homosexuality. Phone sex receives more than three pages of attention. Here the authors adopt the masturbation proviso of Dr. Ruth. If phone sex becomes persistent or too expensive or interferes with actually meeting other men, then avoid it. It can become another intimacy dodge. Pornography still receives favorable reviews despite duly noted feminist objections. The term "promiscuity" connotes "a moral condemnation, and it is used against gays by any group that condemns homosexuality." The term has no empirical referent. On the other hand, Silverstein and Picano do acknowledge the existence of "runaway sex," which they define as the "incessant search" for it regardless of time, place, or appropriateness. Spending one's savings on phone sex is an example. According to the authors, fear of abandonment sparks this behavior, and the incessant search itself becomes a substitute for intimacy and love. Therapy is necessary in this case (126, 127–28, 139–42, 146–48, 150–52).

Just as it infests all of American life, racism exists in gay life too. Alex Comfort in his *Joy* series ignores this issue.[2] Silverstein and Picano restate the conventional feminist linkage of rape with power only to reject it. "'Rape is about power, not about sex' has become a commonly heard statement. Yet sex and power are intimately related. What changes sexual intercourse (in its wildest sense) into rape is not the force used, but rather the lack of consent." Comfort hedges a bit on the relationship between force and consent, while Silverstein and Picano embrace it boldly. The authors, however, do reject the gender binary. "The gay couple has no stake in preserving the male-female dichotomy." Bedroom activity does not translate to the rest of life, and partners often take turns in the different roles anyway. In a repetition of the first edition: "Many gay men dispense with roles altogether, and do not connect fucking, say, with dominance, or sucking with passivity." Pleasure remains the goal, and who does what to whom does not matter all that much. Silverstein and Picano largely reprise the first edition's discussion of sadomasochism. Safe sex is not only medically necessary, but also an expression of how a man feels about himself. The authors supply the standard list of considered safe, considered possibly safe, and considered unsafe activities. They disagree with moralists about sex with animals and decline to "condemn it out of hand"—at least for cows, sheep, and horses. "We hope it doesn't become the *only* sexual contact in a man's life." Curiously, they adjure their readers more sharply about phone sex than bestiality (158–60, 162–63, 171; italics in original).

Silverstein and Picano list the usual suspects in the section on sexually transmitted diseases. Curiously, they neglect to mention that there is a treatment for herpes. They largely repeat the earlier edition's discussion of "sitting on it." "Sleaze" exists in the eyes of the beholder. For some men "sleaze" represents a fashion statement embodying "hardworking, shit-kicking, rock hard masculinity stripped of social pretense and Mama's middle-class morality." Other men engage in "sleaze" as *nostalgie de la boue*. As long as the activity is safe, other factors can be adjusted to taste—a clean rug or STP stained garage floor, for example.

Tragically, as the authors note, one-third of teenage suicides are gay. As a guide to readers, Silverstein and Picano list three special symptoms enumerated by the Centers for Disease Control and Prevention. The authors prefer "backrooms" to "tearooms," but warn that "backrooms" are really unsafe. Silverstein and Picano are aware of the linkages between dysfunctional families and teenage "hustling" or prostitution, but allow some room for intergenerational sex. They refer to some evidence that intergenerational sex leads to "long-lasting love." Silverstein and Picano then supply an anecdote, but not a footnote, to a reliable study. Tenderness still makes sex qualitatively better. "Three-ways" still add spice to the feast, but can cause their own problems (181, 183, 185–86, 189, 191–92, 194).

Before the Stonewall rebellion, top-bottom roles, the gay male reprise of gender, were rigid. As Silverstein and Picano put it, gay men mirrored heterosexual gender roles. As in the first edition, they recommend flexibility. Though some men switch roles, many have a preference. "It's perfectly normal to be solidly top or bottom." Touching and caressing can be a problem for some men. Men are so accustomed to control that its loss can induce anxiety. "Trade," men pretending to be straight, come in two general varieties: rough and commercial. With "trade" self-abasement becomes eroticized, and both parties can revel in humiliation. Homophobia defines these encounters. Silverstein and Picano mainly restate the first edition's teaching about transvestites and transsexuals. They add a reference to the film *Paris Is Burning* as well as some information about family organizations created by many transvestites. "Tricking" can result from boredom, frustration, or surplus libido. Many people put down one-night stands, but the authors simply ask, "Who's being hurt? Probably no one." One-night stands, in fact, can be a way to experiment with different sex roles. Besides, they can be a good way to meet people. On the other hand, one-night stands can become obsessive. The authors end on an optimistic note: "Be safe, be careful, and enjoy yourself." The AIDS crisis necessitates a short section on wills. The text exhausts the alphabet with wrestling: "Such physical combativeness and competition, with its underlying threat of real harm and the possibility of total subjugation, can become the ultimate aphrodisiac" (198–200, 202, 205, 207, 214).

Silverstein and Picano, like Comfort in his 1991 edition, seek to be "permissive" in the age of AIDS. Unlike the first edition of *The Joy of Gay Sex*, *The New Joy of Gay Sex* regards some activities as dangerous not merely because they pose a risk of HIV infection, but also because they might transmit other diseases such as intestinal parasites. The authors do not explicitly endorse any specific activities and trust to the judgment of mature readers. They also, as they well know, censure nothing. They equivocate over intergenerational sex—possibly child abuse by statute— as well as bestiality. Both editions backhandedly endorse promiscuity. The first edition equivocates on promiscuity and blames obsessive "cruising" on internalized homophobia. The second edition is less overtly political in its denunciations of psychiatry and homophobia and resolves the "runaway sex" issue with a distinction of personality types: one seeks autonomy, the other attachment. Coming out, as might be expected, remains a major issue for both editions, but more so in the first one.

Though both editions explicitly valorize flexibility in gender roles, they really accept the premises of the gender binary. Power and sex, as the second edition puts it, are intimately related. One partner has lots of it, the other much less. Though both editions decry this fact and note that some men do not understand intimate behavior this way, both volumes support the powerful/powerless subset of the gender binary. This accounts for the comments on wrestling at the end of both editions. Subjugation, or at least the threat of real harm mixed with combativeness and competition, ensures arousal and fulfillment. Silverstein and Picano accept the gender theory of the origin of homophobia and explicitly call for more flexibility in role playing, though it's all right to be rigid too, but their text teaches that intimacy involves power transactions. In some ways the joy they write about is really the joy of power, and this particular understanding marks the whole series.

Silverstein and Picano also use the term "safe sex" rather than the more conventional designation "safer sex." The term "safer sex" was well established by the time of the book's publication. Safer, as opposed to safe, implies that risk in the age of AIDS exists in many intimate situations. Condoms, as Dr. Ruth will constantly remind us, do break. Very few activities are thoroughly safe. But to admit that a great deal of intimate behavior involves some risk would logically lead to a reappraisal of the promiscuous norm assumed in both volumes.

None of the *Joy* series, Comfort included, is really about joy, the feeling that led Schiller and then Beethoven to compose. Schiller and Beethoven understand joy as a sanctuary that unites men and women as brothers and sisters. They celebrate a divine spark ignited in friendship or marriage that marks all of nature. Silverstein, White, and Picano, on the other hand, distinguish between friends and lovers, while Comfort's casual encounters exclude the celebration of anything other than pleasure. In fact, the entire *Joy* series is actually about pleasure and ways to maximize it. The fundamental dispute among the volumes is not about sexual object choice, but rather which orifices and what combinations of them produce the greatest gratification. In this sense Silverstein, White, and Picano mainly substitute the anus for the vagina, and like Comfort, they understand penetration as a celebration of power, not human togetherness in a sanctuary marked by ecstasy. Comfort, Silverstein, White, and Picano represent aspects of modernity that terrified Kellogg.

The entire *Joy of Sex* series rests on a patriarchal understanding of intimacy that transforms it into a power relationship. Every time Silverstein, White, or Picano state that some men remain uncomfortable with submissiveness, they reinforce the point. They agree with Comfort that power transactions are involved. The issue is to get comfortable with the inferior position, that of women in general. None of the *Joy* series, Comfort included, challenges the fundamental issue of how power informs the gender binary itself. The series merely advocates some role playing or sharing some of the power. Intimate relations, thus, remain rooted in power, ultimately like wrestling—an apt metaphor in this case—as well as combativeness and competition with the threat of harm or even subjugation. As Andrea Dworkin once noted, "too often homosexual relation[s] transgress gender imperatives without transforming them." The first edition's emphasis on androgyny comes closer to the heart of the matter (Dworkin 1974, 185).

In retrospect, Silverstein and White in 1977 wrote in an arcadian time. Though the times were marked by discrimination, persecution, and violence, the authors capture the exuberance of a new movement bursting forth at the end of the 1960s as well as the joy of women and men who would now dare to speak the name of their love. To put this another way, the first edition is an "in your face" type of book. It proclaims self-acceptance and invites others to identify and join in. Except for social sanctions, reasonably assumed to be subject to political change resulting from millions coming out, what harm could be done? Silverstein and White also wrote at the cusp of the antibiotic age when many, if not most, of the diseases listed toward the end of the volume were seen mainly as inconveniences. The earlier, radical agenda of the Gay Liberation Front that called for the elimination of gender itself also informs the work to some extent. Though Silverstein and White do not call for the abolition of gender, their emphasis on androgyny represents a residue of the original goal. Times, however, have changed. They have become a nightmare of disease and death. Silverstein and Picano write at a time when death became part of gay life, as symbolized by the AIDS Memorial Quilt, but they still mainly endorse the pleasure agenda of the whole *Joy* series. Even Jeremy Bentham, who granted no qualitative distinctions between pleasures, would add the possibility of death (condoms do indeed break) to his felicific calculus. Silverstein and Picano want the party to continue, so they tend to minimize medical risks even compared to Comfort's last work, which rules out all anal intercourse. Dr. Ruth, on the other hand, will endorse a different agenda and constantly remind us that condoms do, indeed, break.

Lesbian Joy

Like *The Joy of Gay Sex*, *The Joy of Lesbian Sex* was written in 1977. The authors, Dr. Emily Sisley, a psychologist and educator, and Bertha Harris, a professor and novelist, begin with an introduction to the topic. Lesbianism, for them at least, is like China, vast, uncharted, and separated from society by a great wall. The image that they create of lesbians is one of freedom and erotic abandon. Women are insatiable and inexhaustible, but only the lesbian is free to express this level of eroticism.

Lesbians are the "emblem of eroticism that resists death-by-socialization." Erotic variation is always associated with the feminine (Sisley and Harris 1977, 9, 10).

The second wave of feminism during the twentieth century was having its effect. *The Joy of Lesbian Sex* makes clear that while women are wonderful, it is even better to be a lesbian. In a reversal of the usual biological stereotyping, Sisley and Harris equate men and their efforts in the world to their erections. To be male is to be limited in terms of energy rather than limitless as women are. Men understand things through an all-or-none, black or white lens. But salvation is at hand because at long last, women are finally beginning to form a culture based on their own biology, namely, their orgasms, rather than the purely male experience of tension and release. As described by Sisley and Harris, this is a "system of radiating circles encompassing spirit as well as body." In discussing the penis, the authors note that at best, it is an "accessory to sexual pleasure." At worst it functions as an impediment because it is easily exhausted. In sum, woman is phenomenal, and even "God and Freud wonder at her capacity." In forty short years the accepted view had changed from the notion that nice girls do not usually admit any sexual desires, especially prior to marriage, to a celebration of openly expressed erotic desire. Moreover, women, or at least lesbians, should act on these desires. "Lesbians, like the clitoris, participate in sex for no other reason than the sheer fun of it all," and "there is no other purpose to lesbian sexuality than pleasure" (14–15, 48, 113).

For Sisley and Harris, the relationship between sex and procreation is not important. The lesbian baby boom would not happen for another fifteen years, and then the discussion would revolve around artificial insemination and turkey basters. Sisley and Harris tell us that since the "ovaries and uterus are for procreation, not sex," they will not be discussed, and genitals will be the focus of the book (17).

Like other books in the *Joy* series, *The Joy of Lesbian Sex* is arranged alphabetically by topic, beginning with a caveat about drinking. Like the earlier books in the *Joy* series, this one is not intended to be read in any specific order; rather, the format expects the reader to look for topics that are of interest and read about those. The approach may be intended to provide information in a way that is easy to use, but the overall effect is somewhat choppy. A complete reading of the text illuminates what the authors have to say about a number of topics usually covered in chapter length in more traditionally organized manuals intended for heterosexuals.

While the introductory remarks make it clear that the authors believe that lesbian relationships are, or at least can be, superior to heterosexual ones, lesbian relationships are not without problems. Lesbians cannot advertise their relationships like heterosexual couples can. Instead, most couples will need to hide their love. This is why it is necessary to find other lesbians so that there is at least one group in which to be comfortable and where affection and love can be freely expressed (115–16).

Lesbian relationships are different from heterosexual ones in a number of other ways as well. Sisley and Harris make it clear that in their book they will not be discussing the need to be gentle with a lover, since women know this by their very nature. They do, however, include a section on bondage. Lesbians do not tease—offering, then withholding sexual favors—the way some women do to men. Lesbians, however, do not rush into the bedroom on the first date. Although there is no documentation to support the claim, Sisley and Harris assert that while lesbian couples do fight and occasionally split up, their relationships last longer than heterosexual ones (88, 91).

Sisley and Harris strive to delineate the ways lesbian relationships are better than heterosexual ones. At the same time, they attempt to define a different type of relationship, one that is more open and allows for the possibility of many lovers, while still maintaining a primary relationship with one person. In a theme common to the *Joy* series, "sexual engagement with a stranger or a friend does not indicate promiscuity or disloyalty to the prime lover." Lesbians do not accept the model heterosexual marriage provides, and by and large they do not want it. The concept is too limiting and by definition restricts the individual. Marriage requires fidelity and monogamy and leads to jealousy and possessiveness. Sex outside the primary relationship can be stimulating and can improve the sex between partners in the main couple, providing the extra spice needed to keep things interesting (118).

There also are reasons for having sex outside the relationship besides simple attraction or lust. Couples in relationships in which the sex is gone may choose to nurture their love and wait for desire to return, or if both agree, they may turn to others for the fulfillment of their sexual needs. Of course, this needs to be negotiated with the partner. The person outside the primary relationship must be informed. Women who have an occasional desire for men are entitled to fulfill this sexual need as well, as long as it is discussed with both the other woman and the man. Lesbians need to be honest about these things (21, 31, 122).

Sisley and Harris promote what they consider to be an ideal. They acknowledge that most lesbians do not fully embrace open relationships. In fact, many lesbians are somewhere in between marriage and open relationships in their attitudes and practices. It is difficult to be sexual outside the relationship and not suffer some emotional consequences. Negotiation with your partner does not always work. It would be even worse, however, if you did not try to work it out. The implied message is to try to negotiate, but regardless of the results of the negotiation, do it anyway but discreetly. Many lesbians are finding that the struggle is worth it and they are "having their cake and eating it too." Readers are reminded that jealousy is self-inflicted and is a leftover from the heterosexual conditioning that leads us to believe that we can possess someone and even control them. If you or your partner feels jealous, the best thing to do is to freely admit it and try to move on. Compromises can be negotiated so long as sexual freedom is not too severely restricted (72, 95, 122).

The authors insist that the norm of lifelong partners and heterosexual-style marriage is not a good idea. Only lesbians who do not reject previous sexual systems and rules look for someone to be a lifelong partner. "The prohibitions implicit in such an arrangement usually result in eventual sexual death." Sisley and Harris feel so strongly about this that they include a whole section on what to do when you get to the "afternoon" of love when your sex life becomes routine and then eventually disappears. Fortunately for lesbians, they have a choice in what to do. They can work on renewing their sex life, have sex outside the relationship, or find a new relationship. In any case, as befits a text that begins with a celebration of the unbridled eroticism of women, it is very important to find someone with whom to have sex (20–21, 119).

The Joy of Lesbian Sex covers a great deal of territory. Virtually anything that both partners enjoy is acceptable. There are no real restrictions as long as you enjoy yourselves. The refrain is constant: lesbians have sex for the fun of it. Masturbation is recommended, even during periods of celibacy. Sex is like other activities. We lose our skill and desire if we do not exercise them once in a while. The techniques described are all designed to increase pleasure. There is no discussion about reaching orgasm, since frigidity is "a condition simply unheard of among lesbians." "Lesbians *always* reach orgasm in their lovemaking" (42, 80, 137, 189; italics in original).

Frequency of sex is not an issue here, in contrast to the more conventional marriage manuals. How often and how to have sex are entirely up to the couple. As long as they remember that there are differences between individuals and they negotiate an agreement as to how often and what, then all will be well. As in the discussions of outside sexual affairs, the emphasis is on negotiation and agreement. On the more practical side, the text offers readers advice on kissing (avoid deep kissing without the proper preliminaries), feathers, vibrators, and various types of dildos (77, 80).

Sisley and Harris are invested in presenting a picture of the lesbian woman as different from her straight counterparts. She is much more sexual and liberated, she is working to free herself from the bonds of even the idea of marriage, and she is trying to redefine what it means to be committed to another person. It is more difficult for them to redefine motherhood, and perhaps this is why their comments are essentially negative. It is not that lesbians do not make good mothers. On the contrary, they make terrific mothers, and their children are very well adjusted, probably because of the advantage of being raised in a home where openness and honesty are the rule. However, children who grow up in a lesbian home may be shocked to discover that they are heterosexual and may, Sisley and Harris imply, need reassurance that this is okay. This contrasts with lesbian mothers who maintain the fiction of heterosexuality. Children raised under these circumstances are unemotional and keep their distance because their mothers were unhappy and resentful. Moreover, lesbians decide to have children for better reasons than do heterosexuals. Lesbians truly want to care for and love someone, not merely conform to the societal view of family or to carry on the family name. Lesbian families are freed from the role playing that defines heterosexual families (43–44, 108).

On the other hand, lesbian mothers do have things to contend with. There are the obvious problems with getting pregnant. What method is chosen is something that once again must be negotiated with the partner. Then there can be problems with having a lover who feels neglected after the baby comes. One can solve this problem by negotiating with both children and lover as to how quality and/or private time will be spent with each of them. Eroticism should not be sacrificed just because a woman has children (107–12).

As they do in other areas of lesbian life, Sisley and Harris encourage women to do what they want to as long as they are careful to negotiate with their partner. Thus, children are fine if both partners are quite sure that they really want them, but no woman should feel abnormal if she decides that children are not for her. Either way is perfectly fine, although the authors hint that the desire for children may be a holdover of the way women are socialized and, therefore, a remnant of heterosexual life. But since one of the things that being a lesbian means is that a woman has choices, a lesbian can freely choose to have them or to reject children as an option. It is entirely up to her (112).

Sisley and Harris spend 178 pages expounding on the advantages of a lesbian lifestyle. In contrast to *The Joy of Gay Sex*, there is little discussion of guilt and no section on homophobia. *The Joy of Lesbian Sex* seems to embrace both feminism and the gay liberation movement in one volume. It is wonderful to be lesbian; all things lesbian are good. "Lesbians form the largest percentage of the book buying-public." Lesbians make ideal mothers. Lesbians are always orgasmic and frigidity is unknown. Most lesbians embrace feminism and reject patriarchy without any question. They do not engage in role playing in their relationships except to enhance the sexual fires. "Butch/femme" roles are out of date and may never have been practiced by very many lesbians anyway. Lesbians, like all women, are gentle, and they are rarely interested in bondage games or sadomasochism. Lesbians are working toward rejecting marriage as part of the patriarchy, and most are able to make open relationships work. Above all, lesbians are able to negotiate with their partners, arriving at satisfactory solutions for even the most difficult conflicts (48).

There are few indications that there are any problems associated with a lesbian lifestyle. The only section that is even remotely related to self-help or problem solving is the discussion of consciousness raising. The purpose of CR is described as helping women discover what they have in common, and Sisley and Harris give relatively specific instructions for running CR groups. They emphasize the importance of helping lesbian and straight women understand each other. Of course there is a lack of support for lesbian couples from society as a whole, but all women are basically unsupported by the patriarchy unless they conform to its norms (57–59).

The entire book is a celebration of female sexuality of a certain type, female to female, and it was one of the first books of its kind. It was certainly the first book about lesbian sex that was openly marketed in bookstores for everyone to see, and for those with courage to buy. As in most marriage manuals, the subtext is political. Lesbianism and feminism are warmly embraced in an uncritical view of women that tends to ignore history and, like other marriage manuals, relies on personal opinion and wishful thinking. Given the times, it is not surprising that the book took this tone, but all was not well in lesbianland.

Utopia Revisited

Lesbian Sex by JoAnn Loulan is a book of a quite different type. Written only seven years after *The Joy of Lesbian Sex*, it nevertheless has a very different tone. The introduction makes the purpose of the book clear. It is written so that the reader will be able to change if need be and "achieve the kind of sex life you want." This is a practical book and is not about sexual techniques but rather about issues important to many lesbians. These issues can and often do affect sexuality. Each chapter is coordinated with a set of homework exercises found at the end of the book. The reader is urged to choose those exercises that fit her problems (Loulan 1984, ix).

The author, JoAnn Loulan, works as a lesbian counselor and has conducted many sexuality workshops. Thus it is not surprising that her view is rather different from that of Sisley and Harris. Loulan sees women who are having trouble, and her book is written for any lesbian who wants a better sex life. Her assumptions are far different from those of *The Joy of Lesbian Sex*. While both books assume that women are in control of their own sex lives, Loulan assumes that lesbians sometimes do experience lack of desire or failure to achieve orgasm, something that is totally foreign to Sisley and Harris's point of view.

Sisley and Harris assert that all lesbians are orgasmic and that women always have orgasms during their lovemaking. Seven years later Loulan includes a section in her book entitled "Tyranny of Orgasm." Loulan notes that some women are not orgasmic, and that is okay. All it means is that they did not have an orgasm and does not mean that the experience was not pleasurable. "Orgasm is highly overrated." The goal of sexual behavior is to give and receive pleasure, and it may or may not result in orgasm. Focusing on orgasm is likely to make everyone nervous and may even diminish chances for actually reaching one (71).

Loulan takes far more seriously than Sisley and Harris the existence of barriers women must overcome before they can be truly spontaneous sexual beings. Sexism has caused women to feel weak and powerless, and this carries over into sexual behavior. In contrast to the celebration of unlimited female eroticism espoused by Sisley and Harris, who give only the briefest nod to nonsexual aspects of a lesbian's life, Loulan notes that there are problems with a definition of lesbian that centers on sexual behavior, especially if a woman is feeling inhibited by any of the barriers she identifies. Besides sexism, these barriers include homophobia, trauma, and the burden of being rejected due to some other difference such as race, size, or disability. Homework exercises designed to help women overcome these barriers are provided (3–5, 8).

There are other reasons why a woman may not feel desire, and why she may not be orgasmic. Besides the barriers already mentioned, these include stress, pregnancy, and alcohol and drugs. A final problem is that of too great intimacy with one's partner. Sometimes partners may merge themselves so much that they lose their sense of self. This can also contribute to lack of desire (89, 143, 160–61, 179).

Lesbian Sex also differs from *The Joy of Lesbian Sex* in its view of multiple sex partners. Loulan acknowledges that women interested in casual sex face the problem that many lesbians consider this behavior promiscuous. And single lesbians have problems meeting other lesbians because American culture has not provided places where they can gather. Nor have lesbians had the opportunity to develop the necessary skills to ask women out for dates. Sisley and Harris do not really consider the problems women have finding each other, nor do they consider any sexual relations to be promiscuous. Loulan deals with outside sex only in the section on "sexual addiction," thus making it clear that this is not among the sanctioned types of eroticism. On the other hand, while considering the difficulties of single lesbians, Loulan affirms the right of singles, including lesbian mothers, to do whatever they wish. Lesbian moms are enjoined to educate their children that women have the right to have their sexual needs met. Mothers too are entitled to have both a social and a sexual life (137, 172).

Both volumes struggle to provide some guidelines for lesbians, but neither book achieves its aim. Sisley and Harris attempt to validate nearly any lifestyle a lesbian chooses as long as it is not that of a settled, quasi-married couple. In this attempt, and perhaps without meaning to, they set a new standard. Lesbians always have orgasms and are nearly always interested in sex. In some ways, they have taken the male standard from the *Joy* series and tried to make it work for lesbians. In spite of the clearly feminist bent of the book, the authors have opted for a lesbian sexual pattern of open relationships (regardless of what your partner thinks) and orgasms that is very similar to the pattern more usually thought of as male. Loulan provides the alternative view, that of sexually troubled women who have difficulty with orgasms and are inhibited and generally unhappy with their sex lives. She draws a picture of a rather timid woman who is uninformed about her own body and has difficulty talking to her partner. Neither book has reached the middle ground, but they do provide a description of the poles of lesbian sexuality, at least as it was understood in the late 1970s and early 1980s.

9

Another Reaction
Dr. Ruth Defends Marriage

In her book *Sex for Dummies* in 1995, Dr. Ruth will emphasize the end of the sexual revolution. The political problems faced by Surgeon General C. Everett Koop in getting his AIDS report approved by
President Reagan's White House staff exemplify the changes in America's
sexual ethos.[1] Once Koop drafted his report he had to use a subterfuge to
get approval from the White House's Domestic Policy Council. As he puts
it in his book, "I would have to skate fast on thin ice to get by political ap-
pointees who placed conservative ideology above saving lives." At a meeting Koop provided the council with only a superficial overview, and he
sensed that they had not absorbed the report in any depth. He also presented them with copies printed on expensive paper, because he knew they
would hesitate to make changes so as to save the cost of reprinting the first
one thousand copies. After he presented the report at a press conference
on October 22, 1986, the White House informed Koop that further printings would be delayed pending corrections. A few weeks later, Gary Bauer
and another White House staffer visited him and suggested an "update."

Key White House staffers could accept sexual abstinence as policy, but
they could not bring themselves to endorse the use of condoms. Such an
endorsement would appear to legitimize sex outside marriage as well as
gay male sexuality. It would also ratify the earlier divorce of sex from
procreation, facilitated by the development of the birth control pill in
1960. They responded by reinforcing their perception of social norms.
They sought to support the traditional family together with church and
community. At meetings, according to Koop,

> He [Gary Bauer] dug out his old white notebook containing examples of bad
> semi-pornographic sex education material. . . . I thought it must have made
> the rounds of every meeting in the White House. Bauer said that he did not
> want his . . . [three young daughters] to hear the lurid details of anal inter-
> course. No one had ever suggested that they should learn this, so I spoke up.

The political "sniping" at Koop continued at another meeting of the Domestic Policy Council. This time Koop defended the "integrity of his office" and attacked those who sought to "muzzle" him. Ed Meese, then the attorney general and chair of the Domestic Policy Council, denied any attempts to silence him. "Then those who had tried to muzzle me pretended they knew nothing about it." By the end of the meeting, the council agreed that the government should consult on sex education but not provide it directly. Koop thought that "some crazies had gotten to some members of the cabinet."

Arguments about the surgeon general's report continued at a meeting called to discuss the government's role in sex education. According to Koop the meeting went well until Gary Bauer spoke again.

> Bauer lashed out, saying that Reagan and he (was this a new alliance?) had decided to move further away from me on issues like sex education and condoms. He said the president wanted to say only one thing about AIDS: The nation was facing the problem of AIDS simply because it had abandoned traditional morality, and it would not get out of the situation until we returned to that morality.

It was not until April 1, 1987, that President Reagan declared AIDS "public health enemy Number One" in a speech to the Philadelphia College of Physicians (Cannon 1991, 816). Koop, though, calls this a brief and superficial reference. As President Reagan went up the ramp to Air Force One at the Philadelphia airport, reporters shouted questions about AIDS. His reply: "just say no!" That night NBC News reported that Reagan had not read the surgeon general's report. Margaret Sanger would probably regard all this as antediluvian (Koop 1991, 212, 214, 221–22, 224).

Good Sex in the 1980s

"'Hello, this is Dr. Ruth Westheimer. You're on the air.'" These words greeted listeners to WYNF in New York City on Sunday evenings in the 1980s. Dr. Ruth, as she came to be known, later added a cable TV show, wrote quite a few books, and even hosted a series of Playboy videos. She also writes a syndicated column. Her books claim that she pioneered "media psychology," but she is not trained as a psychologist. Media psychology continues to evolve with Dr. Laura Schlessinger (1996), whose syndicated radio show claims some twenty million listeners, and MTV (Music Television) offers *Loveline* late at night. Dr. Laura offers traditional marital and sexual advice within a moral context, while MTV generally provides more progressive views along with a great deal of irony and humor.

Dr. Ruth's work spans the period from the *Joy of Sex* series and the advent of AIDS to the sexual counterrevolution during the Reagan and Bush presidencies. She continues to publish to this day. In her early works she accepts the premises of *The Joy of Sex*, but continually dampens Comfort's enthusiasms and declines to take his premises to their logical conclusions. She disapproves of swinging, for example. The earlier hippie consciousness of the wondrousness of the natural, of the earthiness and authenticity of sex largely drops out of her 1980s lexicon. Sex, as in Reuben's work, becomes an issue within relationships that lead to marriage. In her later works she explicitly focuses on married lovers and moves farthest away from the premises of the *Joy of Sex* series. As her views mature, they grow more conservative and traditional. Dr. Ruth, ever charming and engaging, is no sex radical, quite the opposite in fact. This chapter will survey several of her major works to discern common themes.

Dr. Ruth's Guide to Good Sex, her first book in 1983, was a spin-off from her radio show. Her shtick proved irresistible. A Jewish grandmother with a German accent and a doctorate from Columbia University spoke frankly about sex on the air. She, of course, quickly became a celebrity and a guest on TV talk shows. Her celebrity status aside, how do her popular works mark the course of America's sexual zeitgeist?

Good Sex picks right up on the gourmet metaphor from the *Joy of Sex* series. Dr. Ruth notes her objective perspective as opposed to a moral one, though she does not disparage religious restrictions on sexuality. She aims to help people discover and map their sexual boundaries and seeks to educate them in an era of sexual permissiveness. She hopes to instill a healthy attitude toward sex and advises readers to avoid offending their families and religion, if such can be reasonably avoided. Ostensibly, she advises, "do your own thing," but she also tells readers to learn all they can because ignorance about sex can only cause problems (Westheimer 1983, 1–13).

As previously remarked, Dr. Ruth explicitly adopts Alex Comfort's premises from the *Joy of Sex* series in *Good Sex*. "Different strokes for different folks indeed!" "In most cases I advise that as long as no one gets hurt, and both people enjoy them, whatever sex games they come up with are fine." In her understanding, this includes "playing rape." She endorses pleasurable activities as long as they cause no harm and both parties consent. She then qualifies with a remark about the dangers of anal sex due to a new disease soon to be called AIDS. Thus she seems to validate all consensual, non–disease transmitting sex games (92, 140–41, 186).

Her premises aside, she does not mean to endorse either swinging or promiscuity, for the 1980s were the era of President Reagan and "just say no" as national policy. Throughout *Good Sex*, Dr. Ruth modifies her premises with her teaching about relationships. Nine out of ten people, according to Dr. Ruth, need a relationship. Long-term relationships offer people qualitative differences over short ones. "Making love with a partner you have had for twenty years, who knows you better than anyone else, who has shared life's ups and downs with you, is a royal pleasure." The main problem in long-term relationships is maintaining sexual stimulation, and the remedy is variety. Sex, as she puts it, involves the mind as well as the body. Closeness, tenderness, and acceptance hold long-term relationships together. Ideally, "when your love mate is the person you like to talk to, the conversation becomes the marriage" (129–30, 132, 242, 354, 382–83).

Besides qualifying the hedonism of "different strokes for different folks" with a relationship criterion, she goes on to add one of guilt. Moral people feel guilty when they transgress. "There is guilt in some sexual activities just as there is in stealing, killing, and so on." Her examples include unwanted pregnancy, infecting another person with herpes, and cheating on a lover or spouse. She concludes that this capacity for guilt makes a person a moral being (380).

Women, according to Dr. Ruth, should take an active role in male arousal. "She can also diplomatically praise his penis and let him know how it arouses her; how she likes it, loves it, finds it noble, handsome, darling, a charming toy, etc." She echoes Comfort once again: "it is as if the penis has a life of its own and can hear the nice things being said about it" (56).

"Women owe it to themselves to have fulfilling orgasms. A woman must educate herself and her partner in how to give her pleasure." Dr. Ruth, however, does not value orgasms in themselves, for a penis is required. Her discussion of vibrators makes this clear. Men cannot duplicate, even with their fingers, the strong stimuli produced by a vibrator. As long as women can avoid getting addicted, however, vibrators serve as a pleasant variation on a theme. She ends this section on a permissive note. "There is no right way or wrong way to use a vibrator. Whatever feels good to you, feels good to you" (110–12).

Though she does not belabor the point, Dr. Ruth considers men sexually active, while women are mainly passive. She encourages role reversal, as does the entire *Joy* series. Men are not only active, but also "skilled love technicians." In her view, one partner, usually the woman, lies on her back and "takes it." Men take risks such as rejection, and women, according to Dr. Ruth, should do the same by occasionally taking the initiative (92, 133, 178–79, 185–86).

Dr. Ruth regards the missionary position as basic, but she nonjudgmentally endorses other possibilities. Exploring eros includes oral and anal sex, as long as both partners are comfortable with it. In this context, she encourages a move away from the idea that every sexual encounter should lead to ejaculation/orgasm. "Sex doesn't have to be only a penis in a vagina. Anything that works and doesn't hurt is worth trying a few times." Oral sex requires a natural, healthy attitude toward the body. Anal sex, as she notes, was formerly considered unnatural, but with adequate lubrication both partners will experience pleasure. Some men even prefer the tighter confines of the anus.

Am I normal? people ask. "Abnormal is a statistical concept. In a country with no cheesecake, a cheesecake addict is abnormal." Her analogy, perhaps especially drawn for New Yorkers, begs the question. Cheesecake is a relatively benign addiction. She does not invite us to consider more extreme sexual behaviors, though she remains willing to endorse rape fantasies. She ends her brief discussion by suggesting that "it is normal to wonder 'Am I normal?'" Given this, one might expect Dr. Ruth to be even more accepting of lesbians and gay men than Comfort and certainly Reuben. But a careful reading of her text suggests equivocation on this point (322).

Dr. Ruth devotes chapter 15 to gay sex. She emphasizes similarities between problems encountered by gays and straights. Young people, regardless of sexual orientation, tend to be promiscuous, and this easily leads to sexual boredom. She suggests that different sexual appetites cause problems for straight relationships as well as gay ones. Overall "if two consenting adults decide to have a homosexual encounter or relationship, whatever feels good between them should be acceptable." But our sexual maven, as in previous cases, will now qualify. Homosexual relationships are more difficult to maintain than heterosexual ones due to societal intolerance. Even if you live in a large city, it is best to act discreetly. Or at least do not come out until you are absolutely certain that you are not in a phase. Then you can be counted as a "soldier in the gay movement." Many people, she notes, go through a "homosexual phase."

Her example of Ray is illuminating. At the age of thirty-two, Ray had experienced sex only with men, but wanted to try being a heterosexual. Dr. Ruth told him to fantasize about men while having sex with a woman. It worked. Subsequent lessons from a female prostitute made him an accomplished lover, and Ray then discovered that he enjoyed heterosexual sex. Shortly after, he married and had two children. Though never unfaithful to his wife with another woman, Ray continued to have occasional liaisons with men. "But Ray was happy being a family man, and his lapses from fidelity grew fewer and further between." Ray, obviously, was not destined to be a soldier in the gay army, but once again Dr. Ruth changes her tone slightly at the end of this chapter. People who are confused will be happier when they find an identity that provides comfort. But what identity provides happiness for Ray besides family man? Since Ray continued liaisons with men, his identity seems to be more that of a bisexual than a heterosexual, or perhaps he should be considered a gay man with a family (217–31, 377).

Unlike Alex Comfort, Dr. Ruth emphasizes the side effects of birth control pills and prefers diaphragms and condoms. She rejects abortion as a form of birth control and terms it "contraceptive failure." Since one cannot hide herpes, a partner should disclose it. Otherwise she recommends silence about occasional infidelities such as Ray's. As is fitting for a work published in 1983, she notes the new incidence of Kaposi's sarcoma among gay men and links it, as was common at the time, to the number of one's partners and anal sex. She recommends caution regarding casual sex and warns of its perils.

> Even though I do believe there is greater happiness in sustained relationships, in not trying to go too long in life overemphasizing sex as just a physical pleasure, something to have with every stimulating person one meets, I do not feel glad that anyone suffers any of the misfortunes that can come to people through sex when it is not enjoyed cautiously, with common sense.

She goes on to reject the notion that diseases serve as punishments for sin. At least in *Good Sex*, relationships are a central norm, much more so than in the *Joy* series (191–200, 203–14).

Teen Sex and the Wisdom of Virgins

In 1985 Dr. Ruth, along with Dr. Nathan Kravetz, published *First Love: A Young People's Guide to Sexual Information.* The authors emphasize the importance of relationships and seek to discourage teenage sex. As befitting more conservative times, the book strikes a cautious note. "Just say no," both to drugs and sex, became a staple of political rhetoric, and the rise of Christian fundamentalism as a political force reintroduced the concept of sin into sexual rhetoric. Like Victorians, fundamentalists believe that God punishes sin in general and finds sexual sins especially heinous.

According to the authors, people have sex to procreate, to express love and unity, and to experience pleasure. Without significant elements of companionship, mutual support, and caring, love affairs become boring. Sex, contrary to much teenage belief, does not keep people together. In fact, Drs. Ruth and Kravetz suggest that the opposite is more likely true. Young people who are strong, self-reliant, and responsible enough to deal with the consequences of sex can make the decision as to when to first experience it. "No young teenager [however] is ready to make that decision." Delaying sex can actually bind two people together. To put it succinctly, "sex is part of love and marriage." Young people, however, need to know about sex so they can make real choices about their lives. Thus the need for a new book specifically addressed to them (Westheimer and Kravetz 1985, 11, 41–43, 45–46).

The authors enumerate the advantages for teenage virgins. When one has sex at a young age, the first time tends to be unpleasant and clumsy. It is qualitatively better if a girl waits. Then she does not have to deceive her parents or worry about herpes or pregnancy. Boys do not experience these fears, but are often too preoccupied to devote time to a sexual relationship. "He has his science-fair projects, his computer mania, his record collection, his sports." All a teenage boy really has time for is occasional masturbation. Of course, religion often plays a role. Drs. Ruth and Kravetz suggest that a young female virgin can be a good friend to her sexually active peers. "Often she knows more about periods, pregnancy, and steps to take when one is in trouble. . . . The virgin has the time to read up on things. And her cooler judgment often makes her the advisor to others." Drs. Ruth and Kravetz do not mention the reading habits of teenage boys. Yet we live in a world, as the authors acknowledge, in which sex before marriage remains widely accepted. Thus they reassure sexually experienced teenagers, foolhardy as they are, that they are still valuable human beings (47–50).

The authors use fear of pregnancy to reinforce their teaching about virginity. Contraception, for example, merely reduces the chance of pregnancy. The pill, however, is more effective than the authors acknowledge. They tell teenagers that until they are ready to deal with the consequences, they should avoid intercourse. For sexually active teenagers they recommend the use of a diaphragm or condom. The authors then use an analogy that summarizes their message. "Somebody hearing a hurricane warning will put out to sea in a canoe. I hope they at least wear a life jacket. Some people are going to have intercourse, some people are going to get pregnant, no matter what *anybody* says to them." Putting out to sea in a canoe even in a mere tropical storm invites death. Is intercourse with a diaphragm and/or a condom really comparable? Some teenagers might not think so. Drs. Ruth and Kravetz, however, are raising the hurricane warnings (69; italics in original).

Aggressiveness in teenage males aggravates the problem of teen sexuality. "Boys may want to 'do it,' and they will 'do it' *with* you. . . . You are no more than the equipment for 'doing it.' A kind of punching bag." Once it happens, you cannot become a virgin again. Girls need to learn to say no (104–6; italics in original).

So what is good sex for teenagers? Good sex, according to the authors, is enjoyable to both partners. It is a way to achieve mutual pleasure and closeness, but should occur within a relationship. "The most satisfactory sex is generally agreed to be between people who have a sustained relationship—who have been together for some time and feel secure in each other's company." Casual sex usually denies emotional closeness, and this definition of good sex excludes it. It does not, however, rule out all teenage liaisons, storm warnings aside (134–35).

Drs. Ruth and Kravetz warn against sexual abuse, and they emphasize what is now called stranger abuse. Rapists, as they explain it, act out anger, hate, and revenge. They do not place sexual assault in the context of patriarchy. They note that the idea of using brute force to get sex is not an ordinary man's idea. Susan Brownmiller, of course, would disagree and argue that sexual assault inheres in the system and becomes a means of social control like lynching in the segregated American South (Brownmiller 1976). The authors advise young women to avoid certain areas like office buildings after hours and, thus, verify Brownmiller's argument.

If rape becomes unavoidable, they advise young women, try to avoid getting hurt unnecessarily. Don't fight, go limp! (142–45).

Chapter 11, entitled "Gay and Straight," deals with lesbians and gay men. Drs. Ruth and Kravetz point out that many lesbians and gay men do not fit the cultural stereotypes and cannot easily be identified by dress and mannerisms. They note the decline of legally sanctioned harassment and observe that gay people have come to accept their sexual orientation as natural. Psychologists, according to Drs. Ruth and Kravetz, now recognize that the origins of homosexuality are much more complex than previously thought. The authors dispute the heterosexual/homosexual binary in a brief discussion of bisexuality. Some can perform only with one sex, others with both. They note that some gay men want to change and that many bisexuals—perhaps Ray is an example—live as heterosexuals due to moral and religious reasons as well as personal comfort levels (200–204).

If approached by an adult homosexual, a teenage male should simply reject any sexual overture. For teenagers who cannot stop worrying about their sexual orientation, they recommend counseling with a minister, doctor, school nurse, or any adult who is trusted. Overall, the authors send an equivocal message: it is all right to be lesbian or gay, but it may be only a phase. Don't rush to join the gay army (200–201).

Diamonds Are a Girl's Best Friend

In 1986 Dr. Ruth wrote *Dr. Ruth's Guide for Married Lovers*. This book clarifies her earlier positions and more explicitly restricts sex to relationships. In this work she moves further from Comfort's premises and explicitly embraces more traditional values.

The current trend, as Dr. Ruth sees it in 1986, is to divorce sex from marriage. Sex had become either a right or merely a pleasurable activity. She sees a need for a new manual that deals with sex within marriage and addresses youthful ignorance. This new manual also needs to take into account Kinsey, Masters and Johnson, and the 1960s sexual revolution. She thus produces a text for "the marrying kind of people" or at least those who seek a meaningful relationship, which she considers a kind of marriage. Regardless, she values monogamous relationships, mainly marriage in its legal sense, which provides for safety, comfort, and pleasure. She then goes on to defend marriage (Westheimer 1986, 2–3, 48–49).

Marriage satisfies adult needs for closeness and sex. It puts sex on a "safe, sane, protected, regular basis. It's like three square meals a day, instead of once in a while if you get lucky." A loving marriage promises sexual bliss. Dr. Ruth, then, distinguishes between marriage and meaningful relationships. As she sees it, the latter term is overly broad and covers her relationships with a variety of people: newspaper vendors, students, and clients, as well as her husband. Overall she prefers "marriage," "a warm, rich, strong word for the union of two people," to the phrase "living together in a stable relationship." She does think of the latter group as married, even if not legally bound together (51).

In a further move away from the *Joy of Sex* series and its delight in sex as a peak experience, Dr. Ruth suggests that sex should not become all-consuming. Sex is not, after all, a religion. "Sex has its time and place, and living for sex alone is not good living and really quite bad for sex." Dr. Ruth teaches that "each person should believe that this creation is here for his or her personal pleasure, avoiding harm to oneself as to others." Sex, in her view, is bound up with spirituality. People are born with spiritual cravings, but not spiritual knowledge. Parents and teachers should supply the latter, but unfortunately many do not. Though she defines herself as a "spiritual pluralist," "there is an inescapable morality to be taught with good sex education. Be responsible. Be loving. Be considerate. Avoid harm to yourself and to others." Dr. Ruth, as her views mature, breaks from the *Joy of Sex* series in that she believes sex is part of a broader spirituality and a general reverence for life. It is not self-sufficient as a subjective "peak experience" (13–14, 59–60).

Dr. Ruth's erotic fantasy-land, like that of Comfort, is amoral and permissive. "In the imagination that is linked with sexual response there is no morality; things are permitted, are harmless, that have very definite drawbacks in the world of reality. Incest, sex with the very young, sex with crazy funky strangers." As long as you do not use illegal and frightening fantasies exclusively, you have nothing to worry about. The forbidden, after all, can spark excitement. Dr. Ruth later notes that aggression is not all bad and that men do try to overwhelm women, though they usually employ indirect means such as charm and gifts. Women, in this sense, are fortresses to be conquered, and teenage males prove especially willing to go once more into the breech (139).

Genitalia belong mutually to both partners. Each one grants the other equity in their body. Comfort in the *Joy of Sex* series grants that women for a moment can share a penis, but it remains essential to male identity and the root of male power. In fact, the penis is another "person" during intercourse. Dr. Ruth, on the other hand, is much more democratic on penis ownership. Then again, she is one of the few female authors of a marriage manual. Though bodies are shared property like a house, each person retains the right to say no (128–29, 132).

Dr. Ruth clearly teaches and emphasizes that orgasms depend on the clitoris. Orgasm results from direct stimulation of the clitoris or penile penetration. In indirect stimulation the penis or some substitute for it serves as an enhancer. A majority of women, however, do not experience orgasm from vaginal intercourse. Since Dr. Ruth, like her predecessors, wishes to valorize penetrative intercourse, she downplays the importance of orgasm. She considers orgasm "overemphasized" and suggests that readers consider the situation of a beautiful woman who cannot have one. Dr. Ruth lists potential compensations: "Wherever she goes men fall all over themselves to help. Headwaiters, stewards on cruise ships, personnel managers where she looks for work all jump to help the pretty woman. If she is a TV star, she has money, jewels for thieves to steal, luxury cars that cost a fortune to keep up. . . . She has all that!" To put it more succinctly: "So the earth doesn't move for her! Who needs it. If she wants the earth to move she can live in Los Angeles." Besides material compensations, Dr. Ruth suggests that physical closeness is enjoyable in itself. Though women are "entitled" to orgasms, fixating on them can hinder good sex. But good sex for whom? Our sexual mensch has supplied another equivocal message. Diamonds can be a girl's best friend; forget orgasms—few women have them anyway. Her compensations consist of a compendium of traditional feminine things reflecting prettiness, what Brownmiller terms the feminine (Westheimer 1986, 97–99, 209–10, 219; Brownmiller 1984 as updated by Wolf 1991).

Women, according to Dr. Ruth, are trapped in a cul-de-sac. Most women, as previously remarked, do not experience orgasms from vaginal intercourse. If they fake one, they cannot then ask their husbands for help after they ejaculate. If women remain honest to their experience and do not pretend, they are "turning the thermostat down and chilling the room." Women have to find their own way through this dilemma. Some of these ways include vibrators and cucumbers and an assortment of other things. Dr. Ruth emphasizes that Kegel exercises focused on the puboccocygeus—adjacent to the vagina—can enhance stimulations that lead to orgasm. On the whole, clitoral stimulation is more easily accomplished in ways other than penile penetration. At best, then, women can increase the likelihood of orgasm from penetration, but the reality is that most will not experience it (98, 216–18).

If the *Joy of Sex* series stands for sexual openness, Dr. Ruth's *Guide for Married Lovers* advocates sexual secrets. Dr. Ruth believes that married lovers should be open to each other about their wants, needs, and feelings, but not about infidelities. People should be silent about their sexual histories. "If you slip and commit an infidelity, that is yours to swallow and digest and do not burden your loving partner with it if it can be avoided." Since one cannot slip past the infectious phase of herpes, one should inform one's partner. Over time, however, as a relationship matures, fewer pretenses are necessary. Then, for example, a wife can reveal that she has been faking orgasms. Relationships, especially the married ones that Dr. Ruth so values, can be built on sexual secrets like that of Ray (55, 231–32).

Good Sex during an Epidemic

In 1992 Dr. Ruth published *Dr. Ruth's Guide to Safer Sex: Exciting, Sensible Directions for the 90s*, which is directed primarily to heterosexuals. She addresses sexually transmitted diseases in general, as well as AIDS, noting that abstinence—a concept foreign to Comfort, Silverstein, White, and Picano—and mutual monogamy provide the only forms of truly safe sex. As she has done in her other works, she calls attention to herpes. Thirty million Americans have it, and there are five hundred thousand new infections every year (Westheimer 1992, 5, 13–15, 33–34, 41).

Safer sex can be terrific sex! It directs our attention away from an exclusive focus on penetration. "For too long, we have been told, explicitly and implicitly, that some kind of *penetration* is the only goal of sex, as if it were a form of drilling." This, of course, contradicts the advice she gives in her *Guide for Married Lovers*. She suggests the term "outercourse," because traditional foreplay now has become an end in itself. Though traditional moral and religious teachings still discourage masturbation, AIDS makes it more acceptable. The imagination, after all, forbids nothing, and the brain is the most powerful sex organ. She now adds zucchini to cucumbers on her list of penis substitutes, and once again recommends exercising the puboccocygeus. She emphasizes abstinence for teenagers once again, since for the most part they cannot handle the emotions stirred up by sexual intimacy (85–86, 98, 102, 105, 110–11, 134; italics in original).

Dr. Ruth does not deal with the politics of AIDS. She does criticize President Bush for his lack of leadership and disapproves of his comment that AIDS is a disease of choice that will not be stopped by the distribution of free condoms. Overall, Dr. Ruth ignores the political context of what is a politicized epidemic (10, 26; Melody 1994a).

Penis Worship

In 1993 Dr. Ruth published *The Art of Arousal*. This work mainly uses Western works of art as well as artifacts from other cultures to depict arousal and the various stages of intercourse. It is her much more genteel version of the explicit drawings and photographs in the *Joy of Sex* series. She does, however, clarify one of her earlier comments. She explicitly notes the historical linkage of the penis with power and virility and notes that men expect women to worship their penises. She goes on to add that women are indifferent and that many of them do not enjoy fellatio (Westheimer 1993, 100). In *Good Sex*, however, she advised women to praise their partner's penis and tell it how wonderful it is. "It is as if the penis has a life of its own and can hear the nice things being said about it."

Dr. Ruth's Evolving Views

In the 1960s American culture evolved to allow more sexual freedom. The availability of the birth control pill in 1960 as well as the conquest of most sexually transmitted diseases through the antibiotic revolution seemed to open the possibility of more erotic gratification. Traditional religious teachings came under assault by advocates of a genteel (and later a more raunchy) hedonism. Supreme Court obscenity rulings allowed much more explicit literature to be sold openly. Court rulings that allowed Americans access to *Lady Chatterley's Lover* were soon extended by sexual entrepreneurs. *Playboy* magazine, scandalous in the 1950s but genteel erotica today, celebrated this new sexual glasnost. Sex, as *Playboy* and its countless imitators depicted it, was a recreational activity, an adults-only sandbox. The American landscape quickly became saturated with XXX bookstores, massage parlors, and swinger's clubs.

The 1960s gave us not only a popular revolt against the Vietnam War, but also a cultural one against the conventional values of the 1950s. Allen Ginsberg's "Howl" captures the angst of the era. According to Ginsberg and other Beats, the values of the 1950s were as shallow and deceptive as the sitcoms that celebrated them. They suffocated the human spirit. Later, members of the antiwar movement incorporated this cultural critique into their political one, and "free sex" became a political claim. Sexual repression came to be viewed as a denial of human freedom and fulfillment. Dr. Ruth, as her views evolve, clearly does not approve.

Dr. Ruth writes explicitly in reaction to this eruption of sexual license. Within the context of providing sexual knowledge, Dr. Ruth structures her advice in terms of an implicit call for more repression. Her views grow more traditional as time passes. She begins with the premises of the *Joy of Sex* but moves slowly toward endorsing sex only in relationships that lead toward marriage. Like Reuben and Comfort, she is also writing popular works and seeks to communicate to a large audience. Many of her readers, regardless of their marital status, had probably come to think of sexual pleasure as a right. On one hand, her books provide practical information and seem to endorse sexual exploration among the unmarried. On the other, her early equivocal messages as well as her later writings suggest that sexual intimacy should be restricted to marriage in its legally defined sense. By offering noncritical readers practical advice together with messages that ostensibly appeal to their preconceptions, she can try to achieve her conservative educational goals and still write best-sellers. She might even convince some of her readers that the sexual revolution is over. On the other hand, Dr. Ruth may merely be inconsistent.

Her earliest work focuses on good sex. A careful reading of the text qualifies this to mean sex within relationships or marriage. Her later works make this linkage explicit. She values relationships of long duration for their security, among other things, and suggests that guilt awaits those who transgress. She also notes that people who have many sexual contacts are immature. She teaches that teenagers should wait before exploring penetrative sex, because they are not ready to deal with the emotional firestorms that result. Yet in a mixed message that is also practical, Dr. Ruth tells teenagers that if they are mature enough in their own estimation, then the decision is theirs. She suggests that teenage women remain "technical virgins," that is, engage in everything but penetration.

She reinforces her restrictive teaching with fear of disease as well as pregnancy. To make her point, Dr. Ruth discounts the effectiveness of birth control pills. Virginal teenage women have time to read books and can serve a vital function in giving advice to their sexually active peers. They should tell their peers to return to "technical virgin" status. Relationships for adults provide a "safe, sane, protected, regular basis" for sex, but Dr. Ruth really means marriage in the legal sense. She rejects the possibilities represented by the term "meaningful relationship" as overly broad and provides an ill-fitting analogy. She claims that the term refers to her relationship with her students and newspaper vendor as well as her husband. Besides defying common usage, her analogy suggests a curious understanding of her relationship with newspaper vendors, not to mention her students. Students typically distinguish between their intimate relationships and those they have with even the most inspiring faculty member. Dr. Ruth rejects the view that sex is merely fun or that it can be justified as recreation or a peak experience. In this assertion, she moves farthest from the *Joy of Sex* series. Dr. Ruth never provides reasons for her preference for marriage as opposed to stable long-term relationships. She also never notes America's evolving family structure. She prefers the traditional marriage commitment and sees sexual boredom as its biggest problem. Her books suggest that sexual variety provides the spice in marriage.

Dr. Ruth also maintains that married partners' genitalia are joint property. Upon marriage, in other words, one acquires an equitable property interest in the genitalia of one's partner, though the partner retains the right to say no to sexual overtures. Just as the house is joint property, so are the penis and vagina. Though she rejects Comfort's premises as her own views mature, she still embraces his view of genitalia as property, but she emphasizes that the penis is a joint possession. In her earlier work, the penis has a life of its own, and women should talk to it—saying only nice things, of course.

Dr. Ruth, like her predecessors, implicitly endorses phallocracy. Women should "take it" in intercourse. Her approval of "taking it," with its implicit reference to power and force, coincides with her endorsement of playing rape as well as the other violent sexual fantasies she endorses. Overall, she suggests the typical patriarchal view: the penis symbolizes power and dominance, and women are mainly acted upon sexually. They "take it." For the most part, Dr. Ruth devalues orgasm—except for her first book in 1983. At one point she even suggests that material rewards can substitute. She also advises women to be prudent when telling their husbands that they have not achieved orgasm. Many women just are not orgasmic in traditional intercourse. Faking it just might be the better solution until the relationship goes on for a while. Though good sex does not require orgasm, a penis certainly is needed. Vibrators, not to mention produce, can certainly make a woman achieve orgasm, but they also cause strong sensations that no man can equal. If women get addicted to these strong stimulations, they may come to view men as inadequate and even turn away from marriage. In her book on safer sex, however, Dr. Ruth gravitates toward a different understanding. She suggests that foreplay, now termed "outercourse," serves as the main event and that the focus on vaginal penetration proves medically dangerous. She compares penetration to drilling. Since most women do not achieve orgasm through vaginal intercourse anyway, this proves no great loss. Men, however, might disagree.

Dr. Ruth is suspicious of lesbians and gay men. Throughout her corpus she emphasizes that homosexual activities can be only a phase, even for someone in their thirties like Ray. She remains uncomfortable about "coming out" and joining the gay army. In her view, this particular army does not offer discharges. Ray, by implication, could more easily deal with his confusion by remaining discreet or "closeted." She endorses Ray's marriage and family, even though Ray still has sex with men on occasion. In other words, traditional marriage and family life are desirable even if built on fraud and infidelity. False heterosexual intimacy is preferable to whatever Ray experienced before his marriage. Dr. Ruth seems to consider gay men as living in arrested development, since they seek so many sexual encounters. They are like teenage males. Ray, on the other hand, did seek help and advice. This suggests that sex therapists like Dr. Ruth should direct unhappy gay men or bisexuals toward heterosexual marriage and family life. The only alternative she sees is joining the gay army—a critical turning point according to *The Joy of Gay Sex*. Dr. Ruth does acknowledge, however, that she knows happy lesbian and gay couples. Though she is not really sympathetic to lesbian and gay relationships, she does proffer her standard norms: be responsible, be considerate, and avoid harm to oneself and others.

Her approach to safer sex rests on the assumption of psychological quarantine. Her work, intended for heterosexuals, suggests avoiding intimate behavior with members of "risk groups" and limiting one's sexual contacts. She assumes, of course, that the HIV virus remains limited to these risk groups and that one can avoid contact with them. The history of AIDS shows that this is not the case. Some gay men—perhaps Ray is an example—are married, and intravenous drug users (IVDUs), mainly heterosexual, have intercourse with women who work as prostitutes. The incidence of AIDS has been spreading rapidly beyond "risk groups." None of Dr. Ruth's advice matters, however, if the one person you are having intercourse with is infected with HIV, and neither knows it. She avoids the issue of HIV testing. Her toleration of occasional infidelities and sexual secrets only compounds this problem. Is Ray, for example, putting his wife at risk? Since herpes cannot be hidden in its infectious stage, Dr. Ruth excludes it as a sexual secret. AIDS, however, can remain hidden for years, but Dr. Ruth does not discuss the issue.

Dr. Ruth, as previously remarked, values the traditional marriage relationship while she makes concessions for occasional infidelities. She generally values stability and intimacy over the long term, even though she accepts Alex Comfort's metaphysics of sexual solipsism. Intertwined lovers certainly have a kind of physical unity, but are really engaging different projections and fantasies that make all intercourse a ballet of strangers and shadows. Since all physical and spiritual intimacy is a pretense in a way, Ray does not present a unique example.

Sexual Solipsism

"Hello, this is Dr. Ruth Westheimer. You're on the air. Do you have a sexual problem?"

"I don't think so, but you might."

"Well, how can I help you?"

"In one of your books you tell women to avoid places where they might be in danger of sexual assault. Doesn't this make it hard for women to hold down jobs where they have to work late? How can a lawyer like Marsha Clark in the O. J. case avoid working late in downtown Los Angeles?"

"You aren't asking a question appropriate for this show, but I'll answer anyway. When I wrote that I was just suggesting common sense."

"But you never acknowledge that sexual assault is a means of keeping women out of public life and punishing those who step outside permitted roles."

"This is not my concern."

"You also suggest that material rewards can compensate women for a lack of sexual fulfillment. Doesn't this deny much of feminist thought since the 1960s? Besides, what about women who are trapped by economic necessity in battering relationships? Do you see your work as reinforcing social inequality between men and women?"

"Of course not! But I didn't write those books for scholars or feminists. The other lines are lighting up so I have to move on. Hello, this is Dr. Ruth Westheimer. You're on the air."

"Hello, Dr. Ruth, my name's Frank. I'm seventeen and only have had sex with other guys. I'm gay, but I'd like to try it with a woman once, but I'm scared to try."

"That's a good question, Frank. Try fantasizing about men when you begin foreplay with a woman. Once you have a good erection, then try penetration. But take things slowly. If you have a good experience, come into my office and we'll talk about it. Joining ACT-UP (AIDS Coalition to Unleash Power, a national activist group) or Queer Nation might be a bit premature for you."

"I really would only be doing it to please my parents and act normal. I'm tired of getting beaten up at school, and I really want to have kids. Will any state let me adopt? Wouldn't I be better off at that special school for gay kids in midtown New York? Do you know anything about it?"

"I don't think any state would let you adopt, but you need to ask a lawyer. Try what I recommended, then get an appointment. Adolescent experimentation is perfectly normal."

"Hello, this is Dr. Ruth Westheimer. You're on the air."

"But Dr. Ruth, since all intimate behavior consists of projections and fantasies, does gender matter much when Frank has sex? Remember what you wrote about vibrators?"

"You again. Where'd you get these ideas about me? Call Howard Stern. He likes to talk about vibrators."

"Hello! Hello! This is Dr. Westheimer. You're on the air."

"Dr. Ruth, I've got a problem. I've stayed in this marriage for years, took care of the kids, helped build his career, and now I'm left with nothing. I've never even had an orgasm. Now he's found a younger woman and wants a divorce. He's hidden all the money and jewelry. He's been having affairs for years, and I never figured it out. What should I do?"

"You need counseling; call for an appointment."

"Hello, this is Dr. Ruth Westheimer. You're on the air."

"Dr. Ruth, it's Ray. It's been a long time, about four years now."

"Hello, Ray. How's your family?"

"Things aren't so good right now."

"Why not, Ray? You were doing wonderfully."

"I've got AIDS and gave it to my wife. She left me and took the kids. She said I betrayed her by having sex with men and never telling her anything. She says I'll never see my kids again. I don't know what to do. My brother cheated with his sister-in-law and like you said he never told and nothing happened to him. Maybe I should have stayed gay and never had kids."

"I'm sad to hear that, Ray. Call my number and get an appointment."

"Hello, this is Dr. Ruth Westheimer. You're on the air . . ." (Brownmiller 1976; MacKinnon 1989, 126–54; 1993, 6, 13, 18, 31).

And Now Sex for Dummies

Dr. Ruth published *Sex for Dummies* in 1995. In this book she brings together many of her earlier themes and writes now from a position of cultural authority. The cover, for example, contains a blurb from *Time* magazine: "Her image is synonymous with sex." The book includes a flyleaf, without page numbers, that can be taken out and posted on a bulletin board, a bedroom door, or even a refrigerator. It includes specific recommendations under six general categories: be loving, be romantic, be surprising, and on the opposite side, be naughty, be spontaneous, be playful. The introduction, as is usual for this genre, includes the conventional observation that sexual misinformation and confusion still abound. Dr. Ruth also notes that old norms have fallen apart, resulting in millions of unwanted pregnancies and single-parent families. Millions more have sexually transmitted diseases. This, she notes, was predictable.

Unlike her earlier books, this volume states her presuppositions directly. She calls herself "old-fashioned" and a "square," and she affirms her belief in God, marriage, and morality. Since she cannot mandate how people act, she will instruct her readers how to enjoy sex safely. Her lessons, if taken to heart, will also reduce unwanted pregnancies as well as sexually transmitted diseases. She encourages readers to establish relationships before sex, though she actually prefers that they wait until marriage. She disapproves of one-night stands, but will supply the appropriate information to keep her readers safe (Westheimer 1995, 4–5).

Dr. Ruth now explicitly links sex to reproduction. Intercourse is "directly related to procreation, propagation, continuing the species, pregnancy, MAKING BABIES!" She recommends abstinence for those who do not intend to procreate. Though contraception allows sex and "making babies" to be separated, the evolutionary purpose of sex remains reproduction. In a chapter addressed to teenagers, she confronts them with their duty as she perceives it. "Part of the job of each new generation is to climb on the shoulders of those who have passed before them and take our civilization one step higher. It's called progress." Today's teenagers face changed circumstances such as the pill and AIDS, but, as she notes, no one has ever died from sexual abstinence (9, 24, 40, 47, 54; uppercase in original).

Dr. Ruth still disapproves of one-night stands. She now argues that sexually transmitted diseases necessitate relationships as a matter of prudence. When it comes to sexually transmitted diseases, Dr. Ruth posits an almost infinite regression. "Joining you . . . is every other person that person has slept with, as well as the partners of their partners. . . . That could easily amount to several hundred people!" She rejects the idea that strangers can really enjoy safer sex and designates this as merely a "potential" for safer sex, provided that all the precautions are taken. Today only "fools" consider scoring an indicator of sexual prowess. "Relying on condoms *can* be enough of a safeguard, but only if you really know the person with whom you're about to have sex." Even oral sex with a condom can be risky. "You can perform oral sex on a man (fellatio) while he's wearing a condom, and provided that you're careful not to bite through the latex, that should be a safer form of sex" (59, 60, 71, 77; italics in original).

Following her more explicit traditional approach in this volume, Dr. Ruth, like the late Victorians, teaches that sexual pleasure functions merely as a lure, not an end in itself. Acknowledging that we live in a post–birth control pill era, she notes that some think this is not a good thing. She then refers to religious leaders and abruptly switches the subject back to one-night stands. She declines, as she puts it, to debate the morality of the sexual revolution. Dr. Ruth once again maintains that sex in a "committed relationship" is better than a one-night stand, but she does not elaborate. Later she defines commitment in terms of an individual's willingness to put their marriage first. Though she equivocates on birth control, she supports abortion and hopes to see the end of unintended pregnancies. She then endorses the use of condoms not as a birth control technique, but rather as a means of protection against sexually transmitted diseases. "If I could snap my fingers and make AIDS and all the other STDs out there disappear I would." Though Dr. Ruth stresses the need for financial resources for single mothers, she really does not approve (78, 80, 82, 96, 103, 112).

Marriage, courtship, and commitment are not "totally dead." One day, she speculates, children might be manufactured, which would destroy the core reason for marriage. Marriage right now still provides the best environment for rearing children. At this point *Sex for Dummies* becomes part of the defense of marriage literature reminiscent of the late 1920s. Dr. Ruth prefers that people wait until marriage to experience sex. She does not expect her readers to do this, however, so she recommends making the first time a moment to treasure. Thus marriage remains best, relationships are a distant second, while one-night stands come in a very distant third (112, 145–47).

Dr. Ruth, as previously remarked, notes the contemporary problems with marriage. Divorce rates have risen and children no longer cement a marriage together. The modern world also surrounds people with temptations. AIDS, however, changes the equation, and married couples now work harder on their relationships. Married couples need romance, which is not the same as sex. Variety helps as well as taking an active role in lovemaking. Take some risks! (195, 201–4).

Dr. Ruth lays out her mixed feelings about homosexuality more fully in this volume. At times she seems fully supportive, at others reluctant. Homosexuality, as she notes, has existed as long as recorded history, but no one knows the real causes. It is true, however, that homosexuality is not a matter of choice. Since homosexuals do not choose to be the way they are, they should be treated equally. Though aware of the traditional biblical injunctions taken to condemn homosexuality, she notes that we all share the same world. Religious groups have no right to proscribe behavior through law.

> Sexual practices between gay men and women when done safely, do no one any harm. Although gay sexuality may not fit the mold used by most people, I believe that we shouldn't criticize gays for behavior over which they may really have no control, and which doesn't harm anyone anyway. Nobody is forcing anyone to be gay, and neither should anyone force someone not to be gay.

She recommends that heterosexuals remain open-minded. Homosexuals, like heterosexuals, should establish a relationship before sex and certainly should engage in safer sex (229).

How does one know if one is a homosexual? According to Dr. Ruth, homosexuals can be aroused only by thinking about members of their own sex. Yet teenagers, as she has written before, often have fantasies about members of their own sex. It's normal, nothing to worry about. Are teenagers, then, in a naturally bisexual stage? She does not discuss bisexuality, or how it complicates the binary she is defending. Though she dismisses Freud on the vaginal orgasm, she does accept the concept that individuals have a true sex that corresponds to identity. Even if a person never engages in gay sex, they may still be essentially lesbian or gay after all. She goes on to list male homosexual activities according to their safety, recommends oral sex with condoms, but drops the warning about biting it. Unlike homosexual men, lesbians tend to be more couple-oriented, and she goes on to list common practices. Lesbians report experiencing more orgasms than heterosexual women.

What does "coming out" mean in the face of all this? "Coming out" at work presents many difficulties. Many lesbians and gay men, as she notes, remain careful about this. Some employers discriminate based on their perception of homosexuality, a fear of AIDS, or the possible reactions of other employees. She does not note that some states and quite a few cities prohibit job discrimination based on sexual orientation. Dr. Ruth adds that discrimination as well as internalized feelings of guilt or inadequacy are never easy to deal with, and she considers this a steep price to pay for admitting one's true identity. Homosexuals in Dr. Ruth's view, especially those fighting in the gay army, are never really happy (227–38).

Though anything goes in fantasies, actually engaging in "deviant sexual behavior" remains problematic. She does not, however, define deviance. Her experience suggests that the end results do not turn out well. Extreme sex, for example, can tear a couple apart. Sex with its powerful feelings needs to be controlled. "Incurable, deadly diseases [AIDS] lie just around the corner." Dr. Ruth suggests the metaphor of a fence with a knothole in it. It is all right to peek through the hole in the fence, but "don't try to climb over it. That fence is there for a good reason, and you should heed the warnings to keep out" (254).

Cybersex represents a relatively new topic in this genre. Just be careful to protect your children and keep track of your downloading time, since cybersex can take a long time and be very expensive. Virtual sex is truly safe, but Dr. Ruth does not know how this will compare to the real thing as more and more people try it. Phone sex is surely safe, but Dr.

Ruth wonders whether children are adequately shielded from access. Videos are preferable to prostitutes and one-night stands, and they can also provide spice for couples. Adultery (Dr. Ruth calls it cheating) is foolish in an era of deadly sexually transmitted diseases. She applauds the efforts of couples to have better relationships, but wishes that better knowledge about good sex sparked it rather than fear of AIDS. Dr. Ruth, however, does use fear of deadly diseases to support her case for monogamy and chastity. Due to changes brought about by the pill, wife swapping was popular in the 1960s and 1970s, but this practice led to jealousy and was not very good for women (254–60, 263–68).

Later in *Sex for Dummies* Dr. Ruth once again announces the end of the sexual revolution. There are now more than thirty sexually transmitted diseases, a "sexual invasion," and one out of four people between fifteen and fifty-five will catch one or more of them. The last-ditch cure for chancroid, for example, is amputation of the penis. Like Silverstein and Picano, she does not mention that medical doctors have a treatment for herpes. Condoms do break. Try a relationship first, it's much safer. Not all of her readers, however, will put prudence ahead of passion. "I don't try to scare people away from having sex. Instead, I want to make sure you have the best possible sex. But an integral part of great sex is healthy sex, protected sex" (271, 273, 276–77, 282, 284).

In the latter part of the text Dr. Ruth elaborates on her defense of marriage and broadens its purpose. People get married, in her view, to have sex as well as a relationship. Marriage also includes companionship and children as well as emotional and financial support. Sex remains a major part of the arrangement. Sexual laws, as she articulates it, developed originally from moral codes, and Dr. Ruth links these to evolutionary necessity. Ages ago, to have a child without a male protector probably meant death for mother and child. While acknowledging that some of these laws are archaic, she supports those penalizing child abuse and incest and requiring consent for marriage. She maintains that sex education should include morality. She once again demurs on date rape, and warns women about climbing into bed naked. "If you get a man too excited, he may not be able to control himself." Prostitution should be made legal and pornography can serve as an outlet for sexual energy. She calls for prohibiting sex videos with violence, children, or animals. Dr. Ruth lists warning signs of sexual abuse in children, but also suggests that America has gone too far trying to uncover it (315–16, 319–20, 323–26, 331–32).

Toward the end of the volume, in a subsection entitled "The More I

Score, the More Pleasure I'll Have," Dr. Ruth addresses promiscuity once again. She reiterates her very conditional acceptance of one-night stands. For some people, the chemistry proves very strong and the opportunity is there. Be fully aware of the risks and protect yourself. "Then a one-night stand may be something that you indulge in once or maybe twice." Some people, however, prefer a series of casual liaisons. For them it remains a matter of quantity, not quality. She terms the idea that more is better "dumb, dumb, and dumb." In the 1990s AIDS and other sexually transmitted diseases mean that multiplying partners also multiplies risks. Safe sex, per se, does not exist; at best it can be merely safer. Every time you have sex, you change the odds. Dr. Ruth believes that people engaging in casual sex are probably doing medically risky things anyway. She reminds women that pregnancy does happen, and then goes on to argue that one-night stands do not provide the best sex. Intimacy, shared feelings, and romance are what makes sex better than masturbating. And what happens the next morning? "Putting another notch on your bedpost is not as satisfying as exchanging the full range of emotions that pass between two people who are making love." Just say no to casual sex and work on developing a relationship (346–47, 353–57).

Defending Marriage

Dr. Ruth's embrace of traditional moral teachings becomes most evident in *Sex for Dummies*. She endorses marriage as the best situation for raising children and grudgingly accepts some nonmarital relationships that include sex. She suggests that couples in a relationship marry once they decide to have children. Dr. Ruth tolerates one-night stands as long as they are extremely infrequent, perhaps once or twice in a lifetime. Like the later Victorians, she deploys fear of disease, especially AIDS, to make her point.

Traditional values have "disintegrated," but Dr. Ruth does not intend to write a work of moral theology. She argues that marriage supplies better sex for couples, and she has to make her case in terms that will persuade her large, popular audience. Like Binkley and Binkley in the 1920s, Dr. Ruth could advocate adapting the institution to changed times. Even as early as the 1920s, Binkley and Binkley saw that birth control necessitated change. The birth control pill as well as changing social norms in the 1960s and 1970s reinforce the prescience of their original observation. Wile and Winn note the new freedom afforded women in their day and advocate that marriage focus more on the relationship between the partners. Groves, on the other hand, notes that birth control has led to the dominance of a pleasure philosophy and prophesies the separation of sex from intimacy. Alex Comfort, of course, makes Groves a true prophet. Dr. Ruth agrees with Groves's diagnosis of the problem, but adopts a different tack. She questions the primacy of pleasure and suggests that marriage, if not long-term relationships, provides for more of it. She reasserts in her later work that marriage exists for "making babies"—a linkage that her predecessors in the 1920s considered sundered. This accounts for her emphasis on condoms as a means of preventing disease transmission rather than pregnancy as well as her lack of enthusiasm for the pill.

Dr. Ruth argues that in a relationship partners know how to please one another better. She never provides reasons why this is so or directly confronts the hedonistic assertions of the entire *Joy of Sex* series that have largely permeated American culture. As Alex Comfort and his imitators note, sometimes sex with strangers is better precisely because the other person is mysterious, strange, and different. In this erotic interplay, a person might even discover a new range of activities, new joys, and new pleasures. Her contention about the embarrassment of waking beside someone whose name you have forgotten is an observation, however true, rather than an argument. Most of her discussion of this issue focuses on the risk of sexually transmitted diseases.

Dr. Ruth's defense of marriage turns on a strategy deployed by the late Victorians. America is in the midst of a "sexual invasion"; life itself is at stake due to the AIDS epidemic. Heterosexuals, as she reminds her readers, can catch this horrific disease. Her approach thus turns on the health risk of casual liaisons. Can one have safer sex, whether oral or vaginal, with condoms? Dr. Ruth maintains that condoms provide for safer sex only when you know the other person. This, of course, implies a relationship and fits with her infinite regression view of sexually transmitted diseases. Though this is true of HIV transmission, it does not hold for many other sexually transmitted diseases. The antibiotic revolution did happen. Many sexually transmitted diseases can be treated and even cured, and thus the infinite regression is broken. Being in a relationship does not guarantee safety, as many gay men found out to their horror early in the AIDS epidemic. If your sexual partner is infected with HIV, unsafe sex is sexual roulette. If a condom breaks, there exists a very real possibility of infection. If your partner is not infected with HIV or other sexually transmitted diseases, then safer sex is positively safe. The safety, in other words, does not depend on how well one knows the other person, though this might help, but on whether or not the other person has a sexually transmitted disease. This undermines the major thrust of Dr. Ruth's argument for relationships. She deploys the full horrors of sexually transmitted diseases, much as the late Victorians used a similar rhetoric to discourage masturbation and prostitution. These diseases promise pain, torment, and sterility, even amputation of the penis. Sexually transmitted diseases in Dr. Ruth's work are not merely a medical matter. They serve a moral agenda. While, Comfort, Silverstein, and Picano understate risk, Dr. Ruth emphasizes it (282, 284).

As Dr. Ruth notes, the norms of the 1960s sexual revolution now inform American culture. The core issue is pleasure. In agreement with the late Victorians, Dr. Ruth teaches that the myriad of pleasures associated with sex serve as an inducement to engage in the activity whose basic purpose is procreation. When she makes this assertion she notes that not everyone would agree, refers to unnamed religious leaders, and then quickly switches the subject to a critique of one-night stands. Whether one-night stands are moral or immoral does not support the case that sexual pleasure is incidental to the act itself, whose real purpose is procreation.

Her homophobia, however implicit, supports this tack. When her books are compared to *The New Joy of Gay Sex*, the judgmental nature of her work stands out. Silverstein and Picano tolerate almost everything, both within and outside relationships, while Dr. Ruth endorses almost nothing outside marriage. Yet what does Dr. Ruth have to say to a teenager who has not "come out"? She knows that the suicide rate for lesbian and gay teenagers remains higher than that for their age cohort (232). Dr. Ruth, however, offers few words of encouragement. She presents a world full of sexually transmitted diseases, especially AIDS, as well as one brimming with discrimination. Dr. Ruth neglects to mention that 165 counties and cities and 11 states prohibit discrimination based on sexual orientation. She fails to note domestic partnership laws as well as the fact that many companies, now including Disney, recognize such relationships ("Law" 1997). She subtly suggests remaining in the closet (Westheimer 1995, 233). Ann Landers, writing for a similar audience, handles the situation differently. When advising a suicidal gay teenager, she begins by noting that about 10 percent of the population consists of lesbians and gay men, and then goes on to recognize their contributions to society, from Michelangelo to Freddie Mercury. Landers notes that people are born this way and then recommends counseling. Dr. Ruth, in contrast, remains terribly aloof; she really does not approve. This coincides with her vague references to "deviant sexual behavior." Since lesbians and gay men do not reproduce—at least in the traditional sense—their only purpose in having sex must be pleasure or relationship building. And this, according to our sexual maven, defies evolution and limits the onward march of progress. Bisexuals who also transgress the gender binary do not even rate a mention (393; Landers 1997).

10

On Penetrative Power

As marriage manuals evolve from the domestic advice literature, medical doctors slowly eclipse the preeminent role of the clergy. In
the late nineteenth century, however, the views of medical writers do not
differ all that much. Typically, late Victorian medical doctors conflate theology, natural philosophy, and science. A shared Christian theology serves
as a common denominator in these works. Science reinforces belief, it certainly does not challenge it. The Bible and St. Paul are authoritative on
these matters as much as, if not more than, any medical authority. Thus
God, nature, and science support the late Victorian sexual regime.

In the early twentieth century theological reasoning mainly falls away in
the literature, but authors still value penetrative vaginal intercourse within
marriage for the purpose of reproduction. This is mainly justified by medical science or psychiatry. Margaret Sanger, however, spills the birth control secret early in the century, and this causes a rupture in the literature.
Some authors, like Van de Velde (in his revised view) and the Stones, endorse birth control as a means of spacing births, while others, like Reuben,
reject it and argue that femininity demands maternity. Only in the 1970s
with Alex Comfort's *Joy of Sex* series do we find an unqualified acceptance
of birth control. Promiscuity becomes the norm as Comfort takes the logic
of effective birth control to its limit. Like Sanger, who had embraced passion many years earlier, he postulates that sex as a peak experience provides the major religious experience of one's life. Promiscuity, the fear of
which was articulated in the defense of marriage literature at the end of the
1920s, finally comes to dominate sexual advice, but is quickly eclipsed by
a much more traditional teaching articulated by Dr. Ruth. As sex becomes
a huge industry in America, the genteel marriage manuals with their indirect expressions evolve into much more explicit sexual ones that focus
mainly on erotic techniques. Though over a century has passed since the
time of the late Victorians, the literature, with the exception of the *Joy of
Sex* series, has not changed all that much in its essentials.

The Power of the Phallus

Power figures prominently in all the works we interrogated. According to the late Victorians, a man displayed his male power by succeeding in business and having children. The late Victorians posit sperm as an élan vital that women both desire and need, and they create a spermatic political economy. This construct continues in the literature through Van de Velde's first edition of *Ideal Marriage*, and a residue can even be found in the 1965 revision. These works focus on controlling male sexual desire and limiting the output of sperm. The oft noted obsession of the late Victorians with masturbation reflects their preoccupation with the spermatic political economy and their view that the fate of the nation rests on the preservation of this élan vital.

Women have either no sexual desires or less desire than men, but to be fulfilled as well as to get sperm they need intercourse and maternity. These views draw significantly on theological beliefs, and the authors posit that in intercourse a man joins with God (gendered as male) in creating new life. Intercourse thus becomes a man's participation in creation, which is viewed as a particularly male thing. Male power becomes linked with divine power, and its instrument is the penis with its flow of élan vital.

Alex Comfort, a medical doctor of a different era, knows better. He transforms the construct, however, rather than doing away with it. Men still experience their masculine power through erections, but in intercourse the penis becomes a third party in the event. It has its own personality and can be shared to some degree. Dr. Ruth, one of the few women to contribute to this genre, also conceives of sex as a power relationship in which men naturally dominate women. Throughout the marriage manual literature this view of power prevails. As many others have noted, the role of women does evolve to some degree, but the underlying power relationship does not vary much. Some commentators become mesmerized by the fact that starting in the 1920s orgasm becomes a substantial concern in the literature. Van de Velde, as all the commentators note, veritably insists on it. The sexual regime seems to change in that women are allowed to demand pleasure, but the fundamental power relationship remains undisturbed.

Penetration equals power. Men penetrate women, men have power over women. Catharine MacKinnon puts it bluntly, as is her wont: "What is sexual is what gives a man an erection. Whatever it takes to make a penis shudder and stiffen with the experience of its potency is what sexuality means culturally" (1989, 137). Almost two decades earlier Kate Millett came to a similar conclusion in *Sexual Politics* (1970). If we take gender as performance we can say that women enact submission, which charges male arousal as MacKinnon suggests. Wolf's survey research points to the same conclusion. Brownmiller suggests that sexuality be understood on a continuum from the typical dominance expressed physiologically in the missionary position to the extreme of sexual assault. The advice literature sanctions dominance and even endorses rape fantasies. In the literature, power engorges penises. Alex Comfort's playful violence, even with his recommendation for changing roles, adds assault to penetrative power, and his proclivity for bondage eroticizes extreme helplessness. In the advice literature, whether late Victorian or more modern, the penis remains the instrument of male power, or as [Pseudo] Aristotle would have it, the rod or staff of authority. The advice literature constructs sex as a powerful male penetrating a less powerful or powerless female. Erection confirms the success of the drama, and intercourse becomes a celebration of male power over women, a conquest. In giving the penis a personality, treating it as a divine instrument, or endowing it with magical qualities, the authors are actually invoking the phallus. Gordon and Shankweiler (1971) note that the fundament of male power remains entrenched in the literature. Even in post–1950s works they do not find fundamental change.

Once medical writers come to understand that the clitoris is the root of female sexual pleasure, they construct an understanding of women's sexuality divorced from physiology (Gordon and Shankweiler 1971, 465). The advice literature does not take into consideration the dichotomy between pleasure and reproduction. Van de Velde, for example, tasks men with providing their wives with pleasure, which he acknowledges results from clitoral stimulation, but he also suggests that ejaculation, jets of sperm striking the vaginal walls, can trigger orgasm. He also writes that women need sperm, the élan vital. Thus he tries to unite the demands of female pleasure with reproduction. Reuben, like Van de Velde, acknowledges that orgasms result from clitoral stimulation, but he then argues that women have maternal needs that necessitate vaginal penetration. Dr. Ruth, writing much later, teaches that the primary purpose of intercourse is reproduction, and she downplays the importance of orgasm. Even though vaginal penetration does not necessarily produce pleasure for women, all the authors of marriage manuals valorize it and thus ratify penetrative power as well as reinforce the linkage between femininity and maternity.

The Joy of Gay Sex could have provided an alternative understanding to penetrative intercourse, since the early proclamations of the Gay Liberation Front condemned traditional gender roles. Yet The Joy of Gay Sex and The New Joy of Gay Sex maintain the traditional power relationship, now translated into top as masculine and bottom as feminine, penetrator and penetrated. These books, however, do recommend role flexibility and advise against rigidity. In a gay male relationship each partner can potentially penetrate the other and experience the fullness of male power. Alex Comfort and Dr. Ruth merely recommend some role playing, for after all only one party can penetrate. Dr. Ruth, curiously enough, often uses rape and power images in her examples of sexual fantasies (Hannibal and his elephants, for example). Only Sisley and Harris in The Joy of Lesbian Sex consider sexual behaviors that do not involve penetration as the path to orgasm. Other authors consider such sexual behavior an alternative to be used when for some reason penetration is impossible or contraindicated. Only among lesbians is there any chance for the power/penetration link to be broken. This may be why the canonical marriage/sex manuals pay so little attention to sex between women, even though at least some of them discuss gay men. Sex without penetration is too subversive to bear intense scrutiny.

Though things do change, the sexual regime remains firmly established. Herbert Marcuse (1955, 1964) might call this an example of repressive tolerance. If women are allowed erotic pleasure, attention is diverted from the more basic repressive structure of the sexual regime, and women become ensnared by newly acceptable powerful pleasures. Attention gets diverted from power to pleasure and gender roles remain firmly in place. As part of socialization, both women and men internalize these norms and, as Foucault reminds us, such internalized norms become largely self-enforcing. These norms not only delimit sexual behavior, but also underpin gender itself. The late Victorian literature makes this correlation explicit, while it often lies implicit in the more modern works. The canonical literature teaches that men experience their power in erections and penetration and publicly display it by succeeding in business and having offspring. Women in this literature are mainly submissive receptacles, though the more modern works allow them to share some power by way of role playing. This sharing, however, can never be equal as long as the basis of male power and identity lies in the penis/phallus. Comfort describes role reversal in bondage as erotic for males because they enjoy the feeling of "becoming one enormous penis." The definition of masculinity remains rooted in power and dominance. Only lesbians, as the literature indicates, can potentially celebrate eros equally and democratically.

In defining normal behavior, the advice literature stigmatizes other behaviors. Both Reuben and Collins demonstrate this power in their teaching about lesbians and gay men. Psychiatrists and medical doctors enforce the norms, and the culture, as Brownmiller and Wolf (among others) point out, supports the sexual regime. College men, as Wolf notes, know well that their task is to dominate women, and they understand that force is central to sex (Wolf 1991, 165). Just as [Pseudo] Aristotle provided somewhat of an alternative to the late Victorian teaching, different views do exist and also inform behavior. Actual behavior, then, reflects a mélange of the canonical views embedded in the advice literature as well as folk wisdom and other popular sources. Behavior would also reflect changes wrought by two sexual revolutions, but the advice literature is already redefining the 1960s sexual revolution and moving toward defending marriage once again.

The Sexual Nature of Woman

Most of the authors believe that there exists a fundamental difference in the sexual natures of women and men. Exactly what this difference is depends on the view of female sexuality held by the author(s). The image of male sexuality remains fairly consistent. Men feel desire, seek release, and are expected to be fully aware of their sexuality. The authors discuss the importance of the élan vital for male and sometimes even female health. Otherwise, advice centers on how frequently a man should have intercourse, and on methods to use to get his wife to comply with his wish for sexual congress. The existence of strong erotic urges is acknowledged, and men are given advice as to how best to control them. The ideal man is able to harness his urges and seek gratification usually within marriage. Women, on the other hand, are described in many different ways. Some early writers see women as passionless and almost asexual, although according to Kevin White, men conceived of women in this way in order to protect them. Passionlessness was "supposed to tame oversexed men" (White 1993, 4). A little later some authors advise that

female sexuality must be awakened and then controlled by a male partner. Still later writers hint at dire results when female sexuality is allowed
to express itself fully. Women are never formally acknowledged to be in
control of their own sexuality. The advice literature systematically provides men with techniques for controlling female sexuality.

These manuals, with only a few exceptions, depict approved sexual
roles for men and women as ordained by either God, biology, or psychology, and all these texts, for the most part, address men. The sexual
knowledge these manuals impart often reflects ingrained sexist gender
norms that have little to do with medical science. These texts teach male
superiority, literally expressed in the missionary position, and use the
rhetoric of medicine/religion/psychoanalysis to normatize their positions.
For example, in the late Victorian period, God, nature, and reason support the phallocentric sexual regime, while today recourse is made to the
normal or to psychological theory. The term "normal" becomes the
rhetorical club that enforces approved practices.

For Guernsey, man embodies truth while woman represents good.
Kellogg justifies a monthly schedule of intercourse through his discussions of the élan vital, the saving (one might say hoarding) of which is
critical for male health. Women have little sexual desire and barely enter
into the discussion except perhaps as necessary beings to carry out God's
plan. In the same vein, Guernsey reaffirms Kellogg's view encouraging
women to submit to the laws of God and nature. Guernsey also asserts
that procreation is male and that in intercourse man joins his power with
God. In a throwback to an earlier century, Guernsey makes an attempt
to wrest away woman's role in procreation. He is not completely successful in his attempt, but he does manage to credit the Father(s) with
transforming both the fetus and the mother as his blood mingles with
theirs.

Writing in the 1920s, and undoubtedly aware of Sanger's work,
Collins provides an exception. He does not endorse the view that male
and female sexual differences are all-important. Instead he writes about
gender equality. What he means by equality is not clear. He may be reflecting the early feminist call for sex rights for women. Early feminists
did not define exactly what they meant by sex rights, but did insist that
basic erotic desires of women be recognized (Cott 1987, 3). Collins supports this view, but portrays it as scientific rather than feminist.

For Collins, nature in both men and women takes the form of instinctual needs that can be modified by reason. In this Collins reflects work on

instincts by Freud and others (e.g., McDougall 1923) as an explanation for behavior. Whatever influenced his opinions, he is among the first authors of marriage/sex manuals to postulate that males and females have the same sexual instincts. This similarity applies only to heterosexuals, however, and he is quite specific about differences between homosexual men and women.

Wile and Winn echo some of what Collins has to say, but they decrease the importance of sex in marriage. As soon as sexual desire is postulated to be the same for men and women, sex in marriage suddenly becomes less important. In their eyes a companionate marriage is the ideal, and partners should share household tasks. Dominance and power, previously a male privilege, now can be shared by partners in life. Nature is not invoked much, but then neither is sex.

Collins and Wile and Winn represent only a brief deviation from the main theme of sexual difference found in the advice literature. The special and different nature of female sexuality, couched in biological terms, becomes an issue once again in the marriage manual written by Marie Stopes. She saw sexual incompatibility as the root of marital difficulty. Sex is a problem, Stopes asserts, because no one takes into account women's Periodicity of Recurrence. With this assertion, Stopes firmly places women's newly acknowledged desire back under the intractable control of biology and nature. Women are at the mercy of their natural tides and can become aroused, on average, for two- or three-day periods every two weeks. The link between arousal, menstruation, fertility, and maternity remains a foregone conclusion. Men have no such periodicity. Arousal is possible on any day. This basic incompatibility need not be a problem. Men must control their own desire and have intercourse on a timetable set by the biological rhythms of their wives. While men control their own bodies, women give themselves up to the ebb and flow of their biological tides.

Van de Velde, one of the most widely read of our authors, has a different view of the sexual nature of woman and criticizes Stopes's version of it. In his view women are responsive any time if only they are wooed properly. Sex arouses feelings of power and domination in men, which wives exult in. The active role is male, and it is the husband's responsibility to satisfy his mate as she revels in his full erection. Interestingly, too much reveling, that is, overly assertive behavior, may cause the erection to wither. Van de Velde fears the consequences if a woman desires sexual pleasure too much. A husband can even smell another man's sperm on his wife's breath. What are we to make of this suggestion except to take it as a warning that adulterous behavior will be discovered? In passionless women adultery is not an issue. Admitting that women have desire raises a whole new set of male anxieties.

Hannah and Abraham Stone's marriage manual is far less explicit than Van de Velde's. It is also the last manual to suggest that the élan vital may have healthful benefits for women (they note that empirical data are lacking on the subject). Nature has made men more sexually aware and active than women. It is good for men to be active sexually from an early age since this correlates with sexual activity in later life. Woman's sexual impulses stay naturally dormant much longer. The husband's job is to awaken his wife's sexuality. Once again, women are depicted as ignorant of this important aspect of their own existence.

Chesser, another popular writer of the 1950s, gives lip service to the changing role of women. Like Collins before him, he notes that women are beginning to want equality. Equality may be all right in some areas, but it should not, according to Chesser, extend to sex. Chesser, too, knows that women and men are naturally different sexually. Those women who think otherwise are in the grip of an infantile wish. Chesser implicitly endorses the Freudian notion that anatomy is destiny. While men may view a sexual event as a mere incident, women are destined to link the sex act with conception, pregnancy, childbirth, lactation, and maternity. Eliminating the concern with conception truncates this chain. Sex without the possibility of conception is not satisfying and causes an increased desire for intercourse, presumably in a futile attempt to achieve true satisfaction. Rape can also stimulate a woman to desire increased intercourse. Chesser implicitly suggests that the aim of intercourse must be conception or else the woman may develop an unnatural desire for intercourse. While many manuals implicitly and explicitly focus on methods men can use to interest their wives in more frequent intercourse, sexual congress initiated by women is mainly viewed as unnatural. The undisciplined nature of female desire is a theme that runs through *Love without Fear*. Men are warned that any woman "can make a pervert of any normal man within six months." Many cultures are concerned with control of female sexuality. Walker and Parmar's *Warrior Marks* (1993), which deals with female genital mutilation, provides a violent example. A fully sexualized woman is a dangerous woman.

Chesser grants more equality while reemphasizing the dangerous, animal nature of womanhood. In contrast, Collins, who also grants women more equality, notes that sex is not particularly important. Woman, it seems, cannot be granted the fully human status of being both sexual and equal.

A marriage/sex manual written in the 1960s might be expected to avoid making some of the distinctions between male and female desire found in earlier ones. This is not the case, however; manuals written in the 1960s and even in later decades represent a backlash. They firmly assert the immutable biological nature of differences in male and female desire. For example, Reuben writes that women have an instinct to breed. Reuben uses this instinctual urge as a basis for asserting that vaginal penetration is the most valued type of sex. Women fulfill their biological destiny and instinctual needs through copulation, regardless of whether or not pregnancy results. Reuben uses a hormonal explanation for role behaviors. Men manifest power through their erections generated by testosterone, which then translates into success in business. Women, lacking testosterone, remain content to be at home taking care of the children that naturally resulted from penetrative vaginal sex. Like Chesser, Reuben is afraid of unleashed female sexuality. Van de Velde had noted earlier that a woman who is too assertive can cause her husband to lose his erection. Reuben cautions that the all-powerful erection is now becoming so fragile that a mere look can cause it to wilt. Impotence is caused by fear of the vagina. In the space of a few decades women have gone from asexuality to wantonness with a kind of supernatural power over the penis—from an innocent virgin to Medusa with *vaginalis dentata*.

Alex Comfort, though writing in the midst of a sexual revolution, does nothing to acknowledge women as sexual beings equal to men, able to experience and control their own desire. Instead, his books in the *Joy of Sex* series reinforce the idea that women's sexuality is scary. He notes that the vulva is magical and the source of most male hang-ups. He acknowledges the power of the vulva, but it is the penis that he identifies as the most valorized organ of the human body. What he means is that the penis is the most positively valorized organ of the human body. The vulva, the source of biologically programmed male anxiety, is clearly invested with negative value.

Perhaps at some level Comfort is aware of the contradictions in his work. He maintains a patriarchal stance, while granting more libidinous freedom to both women and men in the bedroom. Freedom for women, however, comes at a price. When Collins grants greater equality, he diminishes sex. When Chesser grants greater equality, it does not extend to the bedroom, and women are characterized as in thrall to their biological makeup. Comfort grants more sexual freedom, but characterizes women as anxiety provoking in a primitive way. The price that women pay in his formulation is the increased sanctioning of violence in sex play. Violence seems to be part of what one needs to get the most joy from sexual encounters. Women are still depicted as unable to control their biological urges. They must be subdued, not wooed. The subduing enhances sexual experience. While Comfort stops short of Chesser, who says rape can unleash a woman's sexuality, Comfort escalates the level of acceptable violence. The relationship between sex and violence is more fully articulated in Brownmiller's work on sexual assault (1976). The advice literature supports her assertion as well as that of MacKinnon that dominance and power charge male arousal. Femininity, as the advice literature teaches, consists of submission, which corresponds to conclusions drawn by both Brownmiller (1984) and Wolf (1991). The authors of the advice literature seek to control female sexuality. Such control extends on a continuum from the submission and subordination in the literature to the extreme of mutilation decried by Alice Walker (Walker and Parmar 1993). MacKinnon would probably consider the genre pornographic (1993). The missionary position expresses more than merely one option for intercourse. It literally involves male superiority—and invites wrestling metaphors—and is thus a political act as well as a sexual one.

Women as Human

By and large, the marriage manuals reviewed here depict women as "the other." Male sexual experience is better understood by these writers, most of whom are male. The intended audience is male, and in some cases was even supposedly restricted to physicians, as with Van de Velde's early editions.

As "the other," women are characterized as having less sexual knowledge, lower levels of desire, and different mental abilities than men. The consistently negative view of birth control, even in authors writing in the 1970s and 1980s, points to the persistent attempts to maintain the sex/marriage/reproduction link. While the populace may have embraced birth control, thereby linking sex with pleasure rather than or as much as reproduction, the advice literature has not given up maternity.

In all of the literature, either directly or obliquely, it is the penis that is most highly valued. Participation in the phallus, embodied in the penis, is what makes one fully human. Comfort makes this explicit by claiming a personality for the penis. He humanizes a male body part. This stands in sharp contrast to the experience of women, who often find themselves objectified. Brownmiller (1984) and later Wolf (1991) provide the clearest explication of objectification of the female form. No female body part is ever given a personality. Wolf focuses on the plasticity of the female form and how it needs to be surgically modified to fit changing norms.

In the advice literature, everything hinges on the erect penis. For sex to be a peak experience you need a man, a woman, and the third persona, embodied in the penis. Dr. Ruth concurs with Comfort, encouraging women to praise the penis as an arousal technique. While Dr. Ruth does not go so far as to tell us that the penis has its own personality, she does endow it with some human characteristics and recommends praise. The penis/phallus makes the sex act important, just as the possession of the penis/phallus makes the owner fully human. A woman, in this formulation, is not fully human. All the marriage manuals have characterized woman in ways that deprive her of her full humanity. She is most often not in control of her own body, whether it is feeling desire itself or conceiving children. She is not allowed to feel desire, or if she does feel desire it is sporadic or uncontrollable. She is either an innocent who must be taught to experience her own pleasure or a temptress who is wantonly sexual and capable of stealing male potency. The latter is a particularly frightening image for men. The potential for theft is all the more frightening if the erect penis, an image of the phallus, is also symbolic of being fully human.

In all these manuals male sexuality develops without any help. While erections may be fragile, male sexuality is accepted and acceptable. The literature exhibits a uniformity of opinion about male sexuality. His sex, specifically the erect member, defines the man himself. His skill with his penis/phallus translates into success in business. It has a personality and has been endowed with a presence like no other body part. The penis in the literature becomes the phallus. Like an animal, a woman's sexual desire needs to be trained, contained, and restrained for male purposes. Part of male sexual experience is domination, but it is also a demonstration of humanness. This demonstration of phallic power/humanness is heightened when contrasted with the female "other," who has no penis/phallus and thus lacks power as well as an element of humanity.

Gender theory, powerful as it is, supplies only one way of examining the subordination of women. In the advice literature, women are not fully socially alive. Once chattel whose participation in society was mediated through their fathers/husbands, they now have a greater degree of equality. Yet the advice literature clearly demonstrates that women still can make only partial claims to sexual pleasure. The late Victorians conceived of the womb as a locus of male action, divine and human. More modern writers deny women control of their uterus and mandate maternity as an instinctual drive and/or part of feminine nature. Women are denied bodily integrity in the equivocations over birth control found in these manuals, and pleasure remains secondary to maternity. The advice literature, in other words, excludes women from the phallocratic sexual regime. As in everything else, they are acted upon, not actors (see Goldhagen 1996, 1–128). As Dr. Ruth writes, material rewards prove better than orgasms. Diamonds are still a girl's best friend.

Homosexual Subversives

The marriage/sex manuals suggest that participation in the phallus constitutes being fully human, but it is more than mere possession of a penis. The penis must also be used in a specific way. This idea is clarified by the discussions of homosexuality in these manuals. Their approach to the subject illuminates the views of these authors about both female sexuality and humanness as embodied in the penis/phallus. The authors prefer a particular sexual triad: one woman, one man, and one penis. Variations are viewed with varying degrees of perplexity, bemusement, or disgust.

Collins acknowledges the possibility of gay relationships and then attacks them. Male inversion is a genetic defect. Inverts lead unhappy lives, and if they marry they only produce more inverts. Those inverts who do not marry should remain celibate so as to avoid degeneracy and sublimate their sexual desires in their love of ritual. While Collins believes in some tolerance for those inverts who are born defective, he believes that society should not tolerate those who become deviants through seduction or bad habits. He mentions female inverts only briefly. Women do not appear to be subject to the genetic defect. They become inverts from idleness, boredom, and loneliness and are either undersexed or oversexed. Collins has less tolerance for female inverts than he has for male ones. According to him, all female inverts have acquired the vice and are, therefore, more corrupt than genetic ones. The cure for female inversion lies in the acquisition of good habits, presumably through heterosexual sex. In his discussion of inverts, Collins departs from his notion of similar sexual instincts for men and women and regresses to older ideas about female sexuality. Women are sexually malleable. It takes nothing more than boredom for women to look to other women, rather than men, for sexual satisfaction. Sex without a penis, however, is not really sex.

Chesser deals with homosexuality in a chapter on sexual byways. In contrast to Collins, he is more concerned about lesbians than gay men. He has discarded Collins's view of homosexuality as a genetic defect and terms it a predisposition, which may even be activated by rape. Boys may be raped at school and women can be raped by other women, although the effects are quite different. According to Chesser, when a woman is raped, whether by a man or a woman, her sexuality may be unleashed. If raped by a man, the woman may become promiscuous. If raped by a woman, she may become a seducer of others, preying especially on normal girls. Once again, we find a picture of a woman uncontrollably driven by her sexual nature. Rape is particularly interesting as a trigger for unbridled sexuality. The sexual desires of women are portrayed as both so strong and so malleable that a single experience, even a horrific one, can change the course of sexual life.

Reuben refers to hormone imbalances to explain homosexuality, though he offers no empirical evidence to support his thesis. Reuben is affronted by a man who refuses to insert his penis into a vagina. It is hard to know how he feels about a woman who refuses to have sex with a man because Reuben does not consider lesbians worthy of much attention and cannot figure out what they do. Whatever it is, he knows that it does not satisfy and is nothing more than mutual masturbation.

Comfort does not scorn homosexual sex, but he does consider it limited in scope. Perhaps Comfort, who gave the penis a personality, feels that gay men have too many personalities in the bed at the same time. On the other hand, lesbians have too few personalities for good sex.

All these writers characterize homosexual sex as unsatisfying and empty. The penis/phallus is symbolic of dominance, and one person, at least from the traditional point of view, has to dominate. It is too difficult for these male writers to accept a submissive penis/phallus. If, as we suggest, a penis/phallus is also a symbol of humanness, then a submissive phallus is also less than human, a very frightening idea. Lesbians are left with empty, penisless sex. The attitude of these writers seems to be "the less said about that, the better."

The cultural power of the phallus is hard to resist. Once Margaret Sanger came under the influence of Ellis, even she wrote of men as gods and women as fairy princesses. The need to demonstrate one's humanity may account for the disdain with which many of the authors discuss homosexual behavior. Perhaps gay men are too human, or, lacking the contrast effect of a woman, not human enough. Either way, they are subject to extensive discussion and are rarely dealt with neutrally. Lesbians, being women, are not quite fully human and merit little attention. Sex without at least one penis is not to be taken seriously. Butler's formulation of the lesbian phallus is ostensibly about obtaining power (1993, 57–91). Another reading is that it is about lesbians obtaining humanness and authenticity as real people.

The Bisexual Issue

The focus in the literature on reproduction helps to explain the equivocal acceptance of lesbians and gay men, even in recent works like those of Dr. Ruth. Bisexuality is even more difficult for this genre to deal with. In the late nineteenth century Freud postulated bisexuality as a constituent part of the psyche. Freud's ideas as well as those of other psychologists like Ellis start permeating American culture during the 1920s. Despite the fact that humankind's bisexuality has become an assumption among mainstream psychologists, none of the advice literature takes it seriously. Marriage/sex manuals that began with a presumption of bisexuality would then present sexual expression as existing along a continuum. One pole would consist of same-sex expression, while different-sex expression would be at the other pole. Bisexuals would occupy the middle of the continuum and could tend toward one pole or the other. A book that took this point of view could truly be entitled *The Joy of Sex*. Such a construction, however well accepted in depth psychology, would undermine the gender and sex binaries and destigmatize same-sex object choice. Only recently has the cultural view begun to emerge from what Goldhagen might term an eliminationist ideology with regard to gay men, lesbians, and bisexuals (1996). Authors in the marriage manual genre vilify, ignore, and sometimes seek to eliminate sexual minorities.

Collins seeks to limit the increase of inverts, but he neglects to focus on bisexuals. Van de Velde teaches that "man is woman too in his soul, and woman, man." Men tend to repress this part of their psyches, while women act it out in power struggles within marriage. Van de Velde does not dwell on the implications of bisexuality for gender roles in general. In his view, the right man armed with the proper sexual techniques can redeem latent lesbians, thereby eliminating them. Young men experiencing the normal tensions of bisexuality can be recruited by companions or older homosexual men and become impotent and incapable of normal intercourse. Implicit in this is the need to isolate older homosexuals from young men.

Reuben does not focus at all on bisexuals, even though as a psychiatrist he had to be familiar with the concept and its implications. Comfort, unlike the other authors, does address bisexuality. In his first edition he places it in his problems section, while in the 1991 edition he places it in the section on health and other issues. In all his work, Comfort acknowledges that everyone is bisexual by nature, and how people act on this will depend on their particular circumstances. Bisexual behavior in a couples situation is fine, since there is little chance of getting stuck. Presumably he means coming to prefer sex with a same-sex partner. Heterosexuals run no risk of becoming stuck. In *The New Joy of Sex* in 1991 Comfort acknowledges the universality of bisexuality and then begins a discussion of AIDS. He views bisexuals as a transmission vector into what is often termed the general population.

Dr. Ruth does not devote much attention to the subject. *Sex for Dummies*, for example, does not even include bisexuality in the index. In her earlier works she suggests that a bisexual phase is a natural part of the maturation process. Her treatment of Ray suggests that she thinks that bisexuals should be encouraged to form heterosexual marriages, even if they occasionally stray. Bisexuality as a natural part of the human condition, of course, undermines the heterosexual/homosexual binary that all the authors are busily defending. It would also validate relationships that at least in some cases are not marital and do not involve reproduction.

All of the genre with the exception of the lesbian literature celebrates male power/potency. Acknowledgment of bisexuality runs the risk of diluting this power. An even greater threat in the acknowledgment of bisexuality comes from the human/male-nonhuman/female continuum. If to be female is to be less than fully human, then to deal with those bisexual aspects of all of us is to acknowledge either a certain animalism or a certain humanness in each of us. To acknowledge humanness in all of us, however, levels the playing field. To acknowledge the animal elements is to lose the cherished power that comes with possession of the penis/phallus. The strong negative response to bisexuality in men is similar to the response Darwin got when he first suggested that people were actually part of the animal kingdom and not creatures totally different from other animals. Early anti-evolution arguments suggested that God created animals to serve man.[1] Interestingly enough, women and so-called inferior races were also viewed as having been created to serve men.

Bisexuality in women is not dealt with in this literature in much detail. Traditional writers assume that women's desire is malleable, and they recommend good heterosexual sex as a cure. Lesbians, however, take a different view. As both the lesbian sex manuals reviewed here point out, lesbianism is a political orientation as well as a sexual one. Lesbianism does not only involve who a woman has sex with, it also refers to identification with and concern for other women. To be lesbian means to be woman-centered, and in the most radical sense it means the exclusion of men (Johnston 1973). From this perspective, it is difficult for some lesbians to support bisexual activities. Sisley and Harris note that ostracism from the lesbian community can result.

In the final analysis, perhaps bisexuality is both feared and ignored because it undercuts the gender and sex binaries that are so necessary for the organization of society. We cannot conceive of the womanly man and manly woman in each of us, embedded as we are in a culture that is devoted to demonstrating daily that men and women are not only qualitatively different, but that they come from different planets. The uncoupling of sex and reproduction through reproductive technology will continue to pressure existing norms. In spite of a predictable backlash, manifest in still another wave of defense of marriage literature, bisexuality may yet come into its own as a concept and a way of life.

Sex as a Saving Grace

Margaret Sanger dreamed of a perfected world. When women cast off their chains forged by male dominance, free womanhood will burst forth to renew the world. Like most writers in this genre, she freights intimate matters with a tremendous burden. Sexual intimacy involves far more than a relationship between two people. It can be a means to have qualitatively better children, liberate women, and even perfect the world. Sanger is not alone in this belief. The late Victorians believed that even a moral propensity to good or evil could be transmitted to the next generation. Due to their view of humankind's innate propensity to evil, however, their belief in the qualitative improvement of children does not lead them to a vision of a perfected world. Later writers reject the Lamarckian genetics that underlies this view, but a residue of the larger vision remains in the literature.

Van de Velde, writing on the cusp of the 1930s, is one of the first widely read authors to deal with birth control. Though his *Ideal Marriage* endorses only the rhythm method, by his third book birth control combined with the maternal role becomes a substitute for the Lamarckian genetics that underpinned the late Victorian vision of better children. Birth control (really spacing births, in his view) will reduce overpopulation, which, in turn, will remove a cause of war. Sanger had already written that overpopulation causes wars and keeps the lower classes bound in wage slavery, with children competing against their fathers to work for the cheapest rate. Birth control thus becomes the vehicle for world improvement.

By the 1970s and Alex Comfort's *Joy of Sex* series, intimate matters become the foundation for a new religion, also foreseen by Sanger, with an almost endless possibility for peak experiences. These peak experiences become so important that relationships fade in importance. Such peak experiences cannot be shared; much like religious ecstasy, they remain subjective. Comfort, like Dr. Ruth, relies on a psychology that emphasizes the role of perceptions and projections, which ultimately undermines any view of sex as a sharing experience. Both partners can be an occasion for giving the other pleasure, but in the mutual swirl of projections, fantasies, and roles the unique individual quickly gets lost. Like his predecessors, Comfort also freights sex with a burden. In a Dionysian frenzy of playful violence, individuals can discover their true selves. Such acting out offers hope of a better world. As he notes, massacres such as My Lai and the horrors of the Holocaust might even be attenuated. Sex thus becomes a therapeutic event as well as a religious one, and Comfort, despite all his writing about switching roles, really seeks to attenuate male violence. If individual women play along, the world can be a safer place.

The books on lesbian and gay sex dwell on intimate matters as an experience of affirmation in a hostile world. Like Comfort, authors of *The*

Joy of Gay Sex and *The Joy of Lesbian Sex* emphasize pleasure, but they also have a political agenda. They seek to affirm stigmatized, disempowered groups, although they do not reach beyond sex to propound a vision of an improved or perfected world. Dr. Ruth does, and she reasserts this fundament of the genre. In *Sex for Dummies*, which expresses her fully developed views, she teaches that sex should occur within marriage for the purpose of making babies. She believes that couples have a responsibility to continue the species. No longer do authors in this genre write about continuing a particular race. The goal is now the progress of humankind. Perhaps enough time has elapsed since the slaughter of World War II (some fifty million killed worldwide) that this optimism can be taken seriously. Unfortunately, Dr. Ruth does not elaborate. The genre views intimate matters as involving much more than individuals, and many of the authors offer visions of a better or perfected world. Sex, even for Alex Comfort, is never simply sex.

Sexual Revolutions

Alex Comfort's new religion relies on pleasure. This emphasis on pleasure is found to a lesser degree in some of the earlier literature as well. The eruptions of pleasure in the advice genre follow wars and periods of social upheaval. Among many other things, the advice literature from these periods calls for more flexibility in gender roles. After the 1920s, orgasm becomes an expectation, and Comfort invites women to join his new hip religion in the 1970s. Yet both of these eruptions are quickly followed by a defense of marriage literature that reasserts traditional norms. Even though Van de Velde accepts the limited use of birth control to space children, his *Sexual Tensions in Marriage* extols traditional views of womanhood as well as maternity. Marie Stopes, one of the few female voices in this genre, accepts the spermatic political economy, but asserts that women do experience sexual pleasure. Like Van de Velde, however, she charges men with responsibility for their mate's orgasms. Though she advocates that women have an occupation or at least engage in stimulating activities, the purpose of all this is to keep wives interesting to their husbands. Stopes explicitly embraces birth control, but mainly in terms of spacing births, so she is in agreement with Van de Velde's revised view. Overall, she defends marriage and argues that problems reflect sexual ignorance; thus, switching partners will not address the fundamental issue. Like Van de Velde, she restricts sex to the marriage relationship.

Similarly, Dr. Ruth's later works are part of the defense of marriage literature, and she too extols maternity. The genre, with two exceptions, remains basically conservative and traditional. This study of 120 years of the marital/sexual advice literature confirms Gordon's earlier finding. In fact, much of this genre can be considered reactionary in that the authors seek to evade the implications of effective birth control and still task women with maternity. In the earlier period God, nature, and medical science demand it, while the modern authors tend to view maternity as part of feminine nature itself. Biology, in other words, remains destiny. The advice literature, as Weinberg and Hammersmith point out, defines women's status. Certainly a vast amount of social change has taken place since the first sexual revolution in the 1920s, but the advice literature mainly ignores all of this. It propounds a very traditional view of femininity and its corollary in intimate matters. A woman today who takes Dr. Ruth's advice to heart would have beliefs that would not differ all that much from her grandmother's. Dr. Laura Schlessinger, who claims a radio audience of some twenty million, offers marital/sexual advice that is just as traditional as that of Dr. Ruth, and she does, unlike Dr. Ruth, have an explicit moral agenda. Besides hosting a radio show, Dr. Laura has written several books. The full title of one of them suggests her point of view: *How Could You Do That?! The Abdication of Character, Courage, and Conscience* (1996). Dr. Laura, however, is not a clinical psychologist. She holds a doctorate in physiology, but did postdoctoral work in marriage and family counseling. When some of the authors acknowledge that feminism sparked social change, they mainly attack it. Van de Velde, for example, attacks feminists and attributes much mischief to them and their misguided notions. The sexual revolutions are reflected in the literature only in that women are granted the right to pleasure, but little else has changed. Gender roles remain fixed. Male sexuality revolves around power and dominance, and maternity eclipses pleasure.

Birth Control and the Reproductive Matrix

Prior to the Comstock laws, newspapers included advertisements for contraceptives and abortion-inducing tonics. Comstock put an end to this, and Margaret Sanger invited his wrath by spilling the secret. As she notes, it was not all that big a secret anyway. Sanger opened clinics, founded what we know today as Planned Parenthood, and dispensed birth control advice and devices. In these activities she risked jail, and New York state obliged her once. She also drew other women like Katharine McCormick into her criminal conspiracy and arranged financing for research that resulted in the development of the birth control pill. In her own writings, Sanger foresees free womanhood resulting from reproductive control, and liberated women will then spark the creation of a better world. Falling birthrates, among many other things, will reduce wage competition and even remove a cause of war. The marriage/sex manuals, on the other hand, offer only a qualified endorsement—the *Joy of Sex* series providing the exception.

In the days of "restricted shelf" books, Van de Velde's *Ideal Marriage* actually is an anti–birth control tract. Though he later recants, he approves of birth control really as a means of spacing births, and he tasks women with maternity as part of feminine nature. Stopes has no difficulty endorsing birth control, but she accomplishes this within a traditional gender framework. Stopes does not seek to liberate women from reproductive labor or make it a matter of choice; rather, she postulates that all couples desire children. Though effective birth control offers the possibility of free love and sexual pleasure divorced from pregnancy/marriage, Stopes reaffirms the reproductive trinity of sex, marriage, reproduction.

The advice literature in the early part of the century at best grudgingly accepts birth control for the purpose of spacing births; it does not advocate that women take control of the reproductive process. The fear of some of the defense of marriage literature at the end of the 1920s that a wave of hedonism was about to sweep America never came to pass, at least in the advice literature. Even after the development of the birth control pill in 1960, the advice literature remains mostly conservative and reinforces traditional norms. Reuben writing in the heady 1960s certainly gets attention with not only his format aimed at a general audience—no more reserved shelf—but also his frank language and detailed descriptions. His books, however, do not endorse the pill, and he makes readers very aware of harmful side effects. *Any Woman Can*, according to Reuben, but what he means is that any woman can ensnare a man and thus satisfy her maternal instincts. The advice literature does present a shift from the 1930s to the 1960s, but the change does not include an embrace of birth control or reproductive control for women.

Before Sanger risked jail by letting the secret out, frequent intercourse inevitably led to pregnancy. Sanger's own mother, for example, died at age forty-nine after delivering eleven babies and surviving seven miscarriages. Birth control offers the possibility of reproductive choice. The advice literature, however, emphasizes the maternal role of women within marriage and still largely confines sex to marriage. Dr. Ruth, for example, writing several decades after Reuben, comes to embrace maternal needs for the sake of continuing the species as well as civilizational progress. She always notes the side effects of birth control pills and constantly reminds readers that condoms do break. Dr. Ruth employs fear of pregnancy to counsel against premarital sex. In her early writings she is willing to legitimize sexual relationships without benefit of clergy, but in her mature view she teaches that sex should be confined to marriage. According to Dr. Ruth, marriage makes sex better, and in a late work, *Sex for Dummies*, she deplores casual affairs. All through the advice literature the reproductive matrix gets supported, despite the availability of ever more effective birth control.

Among the authors only Alex Comfort in his *Joy of Sex* series embraces the full potential of effective birth control and reaches toward a vision akin to Sanger's original one. Children and maternal instincts receive little attention, and in fact children in a household can easily hinder good sex. Dionysian frenzies involving one or several couples just make too much noise, among other things. About forty years after the defense of marriage literature raises an alarm about rampant sexuality centered on pleasure, Comfort writes a sex manual with this theme in mind. Sex, according to Comfort, focuses on mutually supplied pleasure. Since Comfort never manages to distinguish between long-term relationships and casual ones, he endorses a promiscuous agenda. For example, he has no difficulty accepting swinging.

Though the *Joy of Sex* series enjoyed a run of more than nineteen years, Comfort's work was quickly eclipsed by that of Dr. Ruth, who offers a much more traditional understanding of intimate matters. Along with Dr. Ruth's articulation of the traditional norms comes a new defense of marriage literature, to which conservative social critics like Robert Bork add their voices. Though the 1920s and 1960s witnessed sexual revolutions in behavior, the genre on the whole does not reflect radical changes in the reproductive trinity. Over some 120 years of such advice, a constant theme emerges: sex should take place within marriage for reproductive purposes. The advice literature rarely challenges the prevailing orthodoxy. American sexual practices have undoubtedly changed, and the divorce rate is once again causing cries of alarm, but the advice literature remains constant in its main themes as America enters another era of defending marriage. Dr. Ruth's *Sex for Dummies* does not deal with moral issues, but the text articulates Victorian values for the 1990s.

The advice literature also sounds its traditional themes in a time when reproductive technology offers new challenges to the reproductive trinity. Sperm, ova, and zygotes can now be preserved almost indefinitely outside the body. Though Van de Velde in *Ideal Marriage* allows for virgin births to placate religious authorities, the new technology can make this a reality within human control. Until recently, reproduction required sex or later artificial insemination. Recent technological changes make it possible to unite sperm and ova in a petrie dish and then implant the zygote in a surrogate mother. Though this technology was developed to aid infertile couples, nothing limits its extension except monetary resources. The advice literature, of course, posits the married couple as the reproductive dyad. With the new technology, individuals with enough resources can become parents and reproduce, which challenges the reproductive dyad itself. D'Emilio and Freedman would probably not be surprised if an economic system that fostered consumption and individualism eventually reduced the reproductive matrix to the individual.

This new reproductive technology has already created legal quandaries. In the United States a widow was inseminated with her deceased husband's sperm and later gave birth. A federal district court later decided that the infant was entitled to survivor benefits through Social Security. In this case, the infant's birth certificate has a later date than its father's death certificate. As these changes continue, they promise to further sunder the reproductive matrix. Lesbians have used sperm banks and artificial insemination for years, while the new technology makes it possible for economically privileged gay men to reproduce as individuals. With the past as a guide, the marriage/sex manuals are likely to continue in their conservative vein. All these changes continue to suggest that sex as a reproductive act is different from sex as an occasion for pleasure and a relationship-building experience. Sanger said it long ago.

Expanding Humankind

In her important book *Gender Trouble* (1990), Judith Butler argues that gender essentially consists of a regulatory scheme as well as performance.

She created a powerful and insightful metaphor and has subsequently qualified it in scholarly articles. Her more recent *Bodies That Matter* (1993) not only extends and clarifies her argument about gender as performance, but also probes to new levels of understanding.

Butler begins with the epistemological issue. MacKinnon, of course, also deals with this issue, but she resolves it differently (1989, 3–125). As Butler reformulates the issue: "What are we to make of constructions without which we would not be able to think, to live, to make sense at all, those which have acquired for us a kind of necessity?" In fact, gender constructions that almost serve as Kantian categories of thought underpin the works of these authors. These gender constructions extend from the late Victorians with their spermatic political economy, to Van de Velde, to Comfort's identification of the penis with the phallus, to Dr. Ruth's explicit linkage of sex with power. All our works in this sense are phallocratic and reflect deep-rooted systems of thought (Butler 1993, xi).

Sexuality remains fixed within a field of power, as both Foucault and Butler would say, and this work helps to illuminate the constancy of the regulatory norms, though the justifying ideologies shift. Gender, in this sense, consists of a "ritualized production" and is enforced by "prohibition[s] and taboo[s]." Butler goes further and argues that threats of ostracism and even death shape, but do not totally determine, gender productions. Sexuality cannot be divorced from or even thought about apart from power and the regulations of the sexual regime. "Hegemonic norms" define sex and script performances. Certainly all the texts under consideration reflect this powerful theoretical insight. Sex expresses power. Men have it—through the penis, which partially embodies the phallus and the congruent social system. Women do not. MacKinnon, working from a critique of Marxist theory and using consciousness raising as her epistemological ground, reaches the same conclusion. "What is sexual is what gives a man an erection." Alex Comfort provides an example. The penis, as he told millions, embodies a dominance signal like antlers and even has its own personality. This assertion not only reflects the current hegemonic norms but, more importantly supports the prevailing sexual regime. After the sexual revolution of the 1960s as well as the critiques of gender developed by feminists, the sexual regime needed a revised ideology to maintain the phallus and, thus, the penis as a locus of power. Dr. Ruth, one of the few women writing in this genre, also supports the phallocratic regime and its consequent norms. In Dr. Ruth's work, the penetrating penis, the powerful engorged penis, remains the locus of sex (Butler 1993, 95; MacKinnon 1989, 137).

Butler, unlike MacKinnon, also seeks to ground queer theory and critique the prevailing sexual regime as an ideology/script in support of heterosexuality. This informs the core of *Bodies That Matter* and underpins Butler's assault on the very construction of sexed bodies. As she argues, sex as performed "constitute[s] the materiality of bodies and, more specifically, to materialize the body's sex, to materialize sexual difference in the service of the consolidation of the heterosexual imperative." All our authors, even seemingly progressive writers like Comfort and Dr. Ruth, maintain this imperative.

Collins and Reuben go much further than the equivocations found in Comfort and Dr. Ruth. Both Collins and Reuben, even in his new edition, view lesbians and gay men as the "internally fallen," which quite easily then translates into the enemy within as it did in the 1950s. They propound what Daniel Goldhagen would term an "eliminationist ideology" (1996). Following Goldhagen, Collins and Reuben certainly hold that lesbians and gay men are socially dead, that they do not belong to any legitimate social order. In fact, lesbians and gay men are excluded from the sexual regime. They are, to say the least, defective. Lesbians and gay men are also dishonored; they lack power and have no legitimate social existence. According to our earlier formulation, they are also denied a measure of humanity. In both psychiatric constructions of Collins and Reuben, lesbians and gay men are denied happiness, intimacy, communion, and community. The normative power of psychiatry is then illustrated in its negative construction of lesbians and gay men; it colonizes consciousness and enforces its construction either through a transference neurosis or by electroshock. Psychiatry, as they articulate it, becomes the way for these socially dead, less than human men and women to become socially alive and members of the larger community. This, of course, entails lesbians and gay men ceasing to be what they are. Thus, identity becomes the contested field of power. Goldhagen also argues that an eliminationist ideology can become so ingrained in consciousness and institutions that it can even seem to disappear from popular culture. If we grant this argument, then we can view the homophobia in Comfort and others as a remnant of an eliminationist ideology articulated by Collins and Reuben—however attenuated and changed by lesbian and gay male activists and changing social norms (Goldhagen 1996, 1–128).[2]

The recruitment theory of homosexuality currently propounded by conservative religious groups also presents an implicit eliminationist ideology and draws from the old psychiatric construction. Usually claiming divine authority, these religious leaders generally believe that "homosexuals cannot reproduce—so they must recruit. And to freshen their ranks, they must recruit the youth of America." If homosexuals can be prohibited from teaching in the schools and otherwise isolated from teenagers, this approach implies that their numbers may very well decline and they may very well disappear. Thus, God's will will be served (for an early formulation as well as the citation, see Bryant 1977, 62).

Butler, of course, well knows that the gender binary remains a practical necessity for the gay rights movement, but cannot be defended theoretically. In a limited way, she agrees with Dr. Ruth. The heterosexual/homosexual binary as defended by both sides does recruit lesbian and gay male activists. On a less theoretical level, the dominant constructions of homosexuality also define the current status of the sex, marriage, and reproduction trinity (Butler 1993, 2).

Postmodern works can be playful—full of play in the Platonic sense—and certainly Butler partially intends this in her section on the lesbian phallus. Her argument, however, goes to the core of this book. All our authors except those writing for lesbians privilege the phallus and write in support of the phallocentric sexual regime. Butler calls for "depriviledging the phallus." The phallus remains a powerful symbol of prohibitions and taboos enacted into social structure. Its symbolic force, however, can be appropriated or shifted. As a symbolic force, it can be possessed by lesbians or even by all women. Playfulness aside, Butler calls for reconceptualizing sexuality. "For what is needed is not a new body part, as it were, but a displacement of the hegemonic symbolic of (heterosexist) sexual difference and the critical release of alternative imaginary schemas for constituting sites of erotogenic pleasure." None of our authors, even the modern ones, move beyond the gender and sex binaries to "reconstitute sites of erotogenic pleasure." In fact all the authors, except for Alex Comfort, support the traditional reproductive trinity (Butler 1993, 91). Brownmiller in *Against Our Will* does suggest an alternative way of constructing intimate matters without the phallus. In a sexual regime that eroticizes victimness, Brownmiller writes, "the sex act which can result in pregnancy, has as its *modus operandi* something men call 'penetration.' 'Penetration,' however, describes what the man does. The feminist Barbara Mefrol has suggested that if women were in charge of sex and the language, the same act could be called 'enclosure'—a revolutionary concept" (1976, 372).

In the place of ideas born of the binary, theorists will have to work out a real culture of caring (for an example of the use of feminist principles to reconstruct patriarchal power, see Tronto 1993). Males need to be freed from the tyranny of power and performance and females from their unnatural "natural" selves. Everyone must become fully human. While the binary must be given up to transform the culture as well as individuals, Americans will not have to give up sex. There is merely a need to learn to have sex with each other as two human beings of indeterminantly gendered and sexed selves and bodies.

Notes

1. For a critique of several recent good attempts to get a random sample so scholars could generalize about American sexual behavior, see Lewontin 1995. John Gagnon's work illustrates the problems with the sociological literature. In his work on lesbians and gay men he typically notes that he lacks a random sample. In one case he handed out questionnaires outside gay bars and then proceeded to draw qualified conclusions. Other books then cite his data without his qualifications. Thus sociologists often construct a body of knowledge that becomes ingrained in the scholarly literature but, unfortunately, according to the tenets of empirical research, has no basis in reality.

2. Contrary to Gordon's assertion that the early literature consisted of printed sermons, [Pseudo] Aristotle's *Masterpiece* was first published in America in 1766 and went through more than fifty editions by the late Victorian period. Though the text uses various subterfuges to disguise its true intent, the *Masterpiece* really is a marriage manual. It is one of the few books until this century that acknowledge the role and importance of orgasm in intimate matters.

3. Certainly any socially constructed activity with rules and sanctions could serve as a metaphor, but given the sexual politics, we feel that football is a more apt example.

4. Since the publication of *Gender Trouble*, Butler has clarified her fundamental insight that gender consists of a performance. See, for example, Butler 1998.

5. Wolf's footnotes suggest that the first study was based on a random sample of college men. The methodology of the second study is ambiguous (Wolf 1991, 315).

NOTES TO CHAPTER I

1. We now understand such things as clitoridectomies as heinous child abuse. Kellogg, however, did not.

2. In this edition, the editors at F. A. Davis Company in Philadelphia add a preface noting that the revisions were "relatively slight" and that Dr. Guernsey had "long since gone to his reward" (Guernsey 1915, [vii?]). Therefore, the revised edition need not concern us.

3. Guernsey regards any touching of a child's genitalia as abuse and condemns it as the start of the road to ruin. Today we consider many forms of this touching child abuse. Often its effects are even more psychologically devastating than Guernsey realized.

NOTES TO CHAPTER 4

1. As Van de Velde translates, "only by and through her ovaries, is a woman that which she is."

2. Wolf turns the tables in her book and wonders what would happen if hegemonic gender constructions made men feel inadequate. She catalogs surgical remedies.

Imagine this: penis implants, penis augmentation, foreskin enhancement, testicular silicone injections to correct asymmetry, saline injections with a choice of three sizes, surgery to correct the angle of erection, to lift the scrotum and make it pert. Before and after shots of the augmented penis in Esquire. Risks: Total numbness of the glans. Diminution of sexual feeling. Permanent obliteration of sexual feeling. Gland rigidity, to the consistency of hard plastic. Testicular swelling and hardening, with probable repeat operations, including scar tissue formation that the surgeon must break apart with manual pressure. Implant collapse. Leakage. Unknown long-term consequences. Weeks of recovery necessary during which the penis must not be touched. The above procedures are undergone because they make men sexy to women, or so men are told.

(Wolf 1991, 242–43).

NOTES TO CHAPTER 6

Portions of this chapter have previously been presented as papers at the 1993 and 1994 annual meetings of the American Political Science Association. See Melody 1993, 1994b.

1. The new edition, published in 1999, does not differ substantially in its premises from the first edition.

2. Seeking sexual partners in an anonymous setting might very well be an adaptive reaction to the witch hunts for sexual subversives in the 1950s. Under questioning by the authorities, individuals could not name names or provide addresses they did not know.

3. After the introduction of the pill in 1960, pharmaceutical companies quickly discovered that lower doses proved just as effective as the higher ones and also ensured more safety. The drug companies reduced the dosage from the ten milligrams of the original Enovid formulation. Over time, the amount of es-

trogen declined by two-thirds and progestin by nine-tenths (Asbell 1995, 301–12).

NOTE TO CHAPTER 7

1. Altman (1984, 123) overstates her case about Comfort's table of contents. Comfort does discuss the vulva under starters, but he also includes the penis in this category.

NOTES TO CHAPTER 8

1. White also discusses promiscuity in the 1970s, the clone decade, in *States of Desire* (1980).
2. Though British by birth, Comfort did teach in California and his books were marketed to an American audience. His silence on race cannot be taken as an oversight by a foreign author unfamiliar with American culture.

NOTE TO CHAPTER 9

1. Parts of this section dealing with the surgeon general's report previously appeared in Melody 1994a.

NOTES TO CHAPTER 10

1. Traditional translations of Genesis employ the term "man" rather than "humankind."
2. Goldhagen's book *Hitler's Willing Executioners: Ordinary Germans and the Holocaust* is often referred to as a controversial book. The use of the term "controversial" in this context, however, serves as a de facto *ad hominem* argument. Stating that a work is controversial does nothing to address the argument that such a book makes. Goldhagen basically extends the theoretical work of Orlando Patterson in *Slavery and Social Death* (1982) to include the really or utterly social dead. Goldhagen defines eliminationist ideologies as belief systems that seek the death of groups, and he specifically focuses on the Nazi regime with its eliminationist anti-Semitism. He presents an exhaustive case study, focusing mainly on the murderous activities of one reserve police battalion during the Holocaust. His work, of course, suffers from the limitations of any case study, and much more research needs to be done about other police battalions and their role in the Holocaust. Much of the controversy rages over Goldhagen's imputation of guilt to the German nation, Hitler's beloved Volk. Historians seem especially troubled. Cultural anthropologists, on the other hand, have studied national character ever since Margaret Mead and Ruth Benedict finished their training with Franz Boas at Columbia University. Members of a culture do share

certain fundamental beliefs, and it is possible, though difficult to prove, that such items become so ingrained that they disappear from common sources like newspapers. Goldhagen's book has been well received in Germany. We rely on his theoretical extension of Patterson's argument, which has not drawn the wrath of critics, but we acknowledge the powerful nature of his argument about eliminationist ideologies.

Goldhagen has made a major contribution to political science's understanding of totalitarian governments (Arendt 1958) and ideology and has added an important level of complexity to Arendt's concept of the banality of evil, which unfortunately has become a cliché (Arendt 1965). He has formulated concepts that finally allow political scientists to deal adequately with murderous, genocidal ideologies, which include not only the Holocaust but also the reign of terror of Pol Pot in Cambodia as well as events in the former Yugoslavia (Berghahn 1996; Joffey 1996; Cowell 1996; Elon 1997; Goldhagen 1997).

References

Adam, Barry D. 1987. *The Rise of a Gay and Lesbian Movement*. Boston: Twayne.

Allen, Edward. 1918. *Keeping Our Fighters Fit, for War and After*. New York: Century Company.

Allen, Woody. 1972. *Everything You Always Wanted to Know about Sex*. United Artists Corporation.

Altman, Dennis. 1986. *AIDS in the Mind of America*. Garden City: Doubleday.

Altman, Meryle. 1984. Everything They Always Wanted You to Know: The Ideology of Popular Sex Literature. In Carol Vance, ed., *Pleasure and Danger: Exploring Female Sexuality*. Boston: Routledge and Kegan Paul.

Arendt, Hannah. 1958. *The Origins of Totalitarianism*. Cleveland: World Pubishing Company.

——. 1965. *Eichmann in Jerusalem: A Report on the Banality of Evil*. Rev. ed. New York: Viking.

Arens, W. 1979. *The Man-Eating Myth: Anthropology and Anthropophagy*. Oxford: Oxford University Press.

Asbell, Bernard. 1995. *The Pill: A Biography of the Drug That Changed the World*. New York: Random House.

Bayer, Ronald. 1987. *Homosexuality and American Psychiatry: The Politics of Diagnosis*. Princeton: Princeton University Press.

Beall, Otho T. 1963. Aristotle's Masterpiece in America: A Landmark in the Folklore of Medicine. *William and Mary Quarterly* 20: 207–22.

Berghahn, V. R. 1996. The Road to Extermination. *New York Times Book Review*. 14 April.

Bérubé, Allan. 1990. *Coming Out under Fire: The History of the Gay Men and Women in World War Two*. New York: Free Press.

Binkley, Robert, and Frances Binkley. 1929. *What Is Right with Marriage: An Outline of Domestic Theory*. New York: D. Appleton and Company.

Bloom, Allan, trans. 1968. *The Republic of Plato*. New York: Basic Books.

Bork, Robert H. 1996. *Slouching towards Gomorrah: Modern Liberalism and American Decline*. New York: HarperCollins.

Branch, Taylor. 1988. *Parting the Waters: America in the King Years, 1954–1963*. Vol. 1. New York: Simon and Schuster.

————. 1998. *Pillar of Fire: America in the King Years, 1963–1965*. New York: Simon and Schuster.

Brandt, Allan. 1985. *No Magic Bullet: A Social History of Venereal Disease in the United States since 1880*. New York: Oxford University Press.

Brautigan, Richard. 1964. *A Confederate General from Big Sur*. New York: Grove.

————. 1967. *Trout Fishing in America*. New York: Dell.

————. 1970. *Rommel Drives On into Egypt*. New York: Dell.

Breecher, Edward. 1969. *The Sex Researchers*. Boston: Little, Brown.

Breskin, David. 1991. Oliver Stone. *Rolling Stone*, 4 April.

Brown, Helen Gurley. 1962. *Sex and the Single Girl*. New York: Bernard Geis.

Brownmiller, Susan. 1976. *Against Our Will: Men, Women and Rape*. New York: Bantam Books. Originally published by Simon and Schuster in 1975.

————. 1984. *Femininity*. New York: Simon and Schuster.

Brunt, Rosalind. 1982. An Immense Verbosity: Permissive Sexual Advice in the 1970s. In R. Brunt and C. Rowan, eds., *Feminism, Culture and Politics*. London: Lawrence and Wishart.

Bryant, Anita. 1977. *The Anita Bryant Story*. Old Tappan, NJ: Fleming H. Revell.

Burke, Tom. 1969. The New Homosexuality. *Esquire* 71: 316–18.

Burroughs, William. 1966. *Naked Lunch*. New York: Grove.

Butler, Judith. 1990. *Gender Trouble*. New York: Routledge.

————. 1993. *Bodies That Matter*. New York: Routledge.

————. 1998. How Bodies Come to Matter: An Interview with Judith Butler. By Irene Costera Meijer and Baukje Prins. *Signs* 23, no. 2 (winter).

Cannon, Lou. 1991. *President Reagan: The Role of a Lifetime*. New York: Simon and Schuster.

Chauncey, George. 1994. *Gay New York*. New York: Basic Books.

Chesler, Ellen. 1992. *Woman of Valor: Margaret Sanger and the Birth Control Movement in America*. New York: Anchor Books.

Chesser, Eustace. 1947. *Love without Fear: How to Achieve Sex Happiness in Marriage*. New York: Roy Publishers.

————. 1966. *Unmarried Love*. New York: Simon and Schuster.

Clothing Sales Down; Houses Up: Report for New York, San Francisco, Chicago, Washington. 1950. *U.S. News and World Report*, 14 April, 18–19.

Cochrane, Charles. 1968. *Christianity and Classical Culture*. London: Oxford University Press.

Cohen, Allen, and Michael Bowen, eds. [1967?]. Interview with Alan Watts, Timothy Leary, Gary Snyder and Allen Ginsberg. *Oracle*, 21 March.

Collins, Joseph. 1926. *The Doctor Looks at Love and Life*. New York: George Doran Company.

Comfort, Alex. 1974. *More Joy: A Lovemaking Companion to the Joy of Sex*. New York: Crown.

———. 1991. *The New Joy of Sex*. New York: Crown.

———, ed. 1972. *The Joy of Sex: A Cordon Bleu Guide to Lovemaking*. New York: Crown.

Coontz, Stephanie. 1992. *The Way We Never Were: American Families and the Nostalgia Trap*. New York: Basic Books.

Cott, Nancy F. 1987. *The Grounding of Modern Feminism*. New Haven: Yale University Press.

Cowell, Alan. 1996. Holocaust Writer Debates Irate Historians in Berlin. *New York Times*, 8 September.

DeBenedetti, Charles. 1990. *An American Ordeal: The Antiwar Movement of the Vietnam Era*. Syracuse: Syracuse University Press.

D'Emilio, John. 1983a. Capitalism and Gay Identity. In Ann Snitow et al., eds., *Powers of Desire: The Politics of Sexuality*. New York: Monthly Review Press.

———. 1983b. *Sexual Politics, Sexual Communities: The Making of a Homosexual Minority in the United States, 1940–1970*. Chicago: University of Chicago Press.

D'Emilio, John, and Estelle Freedman. 1988. *Intimate Matters: A History of Sexuality in America*. New York: Harper and Row.

Didion, Joan. 1968. *Slouching towards Bethlehem*. New York: Washington Square Press.

———. 1979. *The White Album*. New York: Simon and Schuster.

Dieckman, Katherine. 1991. Riders on the Storm. *Village Voice*, 26 February.

Doors. 1985. *Dance on Fire*. Video.

Dostoyevsky, Fyodor. 1957. *The Brothers Karamazov*. Trans. Constance Garnett. New York: New American Library.

Douglas, Ann. 1995. *Terrible Honesty: Mongrel Manhattan in the 1920s*. New York: Farrar, Straus and Giroux.

Duberman, Martin. 1991. *Cures: A Gay Man's Odyssey*. New York: Dutton.

———. 1993. *Stonewall*. New York: Dutton.

———. 1994. Stonewall. *Media*, 28 June.

Dworkin, Andrea. 1974. *Woman Hating*. New York: Dutton.

Echols, Alice. 1989. *Daring to Be Bad: Radical Feminism in America, 1967–1975*. Minneapolis: University of Minnesota Press.

Elon, Amos. 1997. The Antagonist as Liberator. *New York Times Magazine*, 26 January.

Epstein, Leslie. 1991. Walking Wounded, Living Dead. In Gerald Howard, ed., *The Sixties*. New York: Paragon House.

Fass, Paula. 1977. *The Damned and the Beautiful: American Youth in the 1920s*. Oxford: Oxford University Press.

Fellman, Anita, and Michael Fellman. 1981. *Making Sense of Self: Medical Advice Literature in Late Nineteenth Century America*. Philadelphia: University of Pennsylvania Press.

Fitzgerald, Frances. 1986. *Cities on a Hill: A Journey through Contemporary American Culture*. New York: Simon and Schuster.

Foucault, Michel. 1977. *Discipline and Punish*. Trans. Alan Sheridan. New York: Vintage Books.

———. 1978. *The History of Sexuality*. Vol. 1. New York: Vintage Books.

———. 1980. Introduction to *Herculine Barbin, Being the Recently Discovered Memoirs of a Nineteenth-Century French Hermaphrodite*. Trans. Richard McDougall. New York: Pantheon.

Friedan, Betty. 1963. *The Feminine Mystique*. New York: Norton.

Friedman, David. 1995. Killing Kids Softly: Rudy Crew's Dangerous AIDS Education Plan. *Village Voice*, 26 December.

Gallagher, Maggie. 1996. Why Make Divorce Easy? *New York Times*, 20 February, op-ed section.

Garber, Marjorie. 1992. *Vested Interests: Cross-Dressing and Cultural Anxiety*. New York: Routledge.

Gay-Bashing by Florida's Good Ol' Boys. 1993. *Miami Herald*, 25 July, 1C.

Gelb, Joyce, and Ethel Klein. 1987. *Women's Movements: Organizing for Change*. Washington, D.C.: American Political Science Association.

Gilmore, Mikal. 1991. The Legacy of Jim Morrison and the Doors. *Rolling Stone*, 4 April.

Gitlin, Todd. 1987. *The Sixties: Years of Hope, Days of Rage*. Toronto: Bantam Books.

Goerner, E. A. 1965. *Peter and Caesar*. New York: Herder and Herder.

Goldhagen, Daniel. 1996. *Hitler's Willing Executioners: Ordinary Germans and the Holocaust*. New York: Knopf.

———. 1997. There Is No Hierarchy among Victims. *New York Times*, 18 January.

Goldstein, Richard. 1991. Jim Morrison Plays Himself: Rescuing the Man from the Myth. *Village Voice*, 26 February.

Gordon, Michael. 1969. The Ideal Husband as Depicted in the Nineteenth Century Marriage Manual. *The Family Coordinator* 18: 226–31.

Gordon, Michael. 1978. From an Unfortunate Necessity to a Cult of Mutual Orgasm: Sex in American Marital Education Literature, 1830–1940. In James Henelin and Edward Sagarin, eds., *The Sociology of Sex*. New York: Schocken Books.

Gordon, Michael, and Charles Bernstein. 1970. Mate Choice and Domestic Life in the Nineteenth-Century Marriage Manual. *Journal of Marriage and the Family* 32: 665–74.

Gordon, Michael, and Penelope Shankweiler. 1971. Different Equals Less: Female Sexuality in Recent Marriage Manuals. *Journal of Marriage and the Family* 33: 459–66 (August).

Grahn, Judy. 1984. *Another Mother Tongue*. Rev. ed. Boston: Beacon Press.

Groves, Ernest R. 1928. *The Marriage Crisis*. New York: Longmans, Green and Company.

Guernsey, Henry. 1882. *Plain Talks on Avoided Subjects*. Philadelphia: F. A. Davis Company.

———. 1915. *Plain Talks on Avoided Subjects*. Rev. ed. [*sic*]. Philadelphia: F. A. Davis Company.

Halberstam, David. 1993. *The Fifties*. New York: Ballantine.

Hanchett, Henry. 1887. *Sexual Health: A Plain and Practical Guide for the People on All Matters Concerning the Organs of Reproduction in Both Sexes and All Ages*. New York: Charles T. Hurlburt.

Hefner, Hugh. 1968. The Legal Enforcement of Morality. *Colorado Law Review* 40: 199–221.

Hill, Bridget, ed. 1986. *The First English Feminist: Reflections upon Marriage and Other Writings by Mary Astell*. New York: St. Martin's.

Himmelfarb, Gertrude. 1995. *The De-Moralization of Society: From Victorian Virtues to Modern Values*. New York: Knopf.

Hinkle, Warren. 1991. A Social History of the Hippies. In Gerald Howard, ed., *The Sixties*. New York: Paragon House.

Hobbes, Thomas. 1962. *Leviathan*. New York: Collier-Macmillan.

Hopkins, Jerry, and Danny Sugarman. 1980. *No One Gets Out Alive*. New York: Warner Books.

Howard, Gerald, ed. 1991. *The Sixties*. New York: Paragon House.

Isaacson, Walter. 1992. *Kissinger*. New York: Simon and Schuster.

Isserman, Maurice. 1987. *If I Had a Hammer: The Death of the Old Left and the Birth of the New Left*. New York: Basic Books.

Jaeger, Werner. 1961. *Early Christianity and Greek Paideia*. London: Oxford University Press.

Joffey, Joseph. 1996. Goldhagen in Germany. *New York Review of Books*, 28 November.

Johnson, Dirk. 1996. No-Fault Divorce Is under Attack. *New York Times*, 12 February, A8.

Johnston, Jill. 1973. *Lesbian Nation: The Feminist Solution*. New York: Touchstone.

Jonas, Hans. 1958. *The Gnostic Religion*. Boston: Beacon Press.

Jones, Dylan. 1990. *Jim Morrison: Dark Star*. New York: Viking Studio Books.

Jones, James. 1981. *Bad Blood: The Scandalous Story of the Tuskegee Experiment—When Government Doctors Played God and Science Went Mad*. New York: Free Press.

Keegan, John. 1976. *The Face of Battle*. New York: Penguin Books.

Kellogg, John Harvey. 1888a. *First Book of Physiology and Hygiene*. Rev. ed. New York: American Book Company.

———. 1888b. *Plain Facts for Old and Young*. Burlington, IA: F. Signer and Company. Reprinted in New York by Arno Press in 1974.

Kennedy, Elizabeth, and Madeline Davis. 1993. *Boots of Leather, Slippers of Gold.* New York: Routledge.

Kelly, Florence Finch. 1931a. Memoirs of a Crusader. *New York Times Book Review,* 4 October.

———. 1931b. *Review of Margaret Sanger's My Fight for Birth Control. New York Times,* 4 October.

Kerouac, Jack. 1958. *On the Road.* New York: Viking.

Kesey, Ken. 1962. *One Flew over the Cuckoo's Nest.* New York: Viking.

Kinsey, Alfred, et al. 1948. *Sexual Behavior in the Human Male.* Philadelphia: W. B. Saunders.

———. 1953. *Sexual Behavior in the Human Female.* Philadelphia: W. B. Saunders.

Kissinger, Henry. 1979. *White House Years.* Boston: Little, Brown.

———. 1982. *Years of Upheaval.* Boston: Little, Brown.

Koop, C. Everett. 1991. *Koop: The Memoirs of America's Family Doctor.* New York: Random House.

Kuhn, Thomas S. 1962. *The Structure of Scientific Revolutions.* Chicago: University of Chicago Press.

Kushner, Tony. 1992. *Angels in America, Part 1: Millennium Approaches.* New York: Theater Communications Group.

Landers, Ann. 1997. Gay Youth Should Seek Counseling. *Miami Herald,* 25 May.

Law Would Provide Legal Recourse, Gays Say. 1977. *Miami Herald,* 16 June.

Lee-Riffe, Nancy M. 1992. Aristotle's Masterpiece. *Bulletin of the Council of Editors of Learned Journals* 11: 29–41.

Lewontin, R. C. 1995. Sex, Lies, and Social Science. *New York Review of Books,* 20 April, 24–29.

Light of Day to Finally Shine on Sordid State Secrets. 1993. *Miami Herald,* 30 June, 17A.

Loulan, JoAnn. 1984. *Lesbian Sex.* San Francisco: Spinsters/Aunt Lute.

Lystra, Karen. 1989. *Searching the Heart.* New York: Oxford University Press.

MacKinnon, Catharine. 1989. *Toward a Feminist Theory of the State.* Cambridge: Harvard University Press.

———. 1993. *Only Words.* Cambridge: Harvard University Press.

Madonna. 1992. *Sex.* New York: Warner Books.

Many Joined Witch Hunt Targeting Gays. 1993. *Miami Herald,* 3 July, 5B.

Mapplethorpe, Robert. 1992. *Mapplethorpe.* New York: Random House.

Marcuse, Herbert. 1955. *Eros and Civilization: A Philosophical Inquiry into Freud.* New York: Vintage Books.

———. 1964. *Dimensional Man: Studies in the Ideology of Advanced Industrial Society.* Boston: Beacon Press.

Maslin, Janet. 1991. Flying and Falling through the '60s: A Life of the Doors. *New York Times,* 1 March, "Living Arts" section.

May, Elaine Tyler. 1988. *Homeward Bound: American Families in the Cold War Era.* New York: Basic Books.

McDougall, W. 1923. *Outline of Psychology.* New York: Scribner.

Melody, M. E. 1993. Breaking through to the Other Side: The Making of "Erotic Politicians." Paper presented at the American Political Science Association annual meeting, Washington, D.C.

———. 1994a. Acting Up Academically: AIDS and the Politics of Disempowerment. In Douglas Feldman, ed., *Global AIDS Policy.* Westport, CT: Bergin and Garver.

———. 1994b. Constructing the Sexuality of the "Other": A (Partial) Explication of the Sexuality of Conquest. Paper presented at the American Political Science Association annual meeting, New York City.

Miles, Barry, ed. 1986. *Allen Ginsberg/Howl.* New York: Harper and Row.

Miller, James. 1987. *Democracy Is in the Streets.* New York: Simon and Schuster.

Millett, Kate. 1970. *Sexual Politics.* Garden City, NY: Doubleday.

Monette, Paul. 1992. *Becoming a Man: Half a Life Story.* New York: Harcourt Brace Jovanovich.

———. 1994. *Last Watch of the Night.* New York: Harcourt Brace.

Morrison, Jim. 1990. *The American Night.* Vol. 2. New York: Villard Books.

Novick, Sheldon. 1989. *Honorable Justice: The Life of Oliver Wendell Holmes.* Boston: Little, Brown.

Papers Show How Gays Were Rooted Out. 1993. *Miami Herald,* 2 July, 1.

Pateman, Carole. 1988. *The Sexual Contract.* Stanford: Stanford University Press.

Patterson, Orlando. 1982. *Slavery and Social Death.* Cambridge: Harvard University Press.

Perry, Charles. 1984. *The Haight-Ashbury.* New York: Vintage Books.

Pfaff, William. 1997. Eugenics, Anyone? *New York Review of Books,* 23 October, 23–24.

Polsky, Andrew. 1991. *The Rise of the Therapeutic State.* Princeton: Princeton University Press.

Porter, Roy, and Lesley Hall. 1995. *The Facts of Life: The Creation of Sexual Knowledge in Britain, 1650–1950.* New Haven: Yale University Press.

[Pseudo] Aristotle. 1796. *Aristotle's Masterpiece.* N.p.: n.p., marked 30th ed.

Race, Jeffrey. 1972. *War Comes to Long An: A Revolutionary Conflict in a Vietnamese Province.* Berkeley: University of California Press.

Reiff, John. 1966. *The Triumph of the Therapeutic.* New York: Harper and Row.

Reuben, David. 1969. *Everything You Always Wanted to Know about Sex, but Were Afraid to Ask.* New York: David McKay.

———. 1999. *Everything You Always Wanted to Know about Sex, but Were Afraid to Ask.* Rev. ed. New York. Harper Collins.

————. 1971. *Any Woman Can! Love and Sexual Fulfillment for the Single, Widowed, Divorced . . . and Married*. New York: David McKay.

Rich, Adrienne. 1983. Compulsory Heterosexuality and Lesbian Existence. In Elizabeth Abel and Emily Abel, eds., *The Signs Reader: Women, Gender and Scholarship*. Chicago: University of Chicago Press.

Rizzo, Arthur. 1969. The Diggers: A Study in the Development of Ideology. M.A. thesis, Department of Sociology [?], San Francisco State University.

Ruskin, Cindy. 1988. *The Quilt: Stories for the Names Project*. New York: Pocket Books.

Sale, Kirkpatrick. 1973. *SDS*. New York: Random House.

Sanger, Margaret. 1914. *Family Limitation*. [New York]: n.p.

————. 1916. *What Every Mother Should Know, or How Six Little Children Were Taught the Truth*. 3d rev. ed. New York: Max N. Maisel.

————. 1917. *The Case for Birth Control*. N.p.: n.p., marked restricted shelf.

————. 1920. *Women and the New Race*. New York: Brentano's.

————. 1921a. *Debate on Birth Control*. Girard, KS: Haldeman-Julius.

————. 1921b. *The Morality of Birth Control*. New York: American Birth Control League.

————. 1922a. *The Pivot of Civilization*. New York: Brentano's.

————. 1922b. *Woman, Morality and Birth Control*. New York: New York Woman's Publishing Company.

————. 1926a. "The Children's Era." In Margaret Sanger, ed., *Religious and Ethical Aspects of Birth Control*. New York: American Birth Control League.

————. 1926b. *Happiness in Marriage*. Cornwall, NY: Cornwall Press.

————. 1928. *Motherhood in Bondage*. New York: Brentano's.

————. 1936. *Woman of the Future*. London: Birth Control Information Center.

Schlessinger, Laura. 1996. *How Could You Do That?! The Abdication of Character, Courage, and Conscience*. New York: HarperCollins.

Sedgwick, Eve Kosofsky. 1990. *Epistemology of the Closet*. Berkeley: University of California Press.

Seelye, Kathyrine. 1995. Gingrich Looks to Victorian Age to Cure Today's Social Failings. *New York Times*, 14 March, A10.

Seidman, Steven. 1989. Constructing Sex as a Domain of Pleasure and Self-Expression: Sexual Ideology in the Sixties. *Theory, Culture and Society* 6: 293–315.

Sense of the Sixties. 1991. WETA (Public Broadcasting System).

Sheehan, Neil. 1988. *A Bright Shining Lie: John Paul Vann and America in Vietnam*. New York: Random House.

Shilts, Randy. 1982. *The Mayor of Castro Street: The Life and Times of Harvey Milk*. New York: St. Martin's.

————. 1987. *And the Band Played On: People and the AIDS Epidemic*. New York: St. Martin's.

———. 1993. *Conduct Unbecoming.* New York: St. Martin's.

Silverstein, Charles, and Felice Picano. 1992. *The New Joy of Gay Sex.* New York: Harper Perennial.

Silverstein, Charles, and Edmund White. 1977. *The Joy of Gay Sex: An Intimate Guide for Gay Men to the Pleasures of a Gay Lifestyle.* New York: Simon and Schuster.

Sisley, Emily L., and Bertha Harris. 1977. *The Joy of Lesbian Sex: A Tender and Liberated Guide to the Pleasures and Problems of a Lesbian Lifestyle.* New York: Simon and Schuster.

Snepp, Frank. 1977. *Decent Interval: An Insider's Account of Saigon's Indecent End Told by the CIA's Chief Strategy Analyst in Vietnam.* New York: Random House.

Spock, Benjamin. 1945. *The Common Sense Book of Baby and Child Care.* New York: Duell, Sloan and Pearce.

Stevens, Jay. 1987. *Storming Heaven: LSD and the American Dream.* New York: Atlantic Monthly Press.

Stone, Hannah M., and Abraham Stone. 1952. *A Marriage Manual: A Practical Guidebook to Sex and Marriage.* New York: Simon and Schuster.

Stone, Oliver. 1991. *The Doors.* Live Home Video, Inc.

Stopes, Marie Carmichael. 1931. *Married Love: A New Contribution to the Solution of Sex Difficulties.* New York: Eugenics Publishing Company.

Strauss, Leo. 1952. *Persecution and the Art of Writing.* Chicago: University of Chicago Press.

Talese, Gay. 1980. *Thy Neighbor's Wife.* New York: Doubleday.

Tronto, Joan. 1993. *Moral Boundaries: A Political Argument for an Ethic of Care.* New York: Routledge.

Van de Velde, Theodore. 1930. *Ideal Marriage: Its Physiology and Technique.* Trans. Stella Browne. New York: Covici Friede.

———. 1931a. *Fertility and Sterility in Marriage: Their Voluntary Promotion and Limitation.* Trans. Stella Browne. New York: Random House.

———. 1931b. *Sexual Tensions in Marriage: Their Origin, Prevention and Treatment.* Trans. Hamilton Marr. New York: Random House.

———. 1965. *Ideal Marriage: Its Physiology and Technique.* Rev. ed. by Margaret Smyth. New York: Random House.

Viorst, Milton. 1979. *Fire in the Streets.* New York: Simon and Schuster.

Voegelin, Eric. 1968. *Science, Politics and Gnosticism.* New York: Henry Regnery.

Walker, Alice, and Pratibha Parmar. 1993. *Warrior Marks.* San Diego: Harcourt Brace.

Walker, Lenore. 1979. *The Battered Woman.* New York: Harper Colophon Books.

———. 1989. *Terrifying Love.* New York: Harper & Row.

Weinberg, Martin, and Sue Hammersmith. 1983. Sexual Autonomy and the Status of Women: Models of Female Sexuality in the U.S. Sex Manuals from 1950 to 1980. *Social Problems* 30: 312–24.

Wells, Tom. 1994. *The War Within: America's Battle over Vietnam*. Berkeley: University of California Press.

Westheimer, Ruth. 1983. *Dr. Ruth's Guide to Good Sex*. New York: Warner Books.

———. 1986. *Dr. Ruth's Guide for Married Lovers*. New York: Warner Books.

———. 1992. *Dr. Ruth's Guide to Safer Sex: Exciting, Sensible Directions for the 90s*. New York: Warner Books.

———. 1993. *The Art of Arousal*. New York: Abbeville Press.

———. 1995. *Sex for Dummies*. Foster City, CA: IDG Books.

Westheimer, Ruth, and Nathan Kravetz. 1985. *First Love: A Young People's Guide to Sexual Information*. New York: Warner Books.

White, Edmund. 1980. *States of Desire*. New York: Penguin.

———. 1997. *The Farewell Symphony*. New York: Knopf.

White, Kevin. 1993. *The First Sexual Revolution: The Emergence of Male Heterosexuality in Modern America*. New York: New York University Press.

Wicker, Tom. 1991. *One of Us: Richard Nixon and the American Dream*. New York: Random House.

Wile, Ira S., and Mary Day Winn. 1929. *Marriage in the Modern Manner*. New York: Century Company.

Williams, Linda. 1989. *Hard Core: Power, Pleasure and the "Frenzy of the Visible."* Berkeley: University of California Press.

Wilmer, Franke, Michael E. Melody, and Margaret Murdock. 1993. Including Native American Perspectives in the Political Science Curriculum. *PS: Political Science and Politics* 27: 269–70.

Wolf, Naomi. 1991. *The Beauty Myth*. New York: William Morrow.

Wolfe, Tom. 1968. *Electric Kool-Aid Acid Test*. New York: Farrar, Straus and Giroux.

Young, Allen. 1971. Out of the Closets. *Ramparts* 10: 52–59.

Young, Perry. 1973. So You Want to Spend a Night at the Tubs. *Rolling Stone*, 128: 48, 50.

Index

About the Authors

M. E. Melody is Professor of Political Science at Barry University. Linda M. Peterson is Professor of Psychology and Coordinator of Women's Studies at Barry University.